NHibernate 3.0 Cookbook

70 incredibly powerful recipes for using the full spectrum of solutions in the NHibernate ecosystem

Jason Dentler

PUBLISHING

BIRMINGHAM - MUMBAI

NHibernate 3.0 Cookbook

First published: October 2010

Production Reference: 1240910

Published by Packt Publishing Ltd.
32 Lincoln Road
Olton
Birmingham, B27 6PA, UK.

ISBN 978-1-84951-304-3

www.packtpub.com

Cover Image by Javier Barria (jbarriac@yahoo.com)

Credits

Author

Jason Dentler

Reviewers

Fabio Maulo

Jose F. Romaniello

Gabriel Nicolas Schenker

Tuna Toksoz

Acquisition Editor

Chaitanya Apte

Development Editor

Rakesh Shejwal

Technical Editor

Paramanand N. Bhat

Indexer

Tejal Daruwale

Editorial Team Leader

Aanchal Kumar

Project Team Leader

Priya Mukherji

Project Coordinator

Prasad Rai

Proofreader

Clyde Jenkins

Graphics

Nilesh Mohite

Production Coordinator

Kruthika Bangera

Cover Work

Kruthika Bangera

About the Author

Jason Dentler grew up in the small Texas town of Mission Valley. He started tinkering with computers as a kid in the late 1980s, and all these years later, he hasn't stopped. He has worked in different industries. Currently, he builds really awesome software for higher education. He's an Eagle Scout and a graduate of the University of Houston – Victoria.

I'd like to thank my family and friends for all their support, and especially my parents, who encouraged and tolerated my computer obsession all those years. Thanks, Mom & Dad. I love you.

About the Reviewers

Fabio Maulo has lived his youth in Montecosaro, a small village in the hills of the Marche in Italy. His first computer was a Mac128 in 1984; since then, he has always followed technology of the moment, trying to learn as much as possible. Since the end of past century, he has followed the evolution of ORM, at first in Delphi's world and then the .NET's world. He joined to NHibernate's team in 2007, and since 2008, is leading the project.

Thanks to my father to let me choose between a motorcycle and a computer (and I did buy a computer with the cost of a motorbike). Thanks to my wife who bears my work.

José Fernando Romaniello is a senior developer with ten years of experience in Microsoft technologies. He currently lives in Argentina, and works for GenWise B.V. José has a strong involvement in various open source projects in .Net world, and he actively contributes to uNhAddins, LinqSpecs, and HqlAddin. He enjoys sharing his knowledge in his blog as well as on mailing lists.

I want to thank Fabio Maulo for sharing long talks with me, for teaching me a lot of things about programming, ORMs, and NHibernate.

I want to thank Jason Dentler for choosing me as a reviewer for this great book.

And finally, I want to thank to my beloved wife and my daughter, I couldn't be here without their help.

Gabriel N. Schenker has been working for over 12 years as an independent consultant, trainer, and mentor, mainly on the .NET platform. He is currently working as lead software architect in a mid-size US company based in Austin, TX providing software and services to the pharmaceutical industry, as well as to many well-known universities throughout the US and in many other countries around the world. Gabriel is passionate about software development, and tries to make life of the developers easier by providing guidelines and frameworks to reduce friction in the software development process.

He has used NHibernate in many different commercial projects—web-based as well as windows-based solutions. Gabriel has written many articles and blog posts about different aspects of NHibernate. He is the author behind the well-known NHibernate FAQ blog.

Gabriel is married, and the father of four children. During his spare, time he likes hiking in the mountains, cooking, and reading.

Tuna Toksoz is currently a graduate student at the Department of Aeronautics and Astronautics at MIT. He mainly concentrates on Software Development and Autonomous Systems. He likes to be involved in OSS projects. He contributes to Nhibernate and Castle projects as a committer, and actively participates in many tech-related mailing groups.

Table of Contents

Preface

This book explains each feature of NHibernate 3.0 in detail through example recipes that you can quickly apply to your applications. These recipes will take you from the absolute basics of NHibernate through its most advanced features and beyond, showing you how to take full advantage of each concept to quickly create amazing database applications.

What this book covers

Chapter 1, Models and Mappings, introduces mappings in XML, Fluent NHibernate, and ConfORM, and includes more advanced topics such as versioning and concurrency.

Chapter 2, Configuration and Schema, explains various methods for configuring NHibernate and generating your database.

Chapter 3, Sessions and Transactions, covers several techniques for proper session and transaction management in your application, including distributed transactions.

Chapter 4, Queries, demonstrates a number of rich query APIs, including the new NHibernate 3.0 LINQ provider and QueryOver API.

Chapter 5, Testing, introduces some techniques you can apply to quickly test your NHibernate applications and includes an introduction to NHibernate Profiler.

Chapter 6, Data Access Layer, shows how to build a flexible, extensible data access layer based on NHibernate and its many query APIs.

Chapter 7, Extending NHibernate, shows a number of ways to customize and extend NHibernate to provide additional services such as audit logging and data encryption.

Chapter 8, NHibernate Contribution Projects, introduces several NHibernate Contribution projects, adding features such as caching, data validation, full text search, geospatial data, and horizontal partitioning of databases.

Appendix, Menu, is designed to guide you to recipes relevant to building different types of applications, such as ASP.NET MVC or WPF applications.

What you need for this book

To complete the recipes in this book, you'll need the following tools:

- ▶ Windows XP or later versions.
- ▶ Visual Studio 2008 or later versions.
- ▶ Microsoft SQL Server 2008 Express edition or later versions.
- ▶ *Chapter 5* requires NHibernate Profiler. A free, 30 day trial version is available on the web at `http://nhprof.com`.

Who this book is for

This book is written for NHibernate users at all levels of experience. Examples are written in C# and XML. Some basic knowledge of SQL is needed.

Beginners will learn several techniques for each of the four core NHibernate tasks – mapping, configuration, session & transaction management, and querying – and which techniques fit best with various types of applications. In short, you will be able to build an application using NHibernate.

Intermediate level readers will learn how to best implement enterprise application architecture patterns using NHibernate, leading to clean, easy-to-understand code, and increased productivity.

In addition to new v3.0 features, advanced readers will learn creative ways to extend NHibernate core, as well as techniques using the NHibernate search, shards, spatial, and validation projects.

Conventions

In this book, you will find a number of styles of text that distinguish between different kinds of information. Here are some examples of these styles, and an explanation of their meaning.

Code words in text are shown as follows: " Create a new class library project called `EncryptedStringExample`" where `EncryptedStringExample` is the code word in text.

A block of code is set as follows:

```
public interface IEncryptor
{
  string Encrypt(string plainText);
  string Decrypt(string encryptedText);
  string EncryptionKey { get; set; }
}
```

When we wish to draw your attention to a particular part of a code block, the relevant lines or items are set in bold:

```
using System.Collections.Generic;

namespace Eg.Core
{
  public class Movie : Product
  {
    public virtual string Director { get; set; }
    public virtual IList<ActorRole> Actors { get; set; }
  }
}
```

New terms and **important words** are shown in bold. Words that you see on the screen, in menus or dialog boxes for example, appear in the text like this: "clicking on the **Next** button moves you to the next screen".

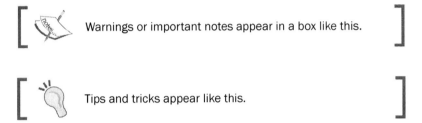

Warnings or important notes appear in a box like this.

Tips and tricks appear like this.

Reader feedback

Feedback from our readers is always welcome. Let us know what you think about this book—what you liked or may have disliked. Reader feedback is important for us to develop titles that you really get the most out of.

To send us general feedback, simply send an e-mail to feedback@packtpub.com, and mention the book title via the subject of your message.

If there is a book that you need and would like to see us publish, please send us a note in the **SUGGEST A TITLE** form on www.packtpub.com or e-mail suggest@packtpub.com.

If there is a topic that you have expertise in and you are interested in either writing or contributing to a book, see our author guide on www.packtpub.com/authors.

Customer support

Now that you are the proud owner of a Packt book, we have a number of things to help you to get the most from your purchase.

Downloading the example code for this book

You can download the example code files for all Packt books you have purchased from your account at http://www.PacktPub.com. If you purchased this book elsewhere, you can visit http://www.PacktPub.com/support and register to have the files e-mailed directly to you.

Errata

Although we have taken every care to ensure the accuracy of our content, mistakes do happen. If you find a mistake in one of our books—maybe a mistake in the text or the code—we would be grateful if you would report this to us. By doing so, you can save other readers from frustration, and help us improve subsequent versions of this book. If you find any errata, please report them by visiting http://www.packtpub.com/support, selecting your book, clicking on the **let us know** link, and entering the details of your errata. Once your errata are verified, your submission will be accepted, and the errata will be uploaded on our website, or added to any list of existing errata, under the Errata section of that title. Any existing errata can be viewed by selecting your title from http://www.packtpub.com/support.

Piracy

Piracy of copyright material on the Internet is an ongoing problem across all media. At Packt, we take the protection of our copyright and licenses very seriously. If you come across any illegal copies of our works, in any form, on the Internet, please provide us with the location address or website name immediately so that we can pursue a remedy.

Please contact us at copyright@packtpub.com with a link to the suspected pirated material.

We appreciate your help in protecting our authors, and our ability to bring you valuable content.

Questions

You can contact us at questions@packtpub.com if you are having a problem with any aspect of the book, and we will do our best to address it.

1
Models and Mappings

In this chapter, we will cover the following topics:

- Mapping a class with XML
- Creating class hierarchy mappings
- Mapping a one-to-many relationship
- Setting up a base entity class
- Bidirectional one-to-many class relationships
- Handling versioning and concurrency
- Creating mappings fluently
- Mapping with ConfORM

Introduction

NHibernate is a popular, mature, open source object / relational mapper (ORM) based on Java's Hibernate project. ORMs, such as LINQ to SQL, Entity Framework, and NHibernate, translate between the database's relational model of tables, columns, and keys to the application's object model of classes and properties.

The NHibernate homepage, `http://NHForge.org`, contains blog posts, a wiki, the complete reference documentation, and a bug tracker. Support is available through the very active nhusers Google group at `http://groups.google.com/group/nhusers`. The NHibernate source code is hosted on SourceForge at `http://sourceforge.net/projects/nhibernate/`. Precompiled binaries of NHibernate releases are also available on SourceForge.

Mapping a class with XML

The suggested first step in any new NHibernate application is mapping the model. In this first example, I'll show you how to map a simple product class.

Getting ready

Before we begin mapping, let's get our Visual Studio solution set up. Follow these steps to set up your solution with NHibernate binaries and schemas.

1. Download the NHibernate 3.0 binaries from SourceForge at `http://sourceforge.net/projects/nhibernate/files/`. The filename should be `NHibernate-3.0.0.GA-bin.zip`, perhaps with a slightly different version number.

2. In Visual Studio, create a new C# class library project named `Eg.Core` with a directory for the solution named **Cookbook**.

3. Delete the `Class1.cs` file.

4. In the Solution Explorer, right-click on the **Cookbook** solution and select **Open Folder in Windows Explorer**. This will open an Explorer window to the `Cookbook` directory.

5. Inside the `Cookbook` folder, create a new folder named `Lib`.

6. Extract the following files from the NHibernate 3 binaries ZIP to the `Lib` folder:

    ❑   All files in the `Required_Bin` folder

    ❑   All files in the `Required_For_LazyLoading\Castle` folder

7. Back in Visual Studio, right-click on the **Solution**, and select **Add | New Solution Folder**.

8. Name the folder `Schema`.

9. Right-click on the **Schema** folder, and select **Add | Existing Item**.

10. Browse to the `Lib` folder, and add two files: `nhibernate-configuration.xsd` and `nhibernate-mapping.xsd`. When the files open in the editor, just close them.

11. Your solution appears as shown in the next screenshot:

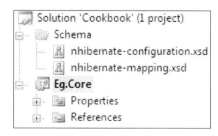

How to do it...

Now, let's start by creating our `Product` class with the following steps:

1. In `Eg.Core`, create a new C# class named `Entity` with the following code:

```
using System;

namespace Eg.Core
{
  public abstract class Entity
  {
    public virtual Guid Id { get; protected set; }
  }
}
```

2. Create a new class named `Product` with the following code:

```
using System;

namespace Eg.Core
{
  public class Product : Entity
  {
    public virtual string Name { get; set; }
    public virtual string Description { get; set; }
    public virtual decimal UnitPrice { get; set; }
  }
}
```

3. Build your application and correct any compilation errors.

Next, let's create an NHibernate mapping for our product class. Follow these steps:

1. In the Solution Explorer window, right-click on your project, and choose **Add | New Item**.
2. Choose the **Data** category on the left pane.
3. Choose **XML file** on the right pane.
4. Name the file **Product.hbm.xml**.
5. In the Solution Explorer, right-click on **Product.hbm.xml**, and choose **Properties**.
6. Change **Build Action** from **Content** to **Embedded Resource**.

7. In the editor, enter the following XML in `Product.hbm.xml`. Let the IntelliSense guide you.

```xml
<?xml version="1.0" encoding="utf-8" ?>
<hibernate-mapping xmlns="urn:nhibernate-mapping-2.2"
    assembly="Eg.Core"
    namespace="Eg.Core">
  <class name="Product">
    <id name="Id">
      <generator class="guid.comb" />
    </id>
    <property name="Name" not-null="true" />
    <property name="Description" />
    <property name="UnitPrice" not-null="true"
      type="Currency" />
  </class>
</hibernate-mapping>
```

How it works...

In this recipe, we begin by creating our model. The **model** is the collection of classes that will be persisted or stored in the database. A **persistent class** is any class that will be persisted. An **entity class** is a persistent class with an ID. An instance of an entity class is called an **entity**. So far, our model only contains the `Product` entity class. We will expand on this model over the next few recipes.

Notice that our `Product` class looks just like any other **Plain Old CLR Object** (**POCO**) class. One of the strongly held design decisions in NHibernate is that all entity classes should be **persistence ignorant**, that is, they should not know about, or be dependent on NHibernate.

Let's examine the `Id` property a little closer. The `Id` property of each `Product` instance will contain the primary key value from the database. In NHibernate, this is named the **persistent object identifier** (**POID**). Just as the primary key value uniquely identifies a row in a database table, the POID will uniquely identify an entity in memory.

If you are new to NHibernate, this protected setter may look strange to you.

```
public virtual Guid Id { get; protected set; }
```

This is a shorthand way to limit access to the `Id` property. Code outside of the `Product` class is unable to change the value of the `Id` property. However, NHibernate sets properties using highly optimized reflection, ignoring the `protected` restriction. This keeps your application from inadvertently altering this value.

Next, we create our mapping for the `Product` entity class. Visual Studio uses the `nhibernate-mapping.xsd` schema to provide IntelliSense while completing this mapping. As a general rule, all NHibernate mapping files end with a `.hbm.xml` extension, and have a build action of **Embedded Resource**. NHibernate searches through the embedded resources in your assembly, loading each one with this extension.

One of the most common mistakes in mapping is forgetting to set the build action to **Embedded Resource**. This leads to the "No Persister for class" `MappingException`.

Let's break down this XML mapping. Every XML mapping document contains a single `hibernate-mapping` element. The `xmlns` attribute sets the XML namespace. Along with the schema in our `Schema` folder, Visual Studio uses this to enable IntelliSense inside NHibernate mappings.

The `assembly` attribute tells NHibernate which assembly, by default, contains our types. Similarly, the `namespace` attribute sets the default .NET namespace types in this mapping file. Together, they allow us to use the simple name `Product` instead of the full assembly qualified name of `Eg.Core.Product, Eg.Core`. Inside the `hibernate-mapping` element, we have a `class` element. The `name` attribute tells NHibernate that this `class` element defines the mapping for our entity class `Product`.

The `Id` element defines the POID. The `name` attribute refers to the `Id` property of our `Product` class. It is case-sensitive, just as in the C# language.

The `generator` element defines how NHibernate will generate POIDs. In this case, we've told NHibernate to use the `guid.comb` algorithm. Several other options exist.

The `property` elements define properties on our `Product` class. Each `name` attribute matches the name of a property on our `Product` class. By default, NHibernate allows null values. Adding `not-null="true"` tells NHibernate to disallow null values.

Avoid redundant mappings

In general, it's best to keep your mappings as short and concise as possible. NHibernate intelligently scans your model and combines this knowledge with the information provided in the mapping. In most cases, specifying the types of properties in your mappings only creates redundancies that must be maintained. The default table name matches the class name, and each column name matches the corresponding property by default. It's not necessary to specify this information again. Similarly, you should avoid setting an attribute in your mapping when it matches an NHibernate default. For example, adding `not-null="false"` to each of your properties is redundant, and makes your mapping difficult to read.

With this mapping, the Microsoft SQL Server database table used to store our **Product** entities appears as shown in the next screenshot. It may differ slightly for other databases.

Product		
Column Name	Data Type	Allow Nulls
🔑 Id	uniqueidentifier	☐
Name	nvarchar(255)	☐
Description	nvarchar(255)	☑
UnitPrice	decimal(19, 5)	☐
		☐

There's more...

There are three main approaches to begin developing an NHibernate application.

▶ With the model-first approach, the path taken in this book, we create our model, map the model, configure NHibernate, and finally generate our database tables from the model and mappings.

▶ The configuration-first approach differs slightly. We build our configuration first, then add each entity class and mapping one at a time. This is a more iterative approach to the model-first approach. Again, the database is generated from the model and mappings.

▶ The database-first approach is only suggested when sharing an existing database with another application. Depending on the database design, this usually requires some advanced mapping techniques. Many NHibernate beginners travel down this path for fresh database applications and end up with mapping and modelling problems well beyond their experience level.

What happens to these mappings?

When it loads, NHibernate will deserialize each of our XML mappings into a graph of hibernate mapping objects. NHibernate combines this data with metadata from the entity classes to create mapping metadata. This mapping metadata contains everything NHibernate must know about our model.

Surrogate keys and natural IDs

A **natural key** is an ID that has semantic meaning or business value. It "means something" to people in the real world. A **surrogate key** is a system generated ID that has no semantic meaning. It is just a value that uniquely identifies data in a database table. NHibernate strongly encourages the use of surrogate keys. There are two reasons for this.

First, the use of natural keys inevitably leads to the use of **composite keys**. Composite keys are multi-field keys composed of the natural keys of other objects. Let's examine the model of a university's course schedule. The natural key for your term or semester entity may be `Fall 2010`. The natural key for the Biology department may be `BIOL`. The natural key for an introductory Biology course would be `BIOL 101`, a composite of the department's natural key and a course number, each stored in a separate field, with proper foreign keys. The natural key for a section or course offering would be the combination of the natural ids from the term, the course, and a section number. You would have a key composed of four distinct pieces of information. The size of the key grows exponentially with each layer. This quickly leads to an incredible amount of complexity.

Second, because natural keys have real-world meaning, they must be allowed to change with the real world. Let's assume you have an `Account` class with a `UserName` property. While this may be unique, it's not a good candidate for use as a key. Suppose usernames are composed of the first initial followed by the last name. When someone changes their name, you'll have to update several foreign keys in your database. If, instead, you use an integer with no meaning for the POID, you only have to update a single `UserName` field.

However, `UserName` would be a great candidate for a **natural id**. A natural id is a property or set of properties that is unique and not null. Essentially, it is the natural key of an entity, though it is not used as the primary key. The mapping for a natural id appears as shown in the following code:

```
<natural-id mutable="true">
    <property name="UserName" not-null="true" />
</natural-id>
```

The `natural-id` element has one attribute: `mutable`. The default value is `false`, meaning that the property or properties contained in this natural id are immutable, or constant. In our case, we want to allow our application to change the `UserName` of an account from time-to-time, so we set `mutable` to `true`. In addition to some subtle improvements in caching, this natural id will create a unique database index on `UserName`.

ID generator selection

NHibernate offers many options for generating POIDs. Some are better than others, and generally fall under these four categories:

The `assigned` generator requires an application to assign an identifier before an object is persisted. This is typical when natural keys are used.

Non-insert POID generators are the best option for new applications. These generators allow NHibernate to assign an identity to a persistent object without writing the object's data to the database, allowing NHibernate to delay writing until the business transaction is complete, reducing round trips to the database. The following POID generators fit in this category:

- ▶ hilo generates an integer using the Hi/Lo algorithm, where an entire range of integers is reserved and used as needed. Once they've all been used, another range is reserved. Because the identity reservation is managed using a database table, this POID generator is safe for use in a database cluster, web farm, client, or server application, or other scenarios where a single database is shared by multiple applications or multiple instances of an application.

- ▶ guid generates a GUID by calling System.Guid.NewGuid(). All of the GUID-based generators are safe for use in a shared-database environment.

- ▶ guid.comb combines 10 bytes of a seemingly-random GUID, with six bytes representing the current date and time to form a new GUID. This algorithm reduces index fragmentation while maintaining high performance.

- ▶ guid.native gets a GUID from the database. Each generation requires a round-trip to the database.

- ▶ uuid.hex generates a GUID and stores it as a human-readable string of 32 hex digits with or without dashes.

- ▶ uuid.string generates a GUID, converts each of the GUID's 16 bytes to the binary equivalent character, and stores the resulting 16 characters as a string. This is not human readable.

- ▶ counter (also known as vm) is a simple incrementing integer. It's initialized from the system clock and counts up. It's not appropriate for shared-database scenarios.

- ▶ increment is also a simple incrementing integer. It's initialized by fetching the maximum primary key value from the database at start-up. It's not appropriate for shared-database scenarios.

- ▶ sequence fetches a single new ID from a database that supports named sequences, such as Oracle, DB2, and PostgreSQL. Each generation requires a round trip to the database. seqhilo provides better performance.

- ▶ seqhilo combines the Hi/Lo algorithm and sequences to provide better performance over the sequence generator.

- ▶ foreign simply copies keys across a one-to-one relationship. For example, if you have contact and customer associated by a one-to-one relationship, a foreign generator on customer would copy the ID from the matching contact.

Post-insert POID generators require data to be persisted to the database for an ID to be generated. This alters the behavior of NHibernate in very subtle ways and disables some performance features. As such, use of these POID generators is strongly discouraged! They should only be used with existing databases where other applications rely on this behavior.

- ▶ identity returns a database-generated ID.

- ▶ select performs a SELECT to fetch the ID from the row after the insert. It uses the natural id to find the correct row.

- ▶ `sequence-identity` returns a database-generated ID for databases that support named sequences.

- ▶ `trigger-identity` returns an ID generated by a database trigger.

Finally, the `native` generator maps to a different POID generator, depending on the database product. For Microsoft SQL Server, DB2, Informix, MySQL, PostgreSQL, SQLite, and Sybase, it is equivalent to `identity`. For Oracle and Firebird, it's the same as `sequence`. On Ingres, it's `hilo`.

See also

- ▶ *Creating class hierarchy mappings*
- ▶ *Mapping a one-to-many relationship*
- ▶ *Setting up a base entity class*
- ▶ *Handling versioning and concurrency*
- ▶ *Creating mappings fluently*
- ▶ *Mapping with ConfORM*

Creating class hierarchy mappings

It's common to have an inheritance hierarchy of subclasses. In this example, I will show you one method for mapping inheritance with NHibernate, called table-per-class hierarchy.

Getting ready

Complete the previous *Mapping a class with XML* example.

How to do it...

1. Create a new class named `Book` with the following code:

```
namespace Eg.Core
{
  public class Book : Product
  {
    public virtual string ISBN { get; set; }
    public virtual string Author { get; set; }

  }
}
```

2. Create a new class named `Movie` with the following code:

```
namespace Eg.Core
{
  public class Movie : Product
  {
    public virtual string Director { get; set; }
  }
}
```

3. Change the `Product` mapping to match the XML shown in the following code:

```xml
<?xml version="1.0" encoding="utf-8" ?>
<hibernate-mapping xmlns="urn:nhibernate-mapping-2.2"
    assembly="Eg.Core"
    namespace="Eg.Core">
  <class name="Product">
    <id name="Id">
      <generator class="guid.comb" />
    </id>
    <discriminator column="ProductType" />
    <natural-id mutable="true">
      <property name="Name" not-null="true" />
    </natural-id>
    <property name="Description" />
    <property name="UnitPrice" not-null="true" />
  </class>
</hibernate-mapping>
```

4. Create a new embedded resource named `Book.hbm.xml` with the following XML:

```xml
<?xml version="1.0" encoding="utf-8" ?>
<hibernate-mapping xmlns="urn:nhibernate-mapping-2.2"
    assembly="Eg.Core"
    namespace="Eg.Core">
  <subclass name="Book" extends="Product">
    <property name="Author"/>
    <property name="ISBN"/>
  </subclass>
</hibernate-mapping>
```

5. Create another embedded resource named `Movie.hbm.xml` with the next XML:

```xml
<?xml version="1.0" encoding="utf-8" ?>
<hibernate-mapping xmlns="urn:nhibernate-mapping-2.2"
    assembly="Eg.Core"
```

```
        namespace="Eg.Core">
    <subclass name="Movie" extends="Product">
     <property name="Director" />
    </subclass>
  </hibernate-mapping>
```

How it works...

In this example, we've mapped a table-per-class hierarchy, meaning data for our entire hierarchy is stored in a single table, as shown in the next screenshot:

Product

	Column Name	Data Type	Allow Nulls
🔑	Id	uniqueidentifier	☐
	ProductType	nvarchar(255)	☐
	Name	nvarchar(255)	☐
	Description	nvarchar(255)	☑
	UnitPrice	decimal(19, 5)	☐
	Director	nvarchar(255)	☑
	Author	nvarchar(255)	☑
	ISBN	nvarchar(255)	☑
			☐

NHibernate uses a discriminator column, **ProductType** in this case, to distinguish among products, books, and movies. By default, the discriminator contains the class name. In this example, that would be `Eg.Core.Product`, `Eg.Core.Book`, or `Eg.Core.Movie`. These defaults can be overridden in the mappings by using a `discriminator-value` attribute on our class and subclass elements.

In our `Book.hbm.xml` mapping, we've defined `Book` as a subclass of `Product` with `Author` and `ISBN` properties. In our `Movie.hbm.xml` mapping, we've defined `Movie` as a subclass of `Product` with a `Director` property.

With table-per-class-hierarchy, we cannot define any of our subclass properties as `not-null="true"`, because this would create a `not-null` constraint on those fields. For instance, if we set up the `Director` property as not null, we wouldn't be able to insert `Product` or `Book` instances, because they don't define a `Director` property. If this is required, use one of the hierarchy mapping strategies listed next.

There's more...

Java refugees may recognize the `extends` attribute, as `extends` is the Java keyword used to declare class inheritance. NHibernate first came to life as a port of Java's Hibernate ORM.

Table-per-class hierarchy is the suggested method for mapping class hierarchies, but NHibernate always gives us other options. However, mixing these options within the same class hierarchy is discouraged, and only works in very limited circumstances.

Table per class

In table-per-class mappings, properties of the base class (`Product`) are stored in a shared table, while each subclass gets its own table for the subclass properties.

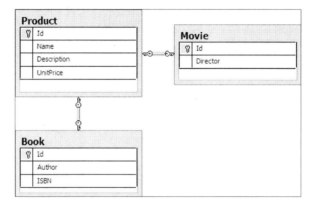

Table per subclass uses the `joined-subclass` element, which requires a `key` element to name the primary key column. As the name implies, NHibernate will use a join to query for this data. Also, notice that our **Product** table doesn't contain a **ProductType** column. Only table-per-class hierarchy uses discriminators. Using table-per-class, our `Movie` mapping will appear as the following code:

```xml
<?xml version="1.0" encoding="utf-8" ?>
<hibernate-mapping xmlns="urn:nhibernate-mapping-2.2"
    assembly="Eg.Core"
    namespace="Eg.Core">
  <joined-subclass name="Movie" extends="Product">
    <key column="Id" />
    <property name="Director" />
  </joined-subclass>
</hibernate-mapping>
```

Table per concrete class

In table-per-concrete-class mappings, each class gets its own table containing columns for all properties of the class and the base class, as shown in the next screenshot:

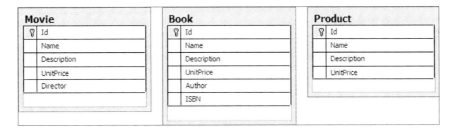

There is no duplication of data. That is, data from a `Book` instance is only written to the **Book** table, not the **Product** table. To fetch `Product` data, NHibernate will use unions to query all three tables. Using table-per-concrete-class, our `Movie` mapping will appear as shown in the following code:

```xml
<?xml version="1.0" encoding="utf-8" ?>
<hibernate-mapping xmlns="urn:nhibernate-mapping-2.2"
    assembly="Eg.Core"
    namespace="Eg.Core">
  <union-subclass name="Movie" extends="Product">
    <property name="Director" />
  </union-subclass>
</hibernate-mapping>
```

See also

- *Mapping a class with XML*
- *Mapping a one-to-many relationship*
- *Setting up a base entity class*
- *Handling versioning and concurrency*
- *Creating mappings fluently*
- *Mapping with ConfORM*

Mapping a one-to-many relationship

It's usually necessary to relate one entity to another. In this example, I'll show you how to map a one-to-many relationship between `Movies` and a new entity class, `ActorRoles`.

Getting ready

Complete the previous *Creating class hierarchy mappings* example.

How to do it...

1. Create a new class named `ActorRole` with the following code:

```
namespace Eg.Core
{
  public class ActorRole : Entity
  {

    public virtual string Actor { get; set; }
    public virtual string Role { get; set; }

  }
}
```

2. Create an embedded resource mapping for `ActorRole` with the following XML:

```xml
<?xml version="1.0" encoding="utf-8" ?>
<hibernate-mapping xmlns="urn:nhibernate-mapping-2.2"
    assembly="Eg.Core"
    namespace="Eg.Core">
  <class name="ActorRole">
    <id name="Id">
      <generator class="guid.comb" />
    </id>
    <property name="Actor" not-null="true" />
    <property name="Role" not-null="true" />
  </class>
</hibernate-mapping>
```

3. Add this `Actors` property to the `Movie` class:

```
using System.Collections.Generic;

namespace Eg.Core
{
  public class Movie : Product
  {

    public virtual string Director { get; set; }
    public virtual IList<ActorRole> Actors { get; set; }

  }
}
```

4. Add the following `list` element to our `Movie` mapping:

```
<subclass name="Movie" extends="Product">
  <property name="Director" />
  <list name="Actors" cascade="all-delete-orphan">
    <key column="MovieId" />
    <index column="ActorIndex" />
    <one-to-many class="ActorRole"/>
  </list>
</subclass>
```

How it works...

Our `ActorRole` mapping is simple. Check out *Mapping a class with XML* for more information. `ActorRole` isn't part of our `Product` hierarchy. In the database, it gets a table of its own, as shown in the next screenshot:

ActorRole		
Column Name	Data Type	Allow Nulls
🔑 Id	uniqueidentifier	☐
Actor	nvarchar(255)	☐
Role	nvarchar(255)	☐
MovieId	uniqueidentifier	☑
ActorIndex	int	☑
		☐

As expected, the **ActorRole** table has fields for the **Id**, **Actor**, and **Role** properties. The **MovieId** and **ActorIndex** columns come from the mapping of our `Actors` list on `Movie`, not the `ActorRole` mapping.

The `Actors` property uses an `IList` collection. Another strong design choice with NHibernate, and a good programming practice in general, is the liberal use of interfaces. This allows NHibernate to use its own list implementation to support lazy loading, discussed later in this recipe.

In our `Movie` mapping, the `Actors` property is mapped with the `list` element. To associate an `ActorRole` with a `Movie` in the database, we store the `Movie`'s Id with each `ActorRole`. The `key` element tells NHibernate to store this in a column named **MovieId**.

We've defined `Actors` as a list, which implies that order is significant. Actors in leading roles get top billing. Our `index` element defines the **ActorIndex** column to store the position of each element in the list. Finally, we tell NHibernate that `Actors` is a collection of `ActorRoles` with `<one-to-many class="ActorRole" />`.

The `all-delete-orphan` value of the `cascade` attribute tells NHibernate to save the associated `ActorRole` objects automatically when it saves a `Movie`, and delete them when it deletes a `Movie`.

There's more...

There are a few items to discuss with this recipe.

Lazy loading collections

To improve application performance, NHibernate supports lazy loading. In short, data isn't loaded from the database until it is required by the application. Let's look at the steps NHibernate will use when our application fetches a movie from the database:

1. NHibernate fetches `Id`, `Name`, `Description`, `UnitPrice`, and `Director` data from the database for a `Movie` with a given `Id`. Notice that we do not load the `Actors` data. NHibernate uses the following SQL query:

```
select
    movie0_.Id as Id1_,
    movie0_.Name as Name1_,
    movie0_.Description as Descript4_1_,
    movie0_.UnitPrice as UnitPrice1_,
    movie0_.Director as Director1_
from Product movie0_
where
    movie0_.ProductType='Eg.Core.Movie' and
    movie0_.Id = 'a2c42861-9ff0-4546-85c1-9db700d6175e'
```

2. NHibernate creates an instance of the `Movie` object.

3. NHibernate sets the `Id`, `Name`, `Description`, `UnitPrice`, and `Director` properties of the `Movie` object with the data from the database.

4. NHibernate creates a special lazy loading object that implements `IList<ActorRole>`, and sets the `Actors` property of the `Movie` object. It is not a `List<ActorRoles>`, but rather a separate, NHibernate-specific implementation of the `IList<ActorRole>` interface.

5. NHibernate returns the `Movie` object to our application.

Then, suppose our application contains the following code. Remember, we haven't loaded any `ActorRole` data.

```
foreach (var actor in movie.Actors)
    Console.WriteLine(actor.Actor);
```

The first time we enumerate the collection, the lazy loading object is initialized. It loads the associated `ActorRole` data from the database with a query as shown:

```
SELECT
    actors0_.MovieId as MovieId1_,
    actors0_.Id as Id1_,
    actors0_.ActorIndex as ActorIndex1_,
    actors0_.Id as Id0_0_,
    actors0_.Actor as Actor0_0_,
    actors0_.Role as Role0_0_
FROM ActorRole actors0_
WHERE
    actors0_.MovieId= 'a2c42861-9ff0-4546-85c1-9db700d6175e'
```

We can disable lazy loading of a collection by adding the attribute `lazy="false"` to the `list` element of our mapping.

Lazy loading proxies

In other circumstances, NHibernate also supports lazy loading through the use of proxy objects. Suppose our `ActorRole` class had a reference back to `Movie`, like the following code:

```
public class ActorRole : Entity
{
    public virtual string Actor { get; set; }
    public virtual string Role { get; set; }
    public virtual Movie Movie { get; set; }
}
```

If we fetch an `ActorRole` from the database, NHibernate builds the `ActorRole` object as we would expect, but it only knows the `Id` of the associated `Movie`. It won't have all the data necessary to construct the entire `Movie` object. Instead, it will create a proxy object to represent the `Movie` and enable lazy loading.

We can, of course, access the `Id` of this `Movie` proxy without loading the movie's data. If we access any other property or method on the proxy, NHibernate will immediately fetch all the data for this movie. Loading this data is completely transparent to the application. The proxy object behaves exactly like a real `Movie` entity.

This proxy object is a subclass of `Movie`. In order to subclass `Movie` and intercept these calls to trigger lazy loading, NHibernate requires a few things from our `Movie` class.

- ► `Movie` cannot be a sealed class.
- ► `Movie` must have a protected or public constructor without parameters.
- ► All public members of `Movie` must be virtual. This includes methods.

NHibernate gives us several choices for the creation of these proxy objects. The traditional choice of NHibernate proxy framework is DynamicProxy, part of the Castle stack of projects. Additionally, NHibernate includes support for LinFu and Spring.NET, and allows you to build your own.

If we specify `lazy="false"` on the class element of our `Movie` mapping, we can disable this behavior. NHibernate will never create a proxy of `Movie`. This will force NHibernate to immediately load the associated movie's data any time it loads an `ActorRole`. Loading data unnecessarily like this can quickly kill the performance of your application, and should only be used in very specific, well-considered circumstances.

Collections

NHibernate supports several collection types. The most common types are as follows:

	Bag	**Set**		**List**	**Map**
Allows Duplicates	Yes	No		Yes	Keys must be unique. Values may be duplicated.
Order is significant	No	No		Yes	No
Type	IList	Iesi.Collections.ISet	IList	IDictionary

All collections may also use the `ICollection` type, or a custom collection type implementing `NHibernate.UserType.IUserCollectionType`. Only bag and set may be used in bidirectional relationships.

Bags

A bag collection allows duplicates, and implies that order is not important. Let's talk about a bag of `ActorRole` entities. The bag may contain actor role 1, actor role 2, actor role 3, actor role 1, actor role 4, and actor role 1. A typical bag mapping appears as shown in the following code:

```
<bag name="Actors">
  <key column="MovieId"/>
  <one-to-many class="ActorRole"/>
</bag>
```

The corresponding `Actors` property may be an `IList` or `ICollection`, or even an `IEnumerable`.

There is no way to identify an individual entry in the bag distinctly with a SQL statement. For example, there is no way to construct a SQL statement to delete just the second entry of actor role 1 from the bag. The SQL statement `delete from Actors where ActorRoleId='1'` will delete all three entries. When an entry is removed, and the updated bag is persisted, the rows representing the old bag contents are deleted, and then entire bag contents are reinserted. For especially large bags, this can create performance issues.

To counter this issue, NHibernate also provides an `idBag` where each entry in the bag is assigned an ID by one of the POID generators. This allows NHibernate to uniquely address each bag entry with queries like `delete from Actors where ActorRoleBagId='2'`.

The mapping for an `idBag` looks like the following code:

```
<idBag name="Actors">
  <collection-id column="ActorRoleBagId" type="Int64">
    <generator class="hilo" />
  </collection-id>
  <key column="MovieId"/>
  <one-to-many class="ActorRole"/>
</idBag>
```

Lists

A list collection also allows duplicates, but unlike a bag, the order is significant. Our list may contain actor role 1 at index 0, actor role 2 at index 1, actor role 3 at index 2, actor role 1 at index 3, actor role 4 at index 4, and actor role 1 at index 5. A typical list mapping looks like the following code:

```
<list name="Actors">
  <key column="MovieId" />
  <list-index column="ActorRoleIndex" />
  <one-to-many class="ActorRole"/>
</list>
```

The corresponding `Actors` property should be an `IList`. Because NHibernate maintains order with the `ActorRoleIndex` column, it can also uniquely identify individual list entries. However, because it maintains order, it also means that these indexes must be reset whenever the list contents change. For example, suppose we have a list of six actor roles and we remove the third actor role. NHibernate updates the `ActorRoleIndex` of each list entry.

Sets

A set collection does not allow duplicates, and the order of a set is not important. In my applications, this is the most common collection type. A set may contain actor role 1, actor role 3, actor role 2, and actor role 4. An attempt to add actor role 1 to the set again will fail. A typical set mapping appears as shown in the following code:

```
<set name="Actors">
  <key column="MovieId" />
  <one-to-many class="ActorRole"/>
</set>
```

The corresponding `Actors` property should be an `ISet` from `Iesi.Collections. dll`. Currently, NHibernate does not directly support the `ISet` interface included in the .NET Framework 4.

An attempt to add an item to an uninitialized lazy-loaded set collection will cause the set to be loaded from the database. This is necessary to ensure uniqueness in the collection. To ensure proper uniqueness in a set, you should override the `Equals` and `GetHashCode` methods, as shown in the next recipe.

Map

Map is another term that crossed over when NHibernate was ported from Java. In .NET, it's known as a dictionary. Each collection entry is a key or value pair. Keys must be unique. Values may not be unique.

```
<map name="Actors" >
  <key column="MovieId" />
  <map-key column="Role" type="string" />
  <element column="Actor" type="string"/>
</map>
```

As you may have guessed, the corresponding `Actors` property must be an `IDictionary<string, string>`, where the key is the name of the movie role, and the value is the actor's name. You are not limited to basic data types as shown here. NHibernate also allows entities for keys and values as shown in the following code:

```
<map name="SomeProperty">
  <key column="Id" />
  <index-many-to-many class="KeyEntity"/>
  <many-to-many class="ValueEntity" />
</map>
```

See also

- ▶ *Mapping a class with XML*
- ▶ *Creating class hierarchy Mappings*
- ▶ *Setting up a base entity class*
- ▶ *Bidirectional one-to-many class relationships*
- ▶ *Handling versioning and concurrency*
- ▶ *Creating mappings fluently*
- ▶ *Mapping with ConfORM*

Setting up a base entity class

In this recipe, I'll show you how to set up a base class to use for your entities.

Getting ready

Complete the previous three recipes.

How to do it...

1. In `Entity.cs`, use the following code for the `Entity` class:

```csharp
public abstract class Entity<TId>
{
  public virtual TId Id { get; protected set; }

  public override bool Equals(object obj)
  {
    return Equals(obj as Entity<TId>);
  }

  private static bool IsTransient(Entity<TId> obj)
  {
    return obj != null &&
           Equals(obj.Id, default(TId));
  }

  private Type GetUnproxiedType()
  {
    return GetType();
  }

  public virtual bool Equals(Entity<TId> other)
  {
    if (other == null)
      return false;

    if (ReferenceEquals(this, other))
      return true;

    if (!IsTransient(this) &&
        !IsTransient(other) &&
        Equals(Id, other.Id))
    {
      var otherType = other.GetUnproxiedType();
      var thisType = GetUnproxiedType();
      return thisType.IsAssignableFrom(otherType) ||
             otherType.IsAssignableFrom(thisType);
    }

    return false;
  }

  public override int GetHashCode()
```

```
    {
      if (Equals(Id, default(TId)))
        return base.GetHashCode();
      return Id.GetHashCode();
    }

}
```

2. To the same file, add an additional `Entity` class as shown in the following code:

```
public abstract class Entity : Entity<Guid>
{
}
```

How it works...

NHibernate relies on the `Equals` method to determine equality. The default behavior defined in `System.Object` uses reference equality for reference types, including classes. That is, `x.Equals(y)` is only true when x and y point to the same object instance. This default works well in most cases.

To support lazy loading, NHibernate uses proxy objects. As we learned in the previous recipe, these proxy objects are subclasses of the real entity class, with every member overridden to enable lazy loading.

This combination of proxy objects and the default `Equals` behavior can lead to subtle and unexpected bugs in your application. An application should not be aware of proxy objects, and therefore would expect that a proxy and a real instance representing the same entity would be equal. A `Product` instance with an ID of 8 should be equal to a different `Product` instance or `Product` proxy with an ID of 8. To handle this, we must override the default `Equals` behavior.

On our `Entity` base class, we override the `Equals` method to determine equality based on POID. In `Equals(Object obj)`, we simply call `Equals(Entity<TId> other)`, attempting to cast the object to `Entity`. If it can't be cast, `null` is passed instead.

If `other` is `null`, the objects are not equal. This serves two purposes. First, `x.Equals(null)` should always return `false`. Second, `someEntity.Equals(notAnEntity)` should also return `false`. Next, we compare references. Obviously, if two variables reference the same instance, they are equal. If `ReferenceEquals(this, other)` returns `true`, we return `true`.

Next, we compare the `Ids` to the default value to determine if the entities are transient. A **transient object** is an object that has not been persisted to the database. `default(TId)` returns whatever the default may be for `TId`. For Guids, the default is `Guid.Empty`. For strings and all other reference types, it's `null`. For numeric types, it's zero. If the `Id` property equals the default value, the entity is transient. If one or both entities are transient, we give up and return `false`.

If both entities are persisted, they both have POIDs. We can compare these POIDs to determine equality. If the POIDs don't match, we know for certain that the two entities are not equal. We return `false`.

Finally, we have one last check. We know that both entities are persistent, and they have the same `Id`. This doesn't quite prove that they're equal. It's perfectly legal for an `ActorRole` entity to have the same POID as a `Product` entity. Our last check is to compare the types. If one type is assignable to the other type, then we know for certain that the two are equal.

Suppose `other` is a proxy of `Product` representing a book entity, and `this` is an actual `Book` instance representing the same entity. `this.Equals(other)` should return `true` because they both represent the same entity. Unfortunately, `other.GetType()` will return the type `ProductProxy12398712938` instead of the type `Product`. As `typeof(ProductProxy12398712938).IsAssignableFrom(typeof(Book))` returns `false`, our `Equals` would fail on this case. However, we can use `other.GetUnproxiedType()` to reach down through the proxy layer and return the entity type. Because `typeof(Product).IsAssignableFrom(typeof(Book))` returns `true`, our `Equals` implementation works.

Because we've overridden `Equals`, we also need to override `GetHashCode` to satisfy the requirements of the .NET Framework. Specifically, if `x.Equals(y)`, then `x.GetHashCode()` and `y.GetHashCode()` should return the same value. The inverse is not necessarily true, however; `x` and `y` may share a hash code even when they're not equal. In our `Entity` base class, we simply use the hash code of `Id`, as this is the basis of our equality check.

There's more...

For more information on `Equals` and `GetHashCode`, refer to the MSDN documentation for these methods at `http://msdn.microsoft.com/en-us/library/system.object.aspx`.

See also

- *Mapping a class with XML*
- *Creating class hierarchy mappings*
- *Mapping a one-to-many relationship*
- *Bidirectional one-to-many class relationships*
- *Handling versioning and concurrency*
- *Creating mappings fluently*
- *Mapping with ConfORM*

Handling versioning and concurrency

For any multiuser transactional system, you must decide between optimistic and pessimistic concurrency to handle concurrent updates and versioning issues. In this recipe, I'll show you how to properly set up versioning and optimistic concurrency with NHibernate.

Getting ready

Complete all the previous recipes including *Setting up a base entity class*.

How to do it...

1. In the `Entity` base class, add a `Version` property, as shown in the following code:

```
public abstract class Entity<TId>
{
  public virtual TId Id { get; protected set; }
  protected virtual int Version { get; set; }

  public override bool Equals(object obj)
  {
    return Equals(obj as Entity<TId>);
  }
}
```

2. In the `Product` mapping, add the version element as shown in the following code:

```
<natural-id mutable="true">
  <property name="Name" not-null="true" />
</natural-id>
<version name="Version" />
<property name="Description" />
<property name="UnitPrice" not-null="true" />
```

3. In the `ActorRole` mapping, add the version element shown here:

```
<id name="Id">
  <generator class="guid.comb" />
</id>
<version name="Version" />
<property name="Actor" not-null="true" />
<property name="Role" not-null="true" />
```

How it works...

Suppose you have a database application with two users. User #1 and user #2 both pull up the same data on their screen and begin making changes. User #1 submits her changes back to the database. A few moments later, user #2 submits his changes. Without any concurrency checking, user #2's changes will silently overwrite user #1's changes. There are two possible ways to prevent this: optimistic and pessimistic concurrency.

Optimistic concurrency is the process where data is checked for changes before any update is executed. In this scenario, user #1 and user #2 both begin their changes. User #1 submits her changes. When user #2 submits his changes, his update will fail because the current data (after user #1's changes) doesn't match the data that user #2 originally read from the database.

In the example shown here, we use the version field to track changes to an entity. Update statements takes the following form:

```
UPDATE  Product
SET     Version = 2 /* @p0 */,
        Name = 'Junk' /* @p1 */,
        Description = 'Cool' /* @p2 */,
        UnitPrice = 100 /* @p3 */
WHERE   Id = '764de11e-1fd0-491e-8158-9db8015f9be5' /* @p4 */
        AND Version = 1 /* @p5 */
```

NHibernate checks that the version is the same value as when the entity was loaded from the database, and then increments the value. If the entity was already updated, the version field will not be 1, and no rows will be updated by this statement. NHibernate detects the zero rows affected and throws a `StaleStateException`, meaning the entity in memory is **stale**, or out of sync with the database.

There's more...

The alternative to optimistic concurrency is pessimistic locking. **Pessimistic locking** is the process where a user obtains an exclusive lock on the data while they are editing it. It takes the pessimistic view that, given the chance, user #2 will overwrite user #1's changes, so it's best not to let user #2 even look at the data. In this scenario, once user #1 pulls up the data, she has an exclusive lock. User #2 will not be able to read that data. His query will wait until user #1 drops the lock or the query times out. Inevitably, user #1 will take a phone call or step away for a cup of coffee while user #2 waits for access to the data. To implement this type of locking with NHibernate, your application must call `session.Lock` within a transaction.

Other methods of optimistic concurrency

In addition to integer version fields, NHibernate also allows you to use `DateTime`-based version fields. However, Micorosoft SQL Server has a `datetime` resolution of about three milliseconds. This may fail when two updates occur almost simultaneously. It's also possible to use SQL Server 2008's `DateTime2` data type, which has a resolution of 100 nanoseconds, or even SQL Server's `timestamp` data type for the version field.

NHibernate allows you to use the more traditional form of optimistic concurrency through the mapping attribute `optimistic-lock`. A simple example would look like the following code:

```
<class name="Product"
        dynamic-update="true"
        optimistic-lock="dirty">
```

In this case, changing a `Product` name from `Stuff` to `Junk` would generate SQL as shown in the following code:

```
UPDATE  Product
SET     Name = 'Junk' /* @p0 */
WHERE   Id = '741bd189-78b5-400c-97bd-9db80159ef79' /* @p1 */
        AND Name = 'Stuff' /* @p2 */
```

This ensures that the `Name` value hasn't been changed by another user because this user read the value. Another user may have changed other properties of this entity.

Another alternative is to set `optimistic-lock` to `all`. In this case, a `Product` update would generate SQL like this:

```
UPDATE  Product
SET     Name = 'Junk' /* @p0 */
WHERE   Id = 'd3458d6e-fa28-4dcb-9130-9db8015cc5bb' /* @p1 */
        AND Name = 'Stuff' /* @p2 */
        AND Description = 'Cool' /* @p3 */
        AND UnitPrice = 100 /* @p4 */
```

As you might have guessed, in this case, we check the values of all properties.

When `optimistic-lock` is set to `dirty`, `dynamic-update` must be `true`. Dynamic update simply means that the update statement only updates **dirty** properties, or properties with changed values, instead of explicitly setting all properties.

See also

- ▶ *Mapping a class with XML*
- ▶ *Creating class hierarchy mappings*
- ▶ *Mapping a one-to-many relationship*
- ▶ *Setting up a base entity class*

▶ *Creating mappings fluently*

▶ *Mapping with ConfORM*

Creating mappings fluently

The Fluent NHibernate project brings strongly-typed C# fluent syntax mappings to NHibernate. In this recipe, I'll show you how to map our `Eg.Core` model using Fluent NHibernate.

Getting ready

Download the Fluent NHibernate binary from the Fluent NHibernate website at `http://fluentnhibernate.org/downloads`. Select a version that's compatible with the specific build of NHibernate you are using. The Fluent NHibernate download also contains the necessary assemblies for NHibernate. You may wish to use them instead.

Extract `FluentNHibernate.dll` from the downloaded ZIP file to the `Lib` folder.

Complete the previous `Eg.Core` model and mapping recipes.

How to do it...

1. Create a new class library project named `Eg.FluentMappings`.

2. Add a reference to `FluentNHibernate.dll`.

3. Copy `Entity.cs`, `Product.cs`, `Book.cs`, `Movie.cs`, and `ActorRole.cs` from `Eg.Core` to the new `Eg.FluentMappings`.

4. In the copied model, change the namespaces from `Eg.Core` to `Eg.FluentMappings`.

5. In `Entity.cs`, change the `Version` property from `protected` to `public`.

6. Add a new folder named `Mappings`.

7. Create a new class named `ProductMapping` with the following code:

```
using FluentNHibernate.Mapping;

namespace Eg.FluentMappings.Mappings
{
  public class ProductMapping : ClassMap<Product>
  {
    public ProductMapping()
    {
      Id(p => p.Id)
        .GeneratedBy.GuidComb();
```

```
            DiscriminateSubClassesOnColumn("ProductType");
            Version(p => p.Version);
            NaturalId()
                .Not.ReadOnly()
                .Property(p => p.Name);
            Map(p => p.Description);
            Map(p => p.UnitPrice)
                .Not.Nullable();
        }

    }
}
```

8. Create a new class named `BookMapping` with the following code:

```
using FluentNHibernate.Mapping;

namespace Eg.FluentMappings.Mappings
{
    public class BookMapping : SubclassMap<Book>
    {

        public BookMapping()
        {
            Map(p => p.Author);
            Map(p => p.ISBN);
        }

    }
}
```

9. Create a new class named `MovieMapping` with the following code:

```
using FluentNHibernate.Mapping;

namespace Eg.FluentMappings.Mappings
{
    public class MovieMapping : SubclassMap<Movie>
    {

        public MovieMapping()
        {
            Map(m => m.Director);
            HasMany(m => m.Actors)
                .KeyColumn("MovieId")
                .AsList(l => l.Column("ActorIndex"));
        }

    }
}
```

10. Create a new class named `ActorRole` with the following code:

```
using FluentNHibernate.Mapping;

namespace Eg.FluentMappings.Mappings
{
  public class ActorRoleMapping : ClassMap<ActorRole>
  {

    public ActorRoleMapping()
    {
      Id(ar => ar.Id)
        .GeneratedBy.GuidComb();
      Version(ar => ar.Version);
      Map(ar => ar.Actor)
        .Not.Nullable();
      Map(ar => ar.Role)
        .Not.Nullable();
    }

  }
}
```

How it works...

Fluent NHibernate provides two methods for mappings: Fluent mapping syntax and auto-mapping. In this recipe, we use the Fluent mapping syntax. Each entity class has a corresponding mapping class.

Because the mapping syntax requires class members to be accessible, we must change the `Version` property from `protected` to `public`. Fluent NHibernate also includes some tricks to work around this issue. They're explained fully in the wiki at http://wiki.fluentnhibernate.org/Fluent_mapping_private_properties.

Mappings for root classes are inherited from `ClassMap`, and subclasses in a class hierarchy inherit from `SubclassMap`. By default, Fluent NHibernate creates a table-per-subclass hierarchy. To use a table-per-class hierarchy instead, we specify `DiscriminateSubClassesOnColumn` in `Product`. Fluent NHibernate doesn't support table-per-concrete-class hierarchies.

When mapping the natural ID of `Product`, we specify `.Not.ReadOnly()`. This is the same as setting `mutable="true"` in the XML mapping.

Properties are mapped using the `Map()` method, which is equivalent to the `property` element in XML mappings.

One-to-many collections are mapped using the `HasMany()` method, followed by `AsMap()`, `AsBag()`, `AsSet()`, or `AsList()`. `AsList` uses the `Column()` method to specify a column name for the list index.

See also

- ▶ *Mapping a class with XML*
- ▶ *Creating class hierarchy mappings*
- ▶ *Mapping a one-to-many relationship*
- ▶ *Setting up a base entity class*
- ▶ *Bidirectional one-to-many class relationships*
- ▶ *Handling versioning and concurrency*
- ▶ *Creating mappings fluently*
- ▶ *Mapping with ConfORM*

Mapping with ConfORM

The ConfORM project brings convention-based mappings to NHibernate. In this recipe, I'll show you how to map your model using ConfORM conventions.

Getting ready

1. Check out the ConfORM source code from Google Code at `http://code.google.com/p/codeconform/source/checkout`.
2. Build the ConfORM project.
3. Complete the previous `Eg.Core` model and mapping recipes.

How to do it...

1. Create a new console project named `Eg.ConfORMMappings`.
2. Add references to the `Eg.Core` model project, `ConfORM.dll` and `ConfORM.Shop.dll`.
3. In `Eg.Core.Entity`, make the `Version` property public.
4. In `Program.cs`, add the following using statements to the beginning of the file:

```
using System;
using System.IO;
using System.Linq;
using System.Xml;
using System.Xml.Serialization;
```

```
using ConfOrm;
using ConfOrm.NH;
using ConfOrm.Patterns;
using ConfOrm.Shop.CoolNaming;
using Eg.Core;
using NHibernate;
using NHibernate.Cfg.MappingSchema;
```

5. Add the following `GetMapping` function to the `Program` class:

```
private static HbmMapping GetMapping()
{
  var orm = new ObjectRelationalMapper();
  var mapper = new Mapper(orm,
    new CoolPatternsAppliersHolder(orm));

  orm.TablePerClassHierarchy<Product>();
  orm.TablePerClass<ActorRole>();

  orm.Patterns.PoidStrategies.Add(
    new GuidOptimizedPoidPattern());
  orm.VersionProperty<Entity>(x => x.Version);
  orm.NaturalId<Product>(p => p.Name);

  orm.Cascade<Movie, ActorRole>(
    Cascade.All | Cascade.DeleteOrphans);

  mapper.AddPropertyPattern(mi =>
    mi.GetPropertyOrFieldType() == typeof(Decimal) &&
    mi.Name.Contains("Price"),
    pm => pm.Type(NHibernateUtil.Currency));

  mapper.AddPropertyPattern(mi =>
    orm.IsRootEntity(mi.DeclaringType) &&
    !"Description".Equals(mi.Name),
    pm => pm.NotNullable(true));

  mapper.Subclass<Movie>(cm =>
    cm.List(movie => movie.Actors,
    colm => colm.Index(
      lim => lim.Column("ActorIndex")), m => { }));

  var domainClasses = typeof(Entity).Assembly.GetTypes()
    .Where(t => typeof(Entity).IsAssignableFrom(t));

  return mapper.CompileMappingFor(domainClasses);
}
```

6. Add the following `WriteXmlMapping` function:

```
private static void WriteXmlMapping(HbmMapping hbmMapping)
{
   var document = Serialize(hbmMapping);
   File.WriteAllText("WholeDomain.hbm.xml", document);
}
```

7. Add the following `Serialize` function:

```
private static string Serialize(HbmMapping hbmElement)
{
   var setting = new XmlWriterSettings { Indent = true };
   var serializer = new XmlSerializer(typeof(HbmMapping));
   using (var memStream = new MemoryStream(2048))
   using (var xmlWriter = XmlWriter.Create(memStream, setting))
   {
      serializer.Serialize(xmlWriter, hbmElement);
      memStream.Flush();
      memStream.Position = 0;
      using (var sr = new StreamReader(memStream))
      {
         return sr.ReadToEnd();
      }
   }
}
```

8. In the `static void Main` method, add the following line:

```
WriteXmlMapping(GetMapping());
```

9. Build and run your application.

10. Browse to the application's `bin\Debug` folder and examine the `WholeDomain.hbm.xml` file. You should find the following familiar mapping:

```
<?xml version="1.0" encoding="utf-8"?>

<hibernate-mapping xmlns:xsi="http://www.w3.org/2001/XMLSchema-
instance" xmlns:xsd="http://www.w3.org/2001/XMLSchema"
namespace="Eg.Core" assembly="Eg.Core" xmlns="urn:nhibernate-
mapping-2.2">

   <class name="Product">
     <id name="Id" type="Guid">
       <generator class="guid.comb" />
     </id>
     <discriminator />
     <natural-id>
       <property name="Name" not-null="true" />
```

```
      </natural-id>
      <version name="Version" />
      <property name="Description" />
      <property name="UnitPrice" type="Currency"
        not-null="true" />
    </class>
    <class name="ActorRole">
      <id name="Id" type="Guid">
        <generator class="guid.comb" />
      </id>
      <version name="Version" />
      <property name="Actor" not-null="true" />
      <property name="Role" not-null="true" />
    </class>
    <subclass name="Book" extends="Product">
      <property name="ISBN" />
      <property name="Author" />
    </subclass>
    <subclass name="Movie" extends="Product">
      <property name="Director" />
      <list name="Actors" cascade="all,delete-orphan">
        <key column="MovieId" />
        <list-index column="ActorIndex" />
        <one-to-many class="ActorRole" />
      </list>
    </subclass>
  </hibernate-mapping>
```

How it works...

With a standard NHibernate application, NHibernate takes each XML mapping and deserializes it into an `HbmMapping` object, then adds the `HbmMapping` object to the NHibernate configuration, as shown in the next diagram:

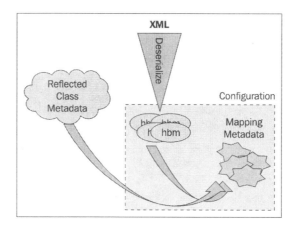

With ConfORM, we skip this deserialization step. The ConfORM mapper outputs an `HbmMapping` object built from our conventions, ready to be added to the configuration.

ConfORM uses conventions and patterns to build a mapping directly from the model. In addition to ConfORM's default patterns, we use a few extra conventions in our model.

1. We begin by specifying our `Product` class hierarchy, which includes `Books` and `Movies`. We also add our `ActorRole` entity class individually.

2. We use the `GuidOptimizedPoidPattern` to find all `Guid` properties named `Id`, and map them as POIDs with the `guid.comb` generator.

3. References from `Movie` to `ActorRole`, such as our `Actors` collection, should use `cascade="all-delete-orphan"`. We set this up with the following bit of code:

   ```
   orm.Cascade<Movie, ActorRole>(
      Cascade.All | Cascade.DeleteOrphans);
   ```

4. Next, we configure a few conventions. All `decimal` properties with the word `Price` in the property name should be mapped as `type="currency"`. We use the following code:

   ```
   mapper.AddPropertyPattern(mi =>
      mi.GetPropertyOrFieldType() == typeof(Decimal) &&
      mi.Name.Contains("Price"),
      pm => pm.Type(NHibernateUtil.Currency));
   ```

5. All properties of root entities, except those named `Description`, are mapped with `not-null="true"`. Remember, we're using the table-per-class hierarchy strategy, so our subclasses shouldn't have `not-null` properties. The code we use is as follows:

```
mapper.AddPropertyPattern(mi =>
    orm.IsRootEntity(mi.DeclaringType) &&
    !"Description".Equals(mi.Name),
    pm => pm.NotNullable(true));
```

6. Finally, we map our `Actors` list in `Movies`, setting the list index column name to `ActorIndex`. We use the following code:

```
mapper.Subclass<Movie>(cm =>
    cm.List(movie => movie.Actors,
    colm => colm.Index(
        lim => lim.Column("ActorIndex")), m => { }));
```

7. The last step in building our `HbmMapping` object is to call `CompileMappingFor`, passing in every `Entity` type, as shown in the following code:

```
var domainClasses = typeof(Entity).Assembly.GetTypes()
    .Where(t => typeof(Entity).IsAssignableFrom(t));

return mapper.CompileMappingFor(domainClasses);
```

8. The resulting mapping object is equivalent to XML mapping contained in `WholeDomain.hbm.xml`.

See also

- ▸ *Mapping a class with XML*
- ▸ *Creating class hierarchy mappings*
- ▸ *Mapping a one-to-many relationship*
- ▸ *Setting up a base entity class*
- ▸ *Bidirectional one-to-many class relationships*
- ▸ *Handling versioning and concurrency*
- ▸ *Creating mappings fluently*

Bidirectional one-to-many class relationships

In some cases, it's useful to have a bidirectional relationship between entities. In this recipe, I'll show you how to set up a bidirectional one-to-many relationship between two entity classes.

How to do it...

1. Create an empty class library project named `ManualRelationships`.

2. Add a reference to `Iesi.Collections.dll` in the `Lib` folder.

3. Add the following `Order` class:

```
public class Order
{
  public virtual Guid Id { get; protected set; }

  public Order()
  {
    _items = new HashedSet<OrderItem>();
  }

  private ISet<OrderItem> _items;
  public virtual IEnumerable<OrderItem> Items
  {
    get
    {
      return _items;
    }
  }

  public virtual bool AddItem(OrderItem newItem)
  {
    if (newItem != null && _items.Add(newItem))
    {
      newItem.SetOrder(this);
      return true;
    }
    return false;
  }

  public virtual bool RemoveItem(
    OrderItem itemToRemove)
  {
    if (itemToRemove != null &&
      _items.Remove(itemToRemove))
    {
      itemToRemove.SetOrder(null);
      return true;
    }
```

```
      return false;
    }
  }
```

4. Add the following mapping as an embedded resource named `Order.hbm.xml`:

```xml
<?xml version="1.0" encoding="utf-8" ?>
<hibernate-mapping xmlns="urn:nhibernate-mapping-2.2"
    assembly="ManualRelationships"
    namespace="ManualRelationships">
  <class name="Order" table="`Order`">
    <id name="Id">
      <generator class="guid.comb" />
    </id>
    <set name="Items"
        cascade="all-delete-orphan"
        inverse="true"
        access="field.camelcase-underscore">
      <key column="OrderId" />
      <one-to-many class="OrderItem"/>
    </set>
  </class>
</hibernate-mapping>
```

5. Add the following `OrderItem` class:

```csharp
public class OrderItem
{
  public virtual Guid Id { get; protected set; }
  public virtual Order Order { get; protected set; }
  public virtual void SetOrder(Order newOrder)
  {
    var prevOrder = Order;
    if (newOrder == prevOrder)
      return;
    Order = newOrder;
    if (prevOrder != null)
      prevOrder.RemoveItem(this);
    if (newOrder != null)
      newOrder.AddItem(this);

  }
}
```

6. Add the following mapping as an embedded resource named `OrderItem.hbm.xml`:

```xml
<?xml version="1.0" encoding="utf-8" ?>
<hibernate-mapping xmlns="urn:nhibernate-mapping-2.2"
    assembly="ManualRelationships"
    namespace="ManualRelationships">
  <class name="OrderItem">
    <id name="Id">
      <generator class="guid.comb" />
    </id>
    <many-to-one name="Order" column="OrderId" />
  </class>
</hibernate-mapping>
```

How it works...

Object relational mappers (ORM) are designed to overcome the impedance mismatch between the object model in the application and the relational model in the database. This mismatch is especially evident when representing a bidirectional one-to-many relationship between entities. In the relational model, this bidirectional relationship is represented by a single foreign key. In the object model, the parent entity has a collection of children, and each child has a reference to its parent.

To work around this mismatch, NHibernate ignores one side of the bidirectional relationship. The foreign key in the database is populated based on either the `OrderItems` reference to the `Order` or the `Orders` collection of `OrderItems`, but not both. We determine which end of the relationship controls the foreign key using the `inverse` attribute on the collection. By default, the `Order` controls the foreign key. Saving a new `Order` with one `OrderItem` will result in the following three SQL statements:

```sql
INSERT INTO "Order" (Id) VALUES (@p0)
INSERT INTO OrderItem (Id) VALUES (@p0)
UPDATE OrderItem SET OrderId = @p0 WHERE Id = @p1
```

When we specify `inverse="true"`, the `OrderItem` controls the foreign key. This is preferable because it eliminates the extra UPDATE statement, resulting in the following two SQL statements:

```sql
INSERT INTO "Order" (Id) VALUES (@p0)
INSERT INTO OrderItem (OrderId, Id) VALUES (@p0, @p1)
```

We are responsible for keeping both sides of our two-way relationship in sync. In a normal class, we would add code in the property setter or the collection's `add` or `remove` methods to update the other end of the relationship automatically. NHibernate, however, throws exceptions when an object is manipulated while NHibernate is initializing it.

For this reason, it's suggested that we prevent direct manipulation of either end of the relationship, and instead use methods specifically written for this purpose, as we've done here with `AddItem`, `RemoveItem`, and `SetOrder`. Notice that we've mapped a set, which implies that order is not significant, and that duplicates are not allowed.

There's more...

Notice the use of backticks in our table name from the `Order` mapping as follows:

```
<class name="Order" table="`Order`">
```

In Microsoft SQL Server, `Order` is a keyword. If we want to use it as an identifier, a table name in this case, NHibernate will need to put quotes around it. The backticks tell NHibernate to surround the identifier with whatever character may be appropriate for the database you're using.

Mappings enumerations

An improperly mapped enumeration can lead to unnecessary updates. In this recipe, I'll show you how to map an enumeration property to a string field.

How to do it...

1. Create a new class library project named `MappingEnums`.

2. Add the following `AccountTypes` enumeration:

```
public enum AccountTypes
{
    Consumer,
    Business,
    Corporate,
    NonProfit
}
```

3. Add the following Account class:

```
public class Account
{
    public virtual Guid Id { get; set; }
    public virtual AccountTypes AcctType { get; set; }
    public virtual string Number { get; set; }
    public virtual string Name { get; set; }
}
```

4. Add an NHibernate mapping document with the following class mapping:

```xml
<class name="Account">
  <id name="Id">
    <generator class="guid.comb" />
  </id>
  <natural-id>
    <property name="Number" not-null="true"  />
  </natural-id>
  <property name="Name" not-null="true" />
  <property name="AcctType" not-null="true" />
</class>
```

5. On the `property` element for `AcctType`, add a `type` attribute with the following value:

```
NHibernate.Type.EnumStringType`1[[MappingEnums.AccountTypes,
MappingEnums]], NHibernate
```

6. Set your mapping as an embedded resource.

How it works...

By default, NHibernate will map an enumeration to a numeric field based on the enumeration's underlying type, typically an `int`. For example, if we set `AcctType` to `AccountTypes.Corporate`, the `AcctType` database field would hold the integer 2. This has one significant drawback. An integer value by itself doesn't describe the business meaning of the data.

One solution is to create a lookup table containing each enumeration value alongside a description, but this must be maintained in perfect sync with the application code because otherwise it can lead to serious versioning issues. Simply rearranging the order of the enumeration in code from one release to the next can have disastrous effects.

Another solution, the one shown here, is to store the name of the enumeration value in a string field. For example, if we set `AcctType` to `AccountTypes.Corporate`, the `AcctType` database field would hold the string value `Corporate`.

By specifying a `type` attribute for `AcctType`, we tell NHibernate to use a custom class for conversion between .NET types and the database. NHibernate includes `EnumStringType<T>` to override the conversion of enumeration values to database values so that the string name is stored, not the numeric value.

The `type` value `NHibernate.Type.EnumStringType`1[[MappingEnums.AccountTypes, MappingEnums]], NHibernate` is the assembly qualified name for `NHibernate.Type.EnumStringType<AccountType>`.

Creating class components

There are cases where a set of properties are used repeatedly. These properties may even have their own business logic, but they don't represent an entity in your application. They are value objects. In this recipe, I'll show you how we can separate these properties and business logic into a component class without creating a separate entity.

How to do it...

1. Create a new class library project named `ComponentExamples`.

2. Add an `Address` class with the following properties:
   ```
   public virtual string Lines { get; set; }
   public virtual string City { get; set; }
   public virtual string State { get; set; }
   public virtual string ZipCode { get; set; }
   ```

3. Add a `customer` class with the following properties:
   ```
   public virtual string Name { get; set; }
   public virtual Address BillingAddress { get; set; }
   public virtual Address ShippingAddress { get; set; }
   ```

4. Add the following mapping document:
   ```xml
   <?xml version="1.0" encoding="utf-8" ?>
   <hibernate-mapping xmlns="urn:nhibernate-mapping-2.2"
       assembly="ComponentExamples"
       namespace="ComponentExamples">
     <class name="Customer">
       <id name="Id">
         <generator class="guid.comb" />
       </id>
       <property name="Name" not-null="true" />
       <component name="BillingAddress" class="Address">
         <property name="Lines" not-null="true" />
         <property name="City" not-null="true" />
         <property name="State" not-null="true" />
         <property name ="ZipCode" not-null="true" />
       </component>
       <component name="ShippingAddress" class="Address">
         <property name="Lines" not-null="true"
                   column="ShippingLines" />
         <property name="City" not-null="true"
   ```

```
                      column="ShippingCity" />
        <property name="State" not-null="true"
                      column="ShippingState" />
        <property name ="ZipCode" not-null="true"
                      column="ShippingZipCode" />
      </component>
    </class>
  </hibernate-mapping>
```

How it works...

In this recipe, we can use the `Address` component class throughout our model without the overhead of maintaining a separate entity. We've used it in our `Customer` class for both billing and shipping address. The resulting database table will appear as shown in the next screenshot:

Our model looks like this:

We get all the reuse benefits without the database work. The **Address** fields are included in every query for **Customer**, and are automatically loaded.

2
Configuration and Schema

In this chapter, we will cover the following topics:

- Configuring NHibernate with `App.config`
- Configuring NHibernate with `hibernate.cfg.xml`
- Configuring NHibernate with code
- Configuring NHibernate with Fluent NHibernate
- Configuring NHibernate using ConfORM Mappings
- Configuring NHibernate logging
- Reducing application startup time
- Generating the database
- Scripting the database
- Using NHibernate Schema Tool

Introduction

NHibernate provides an incredible number of configuration options and settings. The recipes in this chapter demonstrate several methods for configuring NHibernate and generating the necessary database schema.

Configuring NHibernate with App.config

NHibernate offers several methods for configuration and a number of configuration settings.

In this recipe, I'll show you how to configure NHibernate using your application's configuration file with a minimal number of settings to get your application up and running quickly. This recipe also forms the base for several other recipes in this chapter.

Getting ready

1. Complete the `Eg.Core` model and mapping recipes from *Chapter 1, Models and Mappings*.

2. Add a console application project to your solution called `ConfigByAppConfig`.

3. Set it as the **Startup** project for your solution.

4. In the `ConfigByAppconfig` project, add references to `NHibernate.dll` and `NHibernate.ByteCode.Castle.dll` from the `Lib` folder.

5. In `ConfigByAppconfig`, add a reference to the `Eg.Core` project.

6. Add an `App.config` file to your console project.

How to do it...

1. Open the `App.config` file.

2. Declare a section for the NHibernate configuration, as shown here:

```
<configSections>
    <section name="hibernate-configuration" type="NHibernate.Cfg.
ConfigurationSectionHandler, NHibernate"/>
</configSections>
```

3. Add a `connectionStrings` section with a connection string:

```
<connectionStrings>
    <add name="db" connectionString="Server=.\SQLExpress;
Database=NHCookbook; Trusted_Connection=SSPI"/>
</connectionStrings>
```

4. Add your `hibernate-configuration` section:

```
<hibernate-configuration
xmlns="urn:nhibernate-configuration-2.2">
<session-factory>
    <property name="proxyfactory.factory_class">
    NHibernate.ByteCode.Castle.ProxyFactoryFactory, NHibernate.
    ByteCode.Castle
    </property>
    <property name="dialect">
    NHibernate.Dialect.MsSql2008Dialect, NHibernate
    </property>
```

```
        <property name="connection.connection_string_name">
        db
          </property>
        <property name="adonet.batch_size">
        100
          </property>
        <mapping assembly="Eg.Core"/>
      </session-factory>
      </hibernate-configuration>>
```

5. Your completed `App.config` file should look like this:

```xml
<?xml version="1.0" encoding="utf-8" ?>
<configuration>

  <configSections>
    <section name="hibernate-configuration"
        type="NHibernate.Cfg.ConfigurationSectionHandler,
NHibernate"/>
  </configSections>
   <connectionStrings>
    <add name="db" connectionString="Server=.\SQLExpress;
Database=NHCookbook; Trusted_Connection=SSPI"/>
   </connectionStrings>
   <hibernate-configuration
    xmlns="urn:nhibernate-configuration-2.2">
    <session-factory>
      <property name="proxyfactory.factory_class">
        NHibernate.ByteCode.Castle.ProxyFactoryFactory,
        NHibernate.ByteCode.Castle
      </property>
      <property name="dialect">
        NHibernate.Dialect.MsSql2008Dialect,
        NHibernate
      </property>
      <property name="connection.connection_string_name">
        db
      </property>
      <property name="adonet.batch_size">
        100
      </property>
      <mapping assembly="Eg.Core"/>
    </session-factory>
```

```
          </hibernate-configuration>
      </configuration>
```

6. Open `Program.cs` and add `using NHibernate.Cfg;` to the beginning of the file.

7. In your `Main` function, add the following code to configure NHibernate:

```
var nhConfig = new Configuration().Configure();
var sessionFactory = nhConfig.BuildSessionFactory();
Console.WriteLine("NHibernate Configured!");
Console.ReadKey();
```

8. Build and run your application. You will see the text **NHibernate Configured!**.

How it works...

The connection string we've defined points to the NHCookbook database running under the local Microsoft SQL Server Express 2008.

Next, we define a few properties that tell NHibernate how to behave. `proxyfactory.factory_class` specifies the proxy framework we'll use. In this case, we're using Castle's DynamicProxy2. Out of the box, NHibernate also supports the LinFu and Spring frameworks.

The `dialect` property specifies a `dialect` class that NHibernate uses to build SQL syntax specific to a **Relational Database Management System (RDBMS)**. We're using the Microsoft SQL 2008 dialect. Additionally, most dialects set intelligent defaults for other NHibernate properties, such as `connection.driver_class`.

The `connection.connection_string_name` property references our connection string named db. We can name the connection string anything we like, as long as this property matches the connection string's name.

By default, NHibernate will send a single SQL statement and wait for a response from the database. When we set the `adonet.batch_size` property to 100, NHibernate will group up to 100 SQL INSERT, UPDATE, and DELETE statements in a single ADO.NET command and send the whole batch at once. In effect, the work of 100 round trips to the database is combined in one. Because a roundtrip to the database is, at best, an out-of-process call, and at worst, a trip through the network or even the Internet, this improves performance significantly. Batching is currently supported when using the `SqlClientDriver` for Microsoft SQL Server or the `OracleDataClientDriver` for Oracle.

The `mappings` element defines where NHibernate will search for our mappings. In this case, it will search the `Eg.Core` assembly for embedded resources ending in `.hbm.xml`.

There's more...

There are several key components to an NHibernate application, as shown in this diagram:

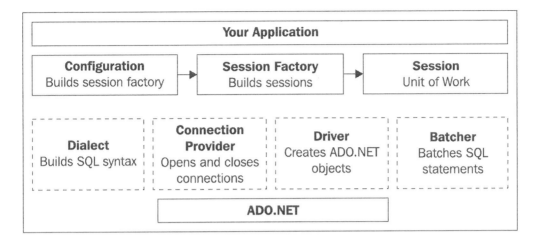

On startup, an NHibernate application builds a `Configuration` object. In this recipe, we build the configuration from settings in the `App.config` file. The `Configuration` object is responsible for loading mappings, reflecting the model for additional information, building the mapping metadata, and finally building a session factory. Building the session factory is an expensive operation, and should be done only once in the life of an application.

The **session factory** is responsible for building sessions. Unlike a session factory, building a session is very cheap.

A **session** represents a unit of work in the application. *Martin Fowler* defines a unit of work as an object that maintains a list of objects affected by a business transaction and coordinates the writing out of changes and the resolution of concurrency problems. An NHibernate session tracks changes to entities and writes those changes back to the database all at once. In NHibernate, this process of waiting to write to the database all at once is called **transactional write-behind**. In addition, the session is the entry point to much of the NHibernate API. More information about the unit of work pattern is available at `http://martinfowler.com/eaaCatalog/unitOfWork.html` and in *Fowler's* book, *Patterns of Enterprise Application Architecture.*

The session acts as an intermediary between our application and several key NHibernate components. A typical application will not interact with these components directly, but understanding them is critical to understanding NHibernate.

A **dialect** is used to build SQL syntax for a specific RDBMS. For example, in Microsoft SQL Server, we begin a select statement with `SELECT TOP 20` to specify a maximum result set size. Only 20 rows will be returned. To do the same in SQLite, we append `LIMIT 20` to the end of the select statement. Each dialect provides the necessary SQL syntax string fragments and other information to build correct SQL strings for the chosen RDBMS.

The **driver** is responsible for building the batcher, creating `IDbConnection` and `IDbCommand` objects, and preparing those commands.

The connection provider is simply responsible for opening and closing database connections.

The batcher manages the batch of commands to be sent to the database and the resulting data readers. Currently, only the `SqlClientDriver` and `OracleDataDriver` support batching. Those drivers that don't support batching provide a `NonBatchingBatcher` to manage `IDbCommands` and `IDataReaders` and simulate the existence of a single logical batch of commands.

NHibernate properties

Here are some of the commonly used NHibernate properties:

Property name	Description
`connection.provider`	Provider class to open and close database connections.
`connection.driver_class`	This is specific to the RDBMS used, and is typically set by the dialect.
`connection.connection_string`	Database connection string.
`connection.connection_string_name`	Name of connection string in `<connectionStrings>` element.
`connection.isolation`	Transaction isolation level.
`dialect`	Required. A class to build RDBMS-specific SQL strings. Typically, this is one of the many dialects from the `NHibernate.Dialect` namespace.
`show_sql`	Boolean value. Set to true to log all SQL statements to `Console.Out`. Alternatively, log4net may be used to log to other locations.
`current_session_context_class`	Class to manage contextual sessions. This is covered in depth in *Chapter 3*.
`query.substitutions`	Comma-separated list of translations to perform on query strings. For example, True=1, Yes=1, False=0, No=0.
`sql_exception_converter`	Class to convert RDBMS-specific ADO.NET Exceptions to custom exceptions.
`prepare_sql`	Boolean value. Prepares SQL statements and caches the execution plan for the duration of the database connection.
`command_timeout`	Number of seconds to wait for a SQL command to complete before timing out.
`adonet.batch_size`	Number of SQL commands to send at once before waiting for a response from the database.

Property name	Description
`generate_statistics`	Enables tracking of some statistical information, such as the number of queries executed and entities loaded.
`proxyfactory.factory_class`	Required. Specifies a factory class for our chosen proxy framework, in this case Castle DynamicProxy2.
`format_sql`	Adds line endings for easier-to-read SQL statements.

Additional information about each of these settings is available in the reference documentation at `http://www.nhforge.org/doc/nh/en/index.html`.

Dialects and drivers

Many dialects set other NHibernate properties to sensible default values, including, in most cases, the `connection.driver_class`. NHibernate includes the following dialects in the `NHibernate.Dialect` namespace and drivers in the `NHibernate.Driver` namespace:

RDBMS	Dialect(s)	Driver(s)
Microsoft SQL Server	`MsSql2008Dialect`	`SqlClientDriver`
	`MsSql2005Dialect`	`SqlServerCEDriver`
	`MsSql2000Dialect`	
	`MsSql7Dialect`	
	`MsSqlCEDialect`	
Oracle	`Oracle10gDialect`	`OracleClientDriver`
	`Oracle9iDialect`	`OracleDataClientDriver`
	`Oracle8iDialect`	`OracleLiteDataDriver`
	`OracleLiteDialect`	
MySql	`MySQLDialect`	`MySqlDataDriver`
	`MySQL5Dialect`	
PostgreSQL	`PostGreSQLDialect`	`NpgsqlDriver`
	`PostGreSQL81Dialect`	
	`PostGreSQL82Dialect`	
DB2	`DB2Dialect`	`DB2Driver`
	`Db2400Dialect`	`DB2400Driver`

RDBMS	Dialect(s)	Driver(s)
Informix	InformixDialect	IfxDriver
	InformixDialect0940	
	InformixDialect1000	
Sybase	SybaseDialect	SybaseClientDriver
	SybaseASA10Dialect	ASAClientDriver
	SybaseASA9Dialect	ASA10ClientDriver
	Sybase11Dialect	SybaseAdoNet12ClientDriver
	SybaseAdoNet12Dialect	
	SybaseAnywhereDialect	
Firebird	FirebirdDialect	FirebirdDriver
		FirebirdClientDriver
SQLite	SQLiteDialect	SQLiteDriver
		SQLite20Driver
Ingres	IngresDialect	IngresDriver

See also

- ▸ *Configuring NHibernate with* hibernate.cfg.xml
- ▸ *Configuring NHibernate with code*
- ▸ *Configuring NHibernate with Fluent NHibernate*
- ▸ *Configuring NHibernate using ConfORM Mappings*

Configuring NHibernate with hibernate.cfg.xml

Another common method for configuring NHibernate uses a separate xml configuration file. In this recipe, I'll show you how to configure NHibernate using hibernate.cfg.xml to provide an identical configuration to the previous recipe.

Getting ready

1. Complete the Eg.Core model and mapping recipes from *Chapter 1*.
2. Add a console application project to your solution named ConfigByXML.
3. Set it as the **Startup** project for your solution.

4. In the `ConfigByXML` project, add references to `NHibernate.dll` and `NHibernate.ByteCode.Castle.dll` in the `Lib` folder.

5. In `ConfigByXML`, add a reference to the `Eg.Core` project.

How to do it...

1. Add an `App.config` file with this configuration:

```xml
<?xml version="1.0" encoding="utf-8" ?>
<configuration>

  <connectionStrings>
    <add name="db" connectionString="Server=.\SQLExpress;
Database=NHCookbook; Trusted_Connection=SSPI"/>
  </connectionStrings>
</configuration>
```

2. Add an XML file named `hibernate.cfg.xml` with this XML:

```xml
<?xml version="1.0" encoding="utf-8" ?>
<hibernate-configuration
  xmlns="urn:nhibernate-configuration-2.2">
  <session-factory>
    <property name="proxyfactory.factory_class">
      NHibernate.ByteCode.Castle.ProxyFactoryFactory,
      NHibernate.ByteCode.Castle
    </property>
    <property name="dialect">
      NHibernate.Dialect.MsSql2008Dialect,
      NHibernate
    </property>
    <property name="connection.connection_string_name">
      db
    </property>
    <property name="adonet.batch_size">
      100
    </property>
    <mapping assembly="Eg.Core"/>
  </session-factory>
</hibernate-configuration>
```

3. On the **Solution Explorer** tab, right-click on **hibernate.cfg.xml** and select **Properties**.

4. Change **Copy to Output Directory** from **Do not copy** to **Copy if newer**.

5. Open `Program.cs` and add `using NHibernate.Cfg;`.

6. In your `Main` function, add the following code to configure NHibernate:

```
var nhConfig = new Configuration().Configure();
var sessionFactory = nhConfig.BuildSessionFactory();
Console.WriteLine("NHibernate Configured!");
Console.ReadKey();
```

7. Build and run your application. You will see the text **NHibernate Configured!**.

How it works...

This recipe works in the same way as the previous recipe. We still use the db connection string defined in the `App.config`. However, in this recipe, we've moved the `hibernate-configuration` element from the `App.config` file to `hibernate.cfg.xml`. Just as with the mappings, we get full IntelliSense from the schema file we added to the solution back in *Chapter 1*. We change **Copy to Output Directory** to ensure that our `hibernate.cfg.xml` file is copied with the build output.

There's more...

By default, NHibernate looks for its configuration in the `hibernate.cfg.xml`. However, we can specify a different configuration file using the following code:

```
var cfgFile = "cookbook.cfg.xml";
var nhConfig = new Configuration().Configure(cfgFile);
```

Additionally, we can embed our configuration file in the assembly. In this case, we pass in the `assembly` containing the resource as well as the embedded resource name.

Finally, we can pass an `XmlReader` to provide our configuration from any other source.

See also

- ▸ *Configuring NHibernate with* `App.config`
- ▸ *Configuring NHibernate with code*
- ▸ *Configuring NHibernate with Fluent NHibernate*
- ▸ *Configuring NHibernate using ConfORM mappings*

Configuring NHibernate with code

We can also configure NHibernate entirely in code. In this recipe, I'll show you how to use the `NHibernate.Cfg.Loquacious` namespace to configure NHibernate.

Getting ready

1. Complete the `Eg.Core` model and mapping recipes from *Chapter 1*.

2. Add a console application project to your solution named `ConfigByCode`.

3. Set it as the **Startup** project for your solution.

4. In the `ConfigByCode` project, add references to `NHibernate.dll` and `NHibernate.ByteCode.Castle.dll` in the `Lib` folder.

5. In `ConfigByCode`, add a reference to the `Eg.Core` project.

How to do it...

1. Add an `App.config` file with this configuration:

```xml
<?xml version="1.0" encoding="utf-8" ?>
<configuration>
    <connectionStrings>
      <add name="db" connectionString="Server=.\SQLExpress;
Database=NHCookbook; Trusted_Connection=SSPI"/>
    </connectionStrings>
</configuration>
```

2. In `Program.cs`, add the following `using` statements:

```csharp
using NHibernate.ByteCode.Castle;
using NHibernate.Cfg;
using NHibernate.Cfg.Loquacious;
using NHibernate.Dialect;
```

3. In your `Main` function, add the following code to configure NHibernate:

```csharp
var nhConfig = new Configuration()
  .Proxy(proxy =>
    proxy.ProxyFactoryFactory<ProxyFactoryFactory>())
  .DataBaseIntegration(db =>
  {
    db.Dialect<MsSql2008Dialect>();
    db.ConnectionStringName = "db";
    db.BatchSize = 100;
  })
  .AddAssembly("Eg.Core");
var sessionFactory = nhConfig.BuildSessionFactory();
Console.WriteLine("NHibernate Configured!");
Console.ReadKey();
```

4. Build and run your application. You should see the text **NHibernate Configured!**.

How it works...

In this recipe, we create an identical NHibernate configuration using extension methods in the NHibernate.Cfg.Loquacious namespace. These methods offer full type safety and improved discoverability over code configurations in the previous version of NHibernate.

We specify proxyfactory.factory_class using the Proxy extension method. Next, we specify dialect, connection.connection_string_name, and adonet.batch_size with the DatabaseIntegration extension method. Finally, we add the embedded resource mappings with the AddAssembly method. AddAssembly isn't an extension method, and has been a part of the NHibernate configuration API for many versions.

There's more...

Notice that we are still referencing the db connection string defined in our App.config file. If we wanted to eliminate the App.config file entirely, we could hardcode the connection string with this code:

```
db.ConnectionString = @"Connection string here...";
```

This, however, is completely inflexible, and will require a full recompile and redeployment for even a minor configuration change.

See also

- ▸ *Configuring NHibernate with App.config*
- ▸ *Configuring NHibernate with XML*
- ▸ *Configuring NHibernate with Fluent NHibernate*
- ▸ *Configuring NHibernate using ConfORM Mappings*

Configuring NHibernate with Fluent NHibernate

In addition to fluent mappings and auto-mappings, the Fluent NHibernate project also brings its own code configuration syntax to NHibernate configuration. In this recipe, I'll show you how to configure NHibernate with the Fluent NHibernate syntax.

Getting ready

1. Complete the Eg.FluentMappings model and mapping from the *Creating Mappings Fluently* recipe in *Chapter 1*.
2. Add a console application project to your solution named ConfigByFNH.

3. Set it as the **Startup** project for your solution.

4. In the `ConfigByFNH` project, add references to `NHibernate.dll`, `NHibernate.ByteCode.Castle.dll`, and `FluentNHibernate.dll` in the `Lib` folder.

5. In `ConfigByFNH`, add a reference to the `Eg.FluentMappings` project.

How to do it...

1. Add an `App.config` file with this configuration:

```xml
<?xml version="1.0" encoding="utf-8" ?>
<configuration>

  <connectionStrings>
    <add name="db" connectionString="Server=.\SQLExpress;
Database=NHCookbook; Trusted_Connection=SSPI"/>
  </connectionStrings>
</configuration>
```

2. In `Program.cs`, add the following `using` statements:

```csharp
using Eg.FluentMappings.Mappings;
using FluentNHibernate.Cfg;
using FluentNHibernate.Cfg.Db;
using NHibernate.ByteCode.Castle;
```

3. In the `Main` method, add this code:

```csharp
var nhConfig = Fluently.Configure()
  .Database(MsSqlConfiguration.MsSql2008
    .ConnectionString(connstr =>
      connstr.FromConnectionStringWithKey("db")
    )
    .ProxyFactoryFactory<ProxyFactoryFactory>()
    .AdoNetBatchSize(100)
  )
  .Mappings(mappings => mappings.FluentMappings
    .AddFromAssemblyOf<ProductMapping>()
  )
  .BuildConfiguration();
var sessionFactory = nhConfig.BuildSessionFactory();
Console.WriteLine("NHibernate configured fluently!");
Console.ReadKey();
```

4. Build and run your application. You should see the text **NHibernate configured fluently!**.

How it works...

Our fluent configuration can be broken down in to three parts. First, we configure these properties:

1. We set the `dialect` property to `MsSql2008Dialect` when we use the `MsSql2008` static property of `MsSqlConfiguration`.

2. `connection.connection_string_name` is set to `db` with a call to `FromConnectionStringWithKey`.

3. When we call `ProxyFactoryFactory`, we set `proxyfactory.factory_class` to the Castle DynamicProxy2 proxy factory.

4. We set `adonet.batch_size` to 100 with a call to `AdoNetBatchSize`.

Next, we load mappings into our configuration. In this recipe, we load our fluent mappings from *Chapter 1*. Fluent NHibernate scans the entire assembly and loads all the fluent mappings it finds. Fluent NHibernate allows you to add any combination of fluent mappings, auto-mappings, and standard `hbm.xml` mappings.

Finally, from the fluent configuration, we build a standard NHibernate configuration.

See also

- ▸ *Configuring NHibernate with* `App.config`
- ▸ *Configuring NHibernate with XML*
- ▸ *Configuring NHibernate with code*
- ▸ *Configuring NHibernate using ConfORM Mappings*

Configuring NHibernate using ConfORM Mappings

As we saw in *Chapter 1*, ConfORM uses conventions to build HbmMapping objects that can be added directly to the NHibernate configuration. In this recipe, I'll show you how to add ConfORM mappings to our NHibernate configuration.

Getting ready

1. Complete *Mapping with ConfORM* recipe in *Chapter 1*.

2. Add a console application project to your solution named `ConfigWithConfORM`.

3. Set it as the **Startup** project for your solution.

4. In the `ConfigWithConfORM` project, add references to `NHibernate.dll` and `NHibernate.ByteCode.Castle.dll` in the `Lib` folder.

5. In `ConfigWithConfORM`, add a reference to the `Eg.ConfORMMappings` project.

How to do it...

1. Add an `App.config` with the following configuration:

```xml
<?xml version="1.0" encoding="utf-8" ?>
<configuration>
  <configSections>
    <section name="hibernate-configuration"
             type="NHibernate.Cfg.ConfigurationSectionHandler,
NHibernate"/>
  </configSections>
  <connectionStrings>
    <add name="db" connectionString="Server=.\SQLExpress;
Database=NHCookbook; Trusted_Connection=SSPI"/>
  </connectionStrings>
  <hibernate-configuration
    xmlns="urn:nhibernate-configuration-2.2">
    <session-factory>
      <property name="proxyfactory.factory_class">
        NHibernate.ByteCode.Castle.ProxyFactoryFactory,
        NHibernate.ByteCode.Castle
      </property>
      <property name="dialect">
        NHibernate.Dialect.MsSql2008Dialect,
        NHibernate
      </property>
      <property name="connection.connection_string_name">
        db
      </property>
      <property name="adonet.batch_size">
        100
      </property>
    </session-factory>
  </hibernate-configuration>
</configuration>
```

2. In `Program.cs`, add the following `using` statements:

```
using Eg.ConfORMMapping.Mappings;
using NHibernate.Cfg;
```

3. In the `Main` method, add the following code:

```
var mappingFactory = new MappingFactory();
var mapping = mappingFactory.CreateMapping();
var nhConfig = new Configuration().Configure();
nhConfig.AddDeserializedMapping(mapping, null);
var sessionFactory = nhConfig.BuildSessionFactory();
Console.WriteLine("NHibernate configured!");
Console.ReadKey();
```

4. Build and run your application. You should see **NHibernate Configured!**.

How it works...

In this recipe, our `App.config` is nearly identical to the `App.config` from our first configuration recipe. We've simply removed the `<mapping>` element that tells NHibernate to load mappings embedded in an assembly. Instead, we use ConfORM to build an `HbmMapping` object containing mappings for our entire model. We new up our `MappingFactory` and call `CreateMapping`.

Next, we build our NHibernate `Configuration` object and load the configuration from `App.config`.

The real trick of this recipe comes when we call `AddDeserializedMapping`. We pass in our `HbmMapping` object. As the method name suggests, it really is a deserialized XML mapping, except that we built it with code, not XML. In fact, we could serialize the `HbmMapping` object with the .NET `XmlSerializer`, and we would get an actual human-readable XML mapping for our model.

There's more...

Because we build our mapping with code, we get a nice speed boost during configuration compared with normal embedded resource XML mappings and even Fluent NHibernate, which serializes its mappings down to XML, then lets NHibernate deserialize them.

See also

▶ *Configuring NHibernate with* `App.config`

▶ *Configuring NHibernate with XML*

▶ *Configuring NHibernate with code*

▶ *Configuring NHibernate with Fluent NHibernate*

Configuring NHibernate logging

NHibernate uses log4net, a highly customizable, open source logging framework. In this recipe, I'll show you a simple log4net configuration to log important NHibernate events to the Visual Studio debug output window.

Getting ready

Complete the earlier *Configuring NHibernate with* `App.config` recipe.

How to do it...

1. Add a reference to `log4net.dll` from the NHibernate download.

2. Open your application configuration file.

3. Inside the `configSections` element, declare a section for the log4net configuration:

```
<section name="log4net"
type="log4net.Config.Log4NetConfigurationSectionHandler,
log4net"/>
```

4. After the hibernate configuration element, add this log4net configuration:

```
<log4net>
<appender name="trace"
        type="log4net.Appender.TraceAppender, log4net">
  <layout type="log4net.Layout.PatternLayout, log4net">
  <param name="ConversionPattern"
      value=" %date %level %message%newline" />
  </layout>
</appender>
<root>
  <level value="ALL" />
  <appender-ref ref="trace" />
</root>
<logger name="NHibernate">
  <level value="INFO" />
</logger>
</log4net>
```

5. At the beginning of your `Main` function, insert the following code to configure log4net:

```
log4net.Config.XmlConfigurator.Configure();
```

6. Run your application.

7. Watch Visual Studio's debug output window.

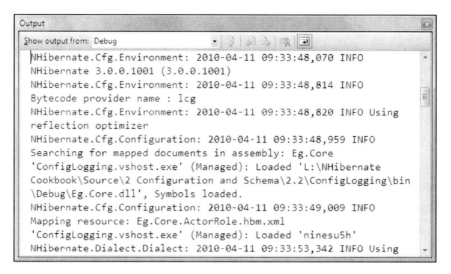

How it works...

log4net uses appenders, layouts, and loggers to format and control log messages from our application, including log messages from NHibernate.

Appenders define destinations for log messages. In this recipe, we've defined a trace appender, which writes our log messages to `System.Diagnostics.Trace`. When we debug our application, Visual Studio listens to the trace and copies each message to the debug output window.

Loggers are the source of log messages. The root element defines values for all loggers, which can be overridden using the logger element. In our configuration, we've declared that all messages should be written to the appender named `trace`.

In log4net, log messages have priorities. In ascending order, they are DEBUG, INFO, WARN, ERROR, and FATAL. In our configuration, we can define a log level with one of these priorities, or with ALL or OFF. A level includes its priority and all the priorities above it. For example, a level of WARN will also log ERROR and FATAL messages. ALL is equivalent to DEBUG: all messages will be logged, and OFF suppresses all messages.

With our configuration, log4net will write messages from NHibernate with a priority of INFO, WARN, ERROR, and FATAL, and ALL messages from other sources.

There's more...

We can use log4net in our own application. Here's a simple example of what some code might look like with log4net logging:

```
using System.IO;
using log4net;
namespace MyApp.Project.SomeNamespace
{
    public class Foo
    {
        private static ILog log = LogManager.GetLogger(typeof(Foo));
        public string DoSomething()
        {
            log.Debug("We're doing something.");
            try
            {
                return File.ReadAllText("cheese.txt");
            }
            catch (FileNotFoundException)
            {
                log.Error("Somebody moved my cheese.txt");
                throw;
            }
        }
    }
}
```

We've defined a simple class named `Foo`. In the `DoSomething()` method, we write the log message, "We're doing something.", with a priority of DEBUG. Then we return the contents of the file `cheese.txt`. If the file doesn't exist, we log an error and throw the exception.

Because we passed in `typeof(Foo)` when getting the logger, `Foo`'s logger is named `MyApp.Project.SomeNamespace.Foo`, the same as the type. This is the typical naming convention when using log4net.

Suppose we were no longer concerned with debug level messages from Foo, but we still wanted to know about warnings and errors. We can redefine the log level with this simple addition to our configuration:

```
<logger name="MyApp.Project.SomeNamespace.Foo">
    <level value="WARN" />
</logger>
```

Alternatively, we can set the log level for the entire namespace or even the entire project with this configuration.

```
<logger name="MyApp.Project">
    <level value="WARN" />
</logger>
```

Using log4net to troubleshoot NHibernate

When we set NHibernate's `show_sql` configuration property to true, NHibernate will write all SQL statements to `Console.Out`. This is handy in some cases, but many applications don't use console output. With log4net, we can write the SQL statements to the trace instead.

NHibernate also writes every SQL statement to a logger named `NHibernate.SQL`. These log messages have `DEBUG` priority. When we add the following snippet to our configuration, we can redefine the log level for this specific logger. We will get every SQL statement in the trace output.

```
<logger name="NHibernate.SQL">
  <level name="DEBUG" />
</logger>
```

See also

- ▸ *Configuring NHibernate with App.config*
- ▸ *Using NHibernate Profiler*

Reducing application startup time

The process of configuring NHibernate is fairly intensive and takes some time. NHibernate has to load, parse, and compile all our mappings and reflect the model. In this recipe, I'll show you how to reduce the startup time of your NHibernate application.

Getting ready

Complete the *Configuring NHibernate with App.config* recipe from the beginning of this chapter.

How to do it...

1. Add a reference to `System.Configuration.dll`.
2. Add a new class named `ConfigurationBuilder`.
3. Add the following using statements:
   ```
   using System;
   using System.Configuration;
   using System.IO;
   using System.Reflection;
   using System.Runtime.Serialization.Formatters.Binary;
   using Configuration = NHibernate.Cfg.Configuration;
   ```
4. In `ConfigurationBuilder`, add a private string constant `SERIALIZED_CFG = "configuration.bin";`

5. Add a method named `Build` with the following code:

```
public Configuration Build()
{
  Configuration cfg = LoadConfigurationFromFile();
  if (cfg == null)
  {
    cfg = new Configuration().Configure();
    SaveConfigurationToFile(cfg);
  }
  return cfg;
}
```

6. Add a method named `LoadConfigurationFromFile` with this code:

```
private Configuration LoadConfigurationFromFile()
{
  if (!IsConfigurationFileValid())
    return null;
  try
  {
    using (var file = File.Open(SERIALIZED_CFG, FileMode.Open))
    {
      var bf = new BinaryFormatter();
      return bf.Deserialize(file) as Configuration;
    }
  }
  catch (Exception)
  {
    // Something went wrong
    // Just build a new one
    return null;
  }
}
```

7. Add a method named `IsConfigurationFileValid` with the following code:

```
private bool IsConfigurationFileValid()
{
  // If we don't have a cached config,
  // force a new one to be built
  if (!File.Exists(SERIALIZED_CFG))
    return false;
  var configInfo = new FileInfo(SERIALIZED_CFG);
```

```
var asm = Assembly.GetExecutingAssembly();
if (asm.Location == null)
  return false;
// If the assembly is newer,
// the serialized config is stale
var asmInfo = new FileInfo(asm.Location);
if (asmInfo.LastWriteTime > configInfo.LastWriteTime)
  return false;
// If the app.config is newer,
// the serialized config is stale
var appDomain = AppDomain.CurrentDomain;
var appConfigPath = appDomain.SetupInformation.
ConfigurationFile;
var appConfigInfo = new FileInfo(appConfigPath);
if (appConfigInfo.LastWriteTime > configInfo.LastWriteTime)
  return false;
// It's still fresh
return true;
}
```

8. Add a method named `SaveConfigurationToFile` with this code:

```
private void SaveConfigurationToFile(Configuration cfg)
{
  using (var file = File.Open(SERIALIZED_CFG, FileMode.Create))
  {
    var bf = new BinaryFormatter();
    bf.Serialize(file, cfg);
  }
}
```

9. In `Program.cs`, replace the NHibernate configuration code with the following code:

```
var nhConfig = new ConfigurationBuilder().Build();
```

How it works...

NHibernate's Configuration class is serializable. Thoroughly validating the mappings and settings takes some effort and time. The very first time our application runs, we can't escape this, but if we serialize our Configuration object to disk, we can deserialize it the next time we run it, saving us all of this busy work.

The `IsConfigurationFileValid` method ensures that the Configuration we've serialized is still fresh. If the executable or the `App.config` has been updated, we need to rebuild our configuration object from scratch.

We compare the last write time of the various files to decide if the serialized configuration is stale. We use a `BinaryFormatter` to serialize and deserialize the configuration.

Actual configuration may vary—batteries not included
In this recipe, we only check the assembly containing our `ConfigurationBuilder` class and the `App.config`. If you store your configuration and mappings elsewhere, you will need to adjust this code accordingly.

There's more...

This technique is especially suited for development and test suites, where we frequently change code, but may not change our mappings or configuration. We can skip all of the extra parsing and get running quickly, and test our changes.

It also works well for desktop NHibernate applications. Because a user is waiting on your application to launch, every second counts. It's not as useful for web applications in production because these basically launch once and stay running.

Generating the database

In *Chapter 1*, we built mappings to map our persistent classes to the database, but we haven't built that database.

In this recipe, I'll show you how to generate all the necessary tables, columns, keys and relationships in your database from your mappings—with two lines of code.

Getting ready

1. Complete the *Configuring NHibernate with App.config* recipe at the beginning of this chapter.
2. Install Microsoft SQL Server 2008 Express on your PC, using the default settings.
3. Create a blank database named NHCookbook.

This recipe works for any RDBMS supported by NHibernate. To use a different system, switch to the dialect for your RDBMS, and use a connection string appropriate for your system.

How to do it...

1. Open `Program.cs`.
2. Add the using statement: `using NHibernate.Tool.hbm2ddl;`.
3. Add the following lines to the end of `Main`.
   ```
   var schemaExport = new SchemaExport(nhConfig);
   schemaExport.Create(false, true);
   ```
4. Build and run your application.
5. Open your database and examine the tables.

How it works...

The hbm2ddl (hibernate mapping to data definition language) tool uses the mapping metadata in the configuration object to build a SQL script of our database objects. It then connects to our database and runs this script.

There's more...

Alternatively, we can use the `hbm2ddl.auto` configuration property to build our database schema automatically whenever our application calls `BuildSessionFactory`. We can set the property to the following values:

- `update`: The `SchemaUpdate` class updates our database schema, avoiding destructive changes. This only works for dialects that implement the `IDataBaseSchema` interface.
- `create`: The `SchemaExport` class creates our database schema from scratch for a fresh database.
- `create-drop`: `SchemaExport` recreates the database schema by first dropping and then creating each table.
- `validate`: The `SchemaValidate` class compares the existing database schema to the schema NHibernate expects, based on your mappings. Like `update`, this requires a dialect that implements `IDataBaseSchema`.

While `create-drop` is immensely helpful during development, only `validate` is suggested for production environments, as the tiniest mistake can have huge consequences. Rather, you should script the database, as shown in the next recipe, and run the script explicitly to set up your production database.

See also

- *Configuring NHibernate with App.config*
- *Scripting the database*

Scripting the database

It's usually not appropriate for your application to recreate database tables each time it runs. In this recipe, we'll generate a SQL script to create your database objects.

Getting ready

1. Complete the *Configuring NHibernate with App.config* recipe at the beginning of this chapter.
2. Install Microsoft SQL Server 2008 Express on your PC, using the default settings.
4. Create a blank database named NHCookbook.

 This recipe works for any RDBMS supported by NHibernate. To use a different system, adjust your connection string and dialect accordingly.

How to do it...

1. Open `Program.cs`.
2. Add the using statement: `using NHibernate.Tool.hbm2ddl;` to the beginning of the file.
3. Add the following lines to the end of `Main`.

```
var schemaExport = new SchemaExport(nhConfig);
schemaExport
  .SetOutputFile(@"db.sql")
  .Execute(false, false, false);
```

4. Build and run your application.
5. Inspect the newly created `db.sql` file.

How it works...

Using the mapping metadata from the configuration object and the current dialect, hbm2ddl builds a SQL script for your entities.

See also

- ▶ *Configuring NHibernate with App.config*
- ▶ *Configuring NHibernate with* `hibernate.cfg.xml`
- ▶ *Configuring NHibernate with code*
- ▶ *Configuring NHibernate with Fluent NHibernate*
- ▶ *Configuring NHibernate Using ConfORM Mappings*
- ▶ *Generating the database*

Using NHibernate Schema Tool

In many cases, you'll want to include building or updating your database in some larger process, such as a build script or installation process. In this recipe, I'll show you how to use this command-line tool to run our hbm2ddl tasks.

Getting ready

Download the latest release of NHibernate Schema Tool from `http://nst.codeplex.com/`.

To install NHibernate Schema Tool, follow these steps:

1. Create a new folder in `C:\Program Files` named `NHibernateSchemaTool`.
2. Copy `nst.exe` to the newly created folder.
3. Add `C:\Program Files\NHibernateSchemaTool` to your `PATH` environment variable.

After the installation of the NHibernate Schema Tool, follow these steps:

1. Complete the *Configuring NHibernate with App.config* recipe from the beginning of this chapter.
2. Install Microsoft SQL Server 2008 Express on your PC, using the default settings.
3. Create a blank database named `NHCookbook`.

 This recipe works for any RDBMS supported by NHibernate. To use a different system, adjust your connection string and dialect accordingly.

How to do it...

1. Add a new file to your project named `hibernate.cfg.xml` with the following code:

```xml
<?xml version="1.0" encoding="utf-8" ?>
<hibernate-configuration
xmlns="urn:nhibernate-configuration-2.2">
<session-factory>
  <property name="proxyfactory.factory_class">
    NHibernate.ByteCode.Castle.ProxyFactoryFactory, NHibernate.
ByteCode.Castle
  </property>
  <property name="dialect">
    NHibernate.Dialect.MsSql2008Dialect, NHibernate
  </property>
  <property name="connection.connection_string">
    Server=.\SQLExpress; Database=NHCookbook; Trusted_
Connection=SSPI
  </property>
</session-factory>
</hibernate-configuration>
```

2. For `hibernate.cfg.xml`, on the properties tab, set **Copy To Output Directory** to **Copy Always**.

3. Build your solution.

4. Open a command prompt window, and switch to the directory containing your compiled mapping assembly and `hibernate.cfg.xml`.

 To open the command prompt window quickly, in Visual Studio, right-click on your project, and choose **Open Folder in Windows Explorer**. Open the `bin` folder. While holding down *Shift,* right-click on the **Debug** folder. Choose **Open Command Window Here**.

5. Run the following command:

   nst /c:hibernate.cfg.xml /a:Eg.Core.dll /o:Create .

How it works...

NHibernate Schema Tool is a command-line wrapper for the hbm2ddl tool. This makes NST ideal for use in build scripts and continuous integration servers.

The `/c` argument specifies the configuration file. It's no mistake that the content of `hibernate.cfg.xml` is nearly identical to the `hibernate-configuration` section in the `app.config`. The `/a` argument specifies the assembly with our classes and mapping embedded resource files. The `/o:Create` option tells NHibernate to create our database objects. It also supports `Update` and `Delete`.

There's more...

NST has several options, enabling a number of creative uses. NST supports these command-line options:

Command-line option	Description
`/c:<path-to-hibernate-config>`	Specifies NHibernate config file to use.
`/a:<assembly[;assembly2`	Path to assembly or semicolon-separated list of assemblies containing embedded `.hbm.xml` files. These assemblies may also contain persistent classes.
`/m:<assembly[;assembly2]>`	Path to assembly or semicolon-separated list of assemblies containing persistent classes.
`/d:<path[;path2]>`	Directory or directories containing `.hbm.xml` mapping files.
`/s`	Generate script, but don't execute. Script is written to the console.
`/v`	Generate script and execute. Script is written to the console.
`/o:<Create|Update|Delete>`	Specifies Create, Update, or Delete operation.

See also

- ▶ *Configuring NHibernate with App.config*
- ▶ *Configuring NHibernate with* `hibernate.cfg.xml`
- ▶ *Configuring NHibernate with code*
- ▶ *Configuring NHibernate with Fluent NHibernate*
- ▶ *Configuring NHibernate Using ConfORM Mappings*
- ▶ *Generating the database*
- ▶ *Scripting the database*

3
Sessions and Transactions

In this chapter, we will cover the following topics:

- ▶ Setting up session per web request
- ▶ Setting up session per presenter
- ▶ Creating a session ASP.NET MVC action filter
- ▶ Creating a transaction ASP.NET MVC action filter
- ▶ Using the Conversation per Business Transaction pattern
- ▶ Using session.Merge
- ▶ Using session.Refresh
- ▶ Using stateless sessions
- ▶ Using dictionaries as entities
- ▶ Using NHibernate with Transaction Scope

Introduction

NHibernate leaves session and transaction management up to the application. There are a number of different ways to manage sessions and transactions, and these depend greatly on the specific application architecture. In addition to a few interesting session methods, the recipes in this chapter show how to handle sessions and transactions for these different types of applications.

Setting up session per web request

Because of its simplicity, the most common pattern used in web applications for managing NHibernate sessions is session-per-request. In this recipe, I'll show you how to set up the session-per-request pattern using NHibernate's contextual sessions feature.

Getting ready

1. Create a new ASP.NET Web Forms or ASP.NET MVC application.

2. Add references to `NHibernate.dll`, `NHibernate.ByteCode.Castle.dll`, `log4net.dll`, and our `Eg.Core` model and mappings project from *Chapter 1*.

3. In the `web.config` file, set up the NHibernate and log4net configuration sections. Refer to the *Configuring NHibernate with App.config* recipes in *Chapter 2*.

How to do it...

1. In the `hibernate-configuration` section of `web.config`, add the `current_session_context_class` property with a value of `web`.

2. If it doesn't exist already, add a new Global application class (`Global.asax`).

3. In `Global.asax`, add these using statements.

```
using NHibernate;
using NHibernate.Cfg;
using NHibernate.Context;
```

4. Create a static property named `SessionFactory`.

```
public static ISessionFactory SessionFactory { get;
private set; }
```

5. In the `Application_Start` method, add the following code.

```
protected void Application_Start(object sender, EventArgs e)
{
  log4net.Config.XmlConfigurator.Configure();
  var nhConfig = new Configuration().Configure();
  SessionFactory = nhConfig.BuildSessionFactory();
}
```

6. In the `Application_BeginRequest` method, add the following code.

```
protected void Application_BeginRequest(object sender, EventArgs e)
{
  var session = SessionFactory.OpenSession();
  CurrentSessionContext.Bind(session);
}
```

7. In the `Application_EndRequest` method, add the following code:

```
protected void Application_EndRequest(object sender, EventArgs e)
{
  var session = CurrentSessionContext.Unbind(SessionFactory);
  session.Dispose();
}
```

How it works...

In web applications, it's common to use a session for each web request. We open the session when the request begins and close it when the request ends.

NHibernate's contextual session feature allows a session to be associated with some application-specific scope that approximates a single unit of work. This context is configured with the `current_session_context_class` property, which specifies an implementation of `NHibernate.Context.ICurrentSessionContext`. In this case, we'll associate it with the web request. `web` is the short name for `NHibernate.Context.WebSessionContext`.

Even with contextual sessions, NHibernate does not open, close or dispose the session for us. We associate and dissociate a session with the current web request using the `CurrentSessionContext.Bind` and `Unbind` methods.

There's more...

To get the NHibernate session for the current web request, we use `SessionFactory.GetCurrentSession()`. In our example web application, it might look something like this:

```
Guid productId = new Guid(Request["id"]);
Eg.Core.Product product;
var session = Global.SessionFactory.GetCurrentSession();
using (var tran = session.BeginTransaction())
{
  product = session.Get<Eg.Core.Product>(productId);
  tran.Commit();
}
Page.Title = product.Name;
Label1.Text = product.Name;
Label2.Text = product.Description;
```

This naive example fetches a product from the database and displays the name and description to the user. In a production-worthy application, we would use dependency injection rather than directly access the singleton. The free TekPub Concepts screencast provides a thorough introduction to dependency injection, and can be found at `http://tekpub.com/view/concepts/1`.

NHibernate sessions are extremely lightweight and cheap to make. Simply opening a session doesn't open a database connection. NHibernate makes every effort to avoid any delay opening a connection. On the other hand, NHibernate goes through great effort to create the session factory. You should only create one session factory for the entire lifecycle of the application.

There are many implementations of session per request using Inversion of Control containers and even HTTP modules. Some use contextual sessions. Others manage the session without NHibernate's help. A complete session per request implementation has four characteristics:

- Create the one and only session factory when the application starts
- Open a session when the web request begins
- Close the session when the request ends
- Provide a standard way to access the current session throughout the data access layer

See also

- *Creating a ASP.NET MVC session action filter*
- *Creating a ASP.NET MVC transaction action filter*
- *Setting up session per presenter.*
- *Using the Conversation per Business Transaction pattern*

Setting up session per presenter

In desktop applications using the model-view-presenter pattern, it's best to use a session for each presenter. This approach can also be adapted to the model-view-view model pattern. More information on these patterns is available at `http://en.wikipedia.org/wiki/Model-view-presenter`.

In this recipe, I'll show you how to implement this session-per-presenter pattern with dependency injection.

Getting ready

You'll need the named scope extension to Ninject available at `http://github.com/remogloor/ninject.extensions.namedscope`.

Download the source code in ZIP format and extract it. Open the `Ninject.Extensions.NamedScope.sln` solution in Visual Studio and build the solution. Copy `Ninject.dll` and `Ninject.Extensions.NamedScope.dll` from the `build\debug` folder to our Cookbook solution's `Lib` folder.

If you're not familiar with the dependency injection concept, a free video tutorial is available from TekPub at `http://tekpub.com/view/concepts/1`.

 This recipe can be completed with other dependency injection frameworks. Just substitute the `NinjectBindings` class with an equivalent configuration for your favorite DI framework.

How to do it...

1. Add a new console project to the solution named `SessionPerPresenter`.

2. Add references to the `Eg.Core` project from *Chapter 1*, `NHibernate.dll`, `NHibernate.ByteCode.Castle.dll`, `Ninject.dll`, and `Ninject.Extensions.NamedScope.dll`.

3. Add an `App.config` file and set up the NHibernate and log4net configuration sections. Refer to the *Configuring NHibernate* and *Configuring NHibernate logging* recipes in *Chapter 2*.

4. Add a folder to the new project named `Data`.

5. In the `Data` folder, create an `IDao<TEntity>` interface with the following code:

```
public interface IDao<TEntity> : IDisposable
  where TEntity : class
{
  IEnumerable<TEntity> GetAll();
}
```

6. Create an implementation with the following code:

```
public class Dao<TEntity> : IDao<TEntity>
  where TEntity : class
{
  private readonly ISessionProvider _sessionProvider;
  public Dao(ISessionProvider sessionProvider)
  {
    _sessionProvider = sessionProvider;
  }
  public void Dispose()
  {
    _sessionProvider.Dispose();
  }
  public IEnumerable<TEntity> GetAll()
  {
    var session = _sessionProvider.GetCurrentSession();
```

```
      IEnumerable<TEntity> results;
      using (var tx = session.BeginTransaction())
      {
        results = session.QueryOver<TEntity>()
          .List<TEntity>();
        tx.Commit();
      }
      return results;
    }
  }
```

7. In the `Data` folder, create an `ISessionProvider` interface with the following code:

```
public interface ISessionProvider : IDisposable
{
  ISession GetCurrentSession();
  void DisposeCurrentSession();
}
```

8. Create an implementation with the following code:

```
public class SessionProvider
  : ISessionProvider
{
  private readonly ISessionFactory _sessionFactory;
  private ISession _currentSession;
  public SessionProvider(ISessionFactory sessionFactory)
  {
    Console.WriteLine("Building session provider");
    _sessionFactory = sessionFactory;
  }
  public ISession GetCurrentSession()
  {
    if (null == _currentSession)
      _currentSession = _sessionFactory.OpenSession();
    return _currentSession;
  }
  public void DisposeCurrentSession()
  {
    _currentSession.Dispose();
    _currentSession = null;
  }
  public void Dispose()
  {
```

```
    if (_currentSession != null)
      _currentSession.Dispose();
    _currentSession = null;
  }
}
```

9. Create a Ninject module named `NinjectBindings` with the following code:

```
public class NinjectBindings : NinjectModule
{
  public override void Load()
  {
    const string presenterScope = "PresenterScope";
    var asm = GetType().Assembly;
    var presenters =
      from t in asm.GetTypes()
      where typeof (IPresenter).IsAssignableFrom(t) &&
            t.IsClass && !t.IsAbstract
      select t;
    foreach (var presenterType in presenters)
      Kernel.Bind(presenterType)
        .ToSelf()
        .DefinesNamedScope(presenterScope);
    Kernel.Bind<ISessionProvider>()
      .To<SessionProvider>()
      .InNamedScope(presenterScope);
    Kernel.Bind(typeof(IDao<>))
      .To(typeof(Dao<>));
  }
}
```

10. In the root of our project, create a `ProductListView` class with the following code:

```
public class ProductListView
{
  private readonly string _description;
  private readonly IEnumerable<Product> _products;
  public ProductListView(
    string description,
    IEnumerable<Product> products)
  {
    _description = description;
    _products = products;
  }
  public void Show()
```

```
    {
      Console.WriteLine(_description);
      foreach (var p in _products)
        Console.WriteLine(" * {0}", p.Name);
    }
}
```

11. Create a public `IPresenter` interface inherited from `IDisposable`. This interface can be left empty.

12. Create a `MediaPresenter` class with the following code:

```
public class MediaPresenter : IPresenter
{
  private readonly IDao<Movie> _movieDao;
  private readonly IDao<Book> _bookDao;
  public MediaPresenter(IDao<Movie> movieDao,
    IDao<Book> bookDao)
  {
    _movieDao = movieDao;
    _bookDao = bookDao;
  }
  public ProductListView ShowBooks()
  {
    return new ProductListView("All Books",
      _bookDao.GetAll().OfType<Product>());
  }
  public ProductListView ShowMovies()
  {
    return new ProductListView("All Movies",
      _movieDao.GetAll().OfType<Product>());
  }
  public void Dispose()
  {
    _movieDao.Dispose();
    _bookDao.Dispose();
  }
}
```

13. Create a `ProductPresenter` class with the following code:

```
public class ProductPresenter : IPresenter
{
  private readonly IDao<Product> _productDao;
  public ProductPresenter(IDao<Product> productDao)
```

```
    {
      _productDao = productDao;
    }
    public ProductListView ShowAllProducts()
    {
      return new ProductListView("All Products",
        _productDao.GetAll());
    }
    public virtual void Dispose()
    {
      _productDao.Dispose();
    }
  }
```

14. In `Program.cs`, in the `Main` method, add the following code:

```
var nhConfig = new Configuration().Configure();
var sessionFactory = nhConfig.BuildSessionFactory();

var kernel = new StandardKernel();
kernel.Load(new Data.NinjectBindings());
kernel.Bind<ISessionFactory>()
  .ToConstant(sessionFactory);

var media1 = kernel.Get<MediaPresenter>();
var media2 = kernel.Get<MediaPresenter>();

media1.ShowBooks().Show();
media2.ShowMovies().Show();

media1.Dispose();
media2.Dispose();

using (var product = kernel.Get<ProductPresenter>())
{
  product.ShowAllProducts().Show();
}

Console.WriteLine("Press any key");
Console.ReadKey();
```

15. If you like, create some test product, book, and movie data in the `NHCookbook` database.

16. Build and run your application. You will see the following output:

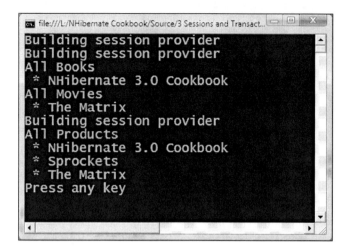

How it works...

There are several interesting items in this recipe to discuss. First, we've set up a slightly complex object graph. For each instance of `MediaPresenter`, our graph appears as shown in the next image:

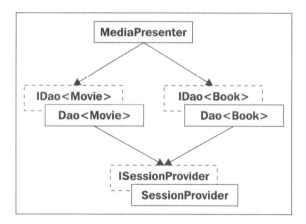

In the previous image, one instance of session provider is shared by both data access objects. This is accomplished with the configuration of Ninject, our dependency injection framework

In our `NinjectBindings`, we match up our service interfaces to their matching implementations. We bind the open generic `IDao<>` interface to `Dao<>`, so that requests for `IDao<Book>` are resolved to `Dao<Book>`, `IDao<Movie>` to `Dao<Movie>`, and so on.

One session per presenter is accomplished with the use of `DefinesNamedScope` and `InNamedScope`. We find all of the `IPresenter` implementations in the assembly. Each presenter is bound and defines the `PresenterScope`. When we bind `ISessionProvider` to `SessionProviderImpl`, we use `InNamedScope("PresenterScope")` to indicate that we will have only one session provider per presenter.

A simple call to `Kernel.Get<MediaPresenter>()` will return a new presenter instance all wired up and ready to use. It will have two data access objects sharing a common session provider. To close the session and release any lingering database connections, be sure to call `Dispose()` when you're finished with the presenter.

A typical `Save` method on a Dao may look something like this:

```
var session = _sessionProvider.GetCurrentSession();
try
{
  session.SaveOrUpdate(entity);
}
catch (StaleObjectStateException)
{
  _sessionProvider.DisposeCurrentSession();
  throw;
}
```

Notice how we are immediately throwing away the session in the catch block. When NHibernate throws an exception from inside a session call, the session's state is undefined. The only remaining operation you can safely perform on that session is `Dispose()`. This allows us to recover gracefully from any exceptions, as the exploded session is already thrown away, so a fresh session can take its place.

You should also take care with entities still associated with this failed session. It's usually a good idea to attach them to the new session, as any operation, including lazy loading, against the failed session will cause further exceptions. The *session.Merge* recipe mentioned later in this chapter discusses a method for accomplishing this.

There's More...

Because the boundaries are not as well-defined as in a web application, there are two very common anti-patterns for handling NHibernate sessions in desktop applications. The first, a singleton session, has the following problems:

- Undefined point for flushing the session to the database
- Untestable interactions between unrelated parts of the application
- It is impossible to recover gracefully from a StaleObjectExceptions or other session-exploding exceptions
- A stateful singleton is always bad architecture

The second, a micro-session, where a session is opened to perform a single operation and then quickly closed loses all of the benefits of the unit of work, most notably the session cache. Entities will be constantly re-fetched from the database.

See also

- *Using the Conversation per Business Transaction pattern*
- *Using session.Merge*

Creating a session ASP.NET MVC action filter

Often, a unit of work maps neatly on to a single controller action. I'll show you how to create an action filter to manage our NHibernate sessions in an ASP.NET MVC application.

Getting ready

Setup an ASP.NET MVC application for NHibernate. The steps are as follows:

1. Create a new ASP.NET MVC application.
2. Add references to `NHibernate.dll`, `NHibernate.ByteCode.Castle.dll`, `log4net.dll`, and our `Eg.Core` project from *Chapter 1*.
3. In the `web.config` file, set up the NHibernate and log4net configuration sections. Refer to the *Configuring NHibernate with App.config* recipes in *Chapter 2*.
4. Set the `current_session_context_class` property to web.
5. In `Global.asax`, create a static property named `SessionFactory`.

   ```
   public static ISessionFactory SessionFactory { get;
   private set; }
   ```

6. In the `Application_Start` method, add this code.

```
log4net.Config.XmlConfigurator.Configure();
var nhConfig = new Configuration().Configure();
SessionFactory = nhConfig.BuildSessionFactory();
```

How to do it...

1. Add the `NHibernateSessionAttribute` class as shown in the following code:

```
[AttributeUsage(AttributeTargets.Method,
AllowMultiple=false)]
public class NHibernateSessionAttribute
  : ActionFilterAttribute
{
  public NHibernateSessionAttribute()
  {
    Order = 100;
  }
  protected ISessionFactory sessionFactory
  {
    get
    {
      return MvcApplication.SessionFactory;
    }
  }
  public override void OnActionExecuting(
    ActionExecutingContext filterContext)
  {
    var session = sessionFactory.OpenSession();
    CurrentSessionContext.Bind(session);
  }
  public override void OnActionExecuted(
    ActionExecutedContext filterContext)
  {
   var session = CurrentSessionContext.Unbind(sessionFactory);
   session.Close();
  }
}
```

2. Decorate your controller actions with the attribute as shown in the following code:

```
[NHibernateSession]
public ActionResult Index()
{
    return View(DataAccessLayer.GetBooks());
}
```

3. Create a dummy data access layer with this code:

```
using System.Collections.Generic;

namespace ActionFilterExample
{
    public static class DataAccessLayer
    {
        public static IEnumerable<Eg.Core.Book> GetBooks()
        {
            var session = MvcApplication.SessionFactory
                .GetCurrentSession();
            using (var tx = session.BeginTransaction())
            {
                var books = session.QueryOver<Eg.Core.Book>()
                    .List();
                tx.Commit();
                return books;
            }
        }
    }
}
```

4. Inside the `Views` folder, create a folder named `Book`

4. In the `Book` folder, add a view using the settings shown in the following screenshot:

6. Open SQL Server Management Studio, connect to the NHCookbook database, and run this SQL code to create some book data:

```
USE NHCookbook

INSERT INTO Product
VALUES (
  NEWID(),
  'Eg.Core.Book',
  0,
  'NHibernate 3 Cookbook',
  'Bridging the gap between database and .NET Application',
  45.99,
  null,
  'Jason Dentler',
  '3043'
)

INSERT INTO Product
VALUES (
  NEWID(),
  'Eg.Core.Book',
  0,
```

```
'NHibernate 2 Beginner's Guide',
'Rapidly retrieve data from your database into .NET objects',
45.99,
null,
'Aaron Cure',
'978-1-847198-90-7'
)
```

7. Build and run your application. You will see the following web page:

Index

	ISBN	Author	Name	Description	UnitPrice	Id
Edit | Details	3043	Jason Dentler	NHibernate 3 Cookbook	Bridging the gap between database and .NET Application	45.99	16554e9d-f172-43fa-b54b-1db3c8997757
Edit | Details	978-1-847198-90-7	Aaron Cure	NHibernate 2 Beginner's Guide	Rapidly retrieve data from your database into .NET objects	45.99	bddef46a-5e39-4a6e-bddb-a1c2e71bbb57

Create New

How it works...

The concept behind this recipe is very similar to our session-per-request recipe at the beginning of the chapter. We are using NHibernate's contextual sessions with a variation of session-per-request.

Before the `Index()` controller action is executed, ASP.NET MVC will run our filter's `OnActionExecuting` method. In `OnActionExecuting`, our action filter opens a session and binds it to this web request using NHibernate's contextual sessions feature.

Similarly, ASP.NET MVC will run our filter's `OnActionExecuted` when `Index()` returns. In `OnActionExecuted`, the filter unbinds the session and closes it. Then, ASP.NET MVC processes the action result. In this case, it renders a view to display a list of books.

The `Order` property of an action filter determines in what order that action filter executes. For `Executing` events, all action filters with an unspecified `Order` are executed first. Then, those with a specific `Order` are executed, starting with zero, in ascending order. For `Executed` events, the process works in reverse. Essentially, it allows us to stack action filters - last in, first out. This provides a determinate order, so we can combine it with session-dependent filters with higher `Order` values.

There's more...

NHibernate requires an NHibernate transaction around every database interaction, whether it be a direct method call on the session or an action that triggers lazy loading. With this implementation, it is very difficult to capture lazy loading calls in a transaction. As we will see in the next recipe, we can combine the proper use of sessions and transactions in a single action filter to allow for lazy loading elsewhere in the controller action.

Be sure an action loads all of the data required by the view. The session is not open anymore when the action result (a view, in this case) is rendered.

 Because the session has already been closed, if a view attempts to access a lazy-loaded collection that wasn't loaded by the controller action, you will get a `LazyInitializationException`.

Even with more lenient implementations, it's not recommended to access the database from the view. Views are usually dynamic and difficult to test.

View models

To avoid this issue and many others, many ASP.NET MVC applications use view models. A view model class is defined for each view, and contains exactly the data required by that view, and nothing more. Think of it as a data transfer object between the controller and the view.

Rather than write pages of plumbing code to copy data from entities to view models, you can use an open source project, AutoMapper. When combined with an action filter attribute, this process becomes dead simple. A good example of this can be found in Jimmy Bogard's blog post at `http://www.lostechies.com/blogs/jimmy_bogard/archive/2009/06/29/how-we-do-mvc-view-models.aspx`.

Pay attention to the `Order` property on the AutoMapper attribute. To allow for lazy loading when translating from entities to view models, the `Order` should be even higher than our session attribute. This ensures that the session is open when AutoMapper is translating.

See also

▶ *Setting up session per web request*

▶ *Creating a transaction ASP.NET MVC action filter*

Creating a Transaction ASP.NET MVC action filter

We can extend the concepts of the previous recipe to NHibernate transactions as well. In this recipe, I'll show you how to create an action filter to manage our NHibernate sessions and transactions.

Getting ready

Complete the previous recipe, *Creating a Session ASP.NET MVC action filter*.

How to do it...

1. Add the `NeedsPersistenceAttribute` class as shown on the following lines of code:

```
[AttributeUsage(AttributeTargets.Method,
  AllowMultiple=true)]
public class NeedsPersistenceAttribute
  : NHibernateSessionAttribute
{
  protected ISession session
  {
    get
    {
      return sessionFactory.GetCurrentSession();
    }
  }

  public override void OnActionExecuting(
    ActionExecutingContext filterContext)
  {
    base.OnActionExecuting(filterContext);
    session.BeginTransaction();
  }

  public override void OnActionExecuted(
    ActionExecutedContext filterContext)
  {
    var tx = session.Transaction;
    if (tx != null && tx.IsActive)
```

```
session.Transaction.Commit();

    base.OnActionExecuted(filterContext);
    }

}
```

2. Decorate your controller actions with the attribute as shown in the following lines of code:

```
[NeedsPersistence]
public ActionResult Index()
{
    return View(DataAccessLayer.GetBooks());
}
```

3. Update the `DataAccessLayer.GetBooks()` method to use the following code:

```
var session = MvcApplication.SessionFactory
    .GetCurrentSession();
var books = session.QueryOver<Eg.Core.Book>()
    .List();
return books;
```

4. Build and run your application. Again, you will see the following screenshot:

Index

	ISBN	Author	Name	Description	UnitPrice	Id
Edit | Details	3043	Jason Dentler	NHibernate 3 Cookbook	Bridging the gap between database and .NET Application	45.99	16554e9d-f172-43fa-b54b-1db3c8997757
Edit | Details	978-1-847198-90-7	Aaron Cure	NHibernate 2 Beginner's Guide	Rapidly retrieve data from your database into .NET objects	45.99	bddef46a-5e39-4a6e-bddb-a1c2e71bbb57

Create New

How it works...

Before ASP.NET MVC executes the controller action, our `NeedsPersistence` action filter starts a new session and NHibernate transaction. If everything goes as planned, as soon as the action is completed, the filter commits the transaction. If the controller action rolls back the transaction, no action is taken.

Notice that we no longer need to use a transaction in our data access layer, as the entire controller action is wrapped in a transaction.

There's more...

This attribute inherits from our session action filter defined in the previous recipe. If you're managing your session differently, such as session-per-request, inherit from `ActionFilterAttribute` instead.

Using the Conversation per Business Transaction pattern

Another common pattern for session management in desktop applications is Conversation per Business Transaction, often abbreviated as CpBT. In this recipe, I'll show you how to use the CpBT implementation available from the unofficial NHibernate AddIns project, one of many active NHibernate-related open source projects. uNhAddIns was started by NHibernate project leader, *Fabio Maulo*, and is maintained by several well-known NHibernate contributors.

Getting ready

You'll need to download the latest uNhAddIns project binaries from the project website at `http://code.google.com/p/unhaddins/`. Extract those binaries from the ZIP file to your solution's `Lib` folder.

How to do it...

1. Create a new console application named CpBT.

2. Add references to `Castle.Core`, `Castle.Windsor`, `log4net`, `NHibernate`, `NHibernate.ByteCode.Castle`, `uNhAddIns`, `uNhAddIns.Adapters`, `uNhAddIns.CastleAdapters`, and our `Eg.Core` project from *Chapter 1*.

3. Add an `application configuration` file with standard `log4net` and `hibernate-configuration` sections, just as we did in *Chapter 2*.

4. In the `hibernate-configuration session-factory` element, set `current_session_context_class` to `uNhAddIns.SessionEasier.Conversations.ThreadLocalConversationalSessionContext, uNhAddIns`

5. Add a new folder named `DataAccess`.

6. To the `DataAccess` folder, add an `IDao<TEntity>` interface with these two methods:

```
TEntity Get(Guid Id);
void Save(TEntity entity);
```

7. Add an implementation of `IDao<TEntity>` named `Dao<TEntity>` with this code:

```
private readonly ISessionFactory _sessionFactory;

public Dao(ISessionFactory sessionFactory)
{
  _sessionFactory = sessionFactory;
}

protected ISession Session
{
  get { return _sessionFactory.GetCurrentSession(); }
}

public TEntity Get(Guid Id)
{
  return Session.Get<TEntity>(Id);
}

public void Save(TEntity entity)
{
  Session.SaveOrUpdate(entity);
}
```

8. To the CpBT project, add a new folder named `ApplicationServices`.

9. To the `ApplicationServices` folder, add an `IEditMovieModel` interface with the following methods:

```
Movie GetMovie(Guid movieId);
void SaveMovie(Movie movie);
void SaveAll();
void CancelAll();
```

10. Add an implementation of `IEditMovieModel` named `EditMovieModel` with this code:

```
private readonly IDao<Movie> _movieDao;

public EditMovieModel(IDao<Movie> movieDao)
{
  _movieDao = movieDao;
}

public virtual Movie GetMovie(Guid movieId)
{
  return _movieDao.Get(movieId);
}

public virtual void SaveMovie(Movie movie)
```

```
{
  _movieDao.Save(movie);
}

public virtual void SaveAll()
{
}

public virtual void CancelAll()
{
}
```

11. Add this using statement: `using uNhAddIns.Adapters;`

12. Decorate the `EditMovieModel` class with the following attribute:

    `[PersistenceConversational`

13. Decorate the `SaveAll` method with the following attribute:

    `[PersistenceConversation(ConversationEndMode=EndMode.End)]`

14. Decorate the `CancelAll` method with the following attribute:

    `[PersistenceConversation(ConversationEndMode=EndMode.Abort)]`

15. Add a public static class named `ContainerProvider`, and add the following using statements:

    ```
    using Castle.Facilities.FactorySupport;
    using Castle.MicroKernel.Registration;
    using Castle.Windsor;
    using CpBT.ApplicationServices;
    using CpBT.DataAccess;
    using NHibernate;
    using NHibernate.Engine;
    using uNhAddIns.CastleAdapters;
    using uNhAddIns.CastleAdapters.AutomaticConversationManagement;
    using uNhAddIns.SessionEasier;
    using uNhAddIns.SessionEasier.Conversations;
    ```

16. To configure Castle Windsor for NHibernate and CpBT, add the following code to `ContainerProvider`:

    ```
    private static readonly IWindsorContainer _container;

    public static IWindsorContainer Container
    {
      get
      {
        return _container;
      }
    ```

```csharp
}
static ContainerProvider()
{
  _container = new WindsorContainer();
  _container
    .AddFacility<PersistenceConversationFacility>();
  _container
    .AddFacility<FactorySupportFacility>();

  _container.Register(
    Component.For<ISessionFactoryProvider>()
    .ImplementedBy<SessionFactoryProvider>());

  _container.Register(
    Component.For<ISessionFactory>()
      .UsingFactoryMethod(
        () => _container
                .Resolve<ISessionFactoryProvider>()
                .GetFactory(null))
    );

  _container.Register(
    Component.For<ISessionWrapper>()
    .ImplementedBy<SessionWrapper>());

  _container.Register(
    Component.For<IConversationFactory>()
    .ImplementedBy<DefaultConversationFactory>());

  _container.Register(
    Component.For<IConversationsContainerAccessor>()
    .ImplementedBy<NhConversationsContainerAccessor>());

  _container.Register(
    Component.For(typeof(IDao<>))
      .ImplementedBy(typeof(Dao<>)));

  _container.Register(
    Component.For<IEditMovieModel>()
      .ImplementedBy<EditMovieModel>()
      .LifeStyle.Transient);
}
```

17. Add the `CreateMovie` method to the `Program` class:

```
static Movie CreateNewMovie()
{
  return new Movie()
  {
  Name = "Hackers",
  Description = "Bad",
  UnitPrice = 12.59M,
  Director = "Iain Softley",
  Actors = new List<ActorRole>()
  {
    new ActorRole()
    {
    Actor = "Jonny Lee Miller",
    Role="Zero Cool"
    },
    new ActorRole()
    {
    Actor = "Angelina Jolie",
    Role="Acid Burn"
    }
  }
  };
}
```

18. Finally, add the following code to your `main` method:

```
log4net.Config.XmlConfigurator.Configure();
var container = ContainerProvider.Container;

Movie movie = CreateNewMovie();
Guid movieId;

var model = container.GetService<IEditMovieModel>();

model.SaveMovie(movie);
movieId = movie.Id;
model.SaveAll();
movie = null;

movie = model.GetMovie(movieId);
movie.Description = "Greatest Movie Ever";
model.CancelAll();
movie = null;
```

How it works...

Conversation per Business Transaction (CpBT) introduces the idea of a long-running unit of work with multiple transactions. A single session is held open, perhaps allowing the user several opportunities to interact with the application. Within that session, we may open and commit several transactions, while waiting to save the entire set of changes on the final commit. A typical NHibernate application uses `FlushMode.Commit`, which means that the unit of work is persisted when the transaction is committed. CpBT uses `FlushMode.Never`, which means that the unit of work is not automatically persisted when a transaction is committed. Instead, CpBT will explicitly call `session.Flush()` to persist the unit of work when the conversation has ended.

In a typical use of CpBT, we have a class representing a business transaction, or unit of work, and encapsulating the associated business logic. Each instance serves as a context for our conversation with the database. The conversation can be started, paused, resumed, and either ended or aborted, as shown in this image:

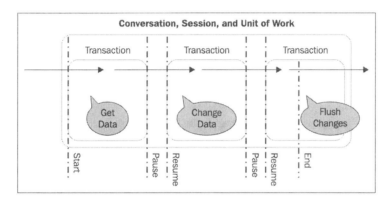

The following five conversation actions each handle distinct tasks in our persistent conversation:

- **Start** aborts any previous active conversation in this context, then begins a new session and transaction.

- **Resume** first starts a conversation if one doesn't already exist in this context, and then starts a new transaction.

- **Pause** commits the transaction. Because CpBT uses `FlushMode.Never`, the unit of work continues and no changes are persisted.

- **End** flushes the changes to the database, commits the final transaction, and closes the session.

- Abort rolls back the transaction and disposes the session.

In this implementation of CpBT, resume is implied at the beginning of each method, as is pause at the end of each method not decorated with end or abort. This automatic CpBT handling is accomplished with the `PersistentConversationFacility` set up in the `ContainerProvider`. If Castle would normally return a class decorated with a `PersistenceConversational` attribute, it will instead return a proxy object. This proxy object handles all of the CpBT actions for us. Thanks to this powerful bit of aspect-oriented programming, we can simply call our business logic methods normally without caring much for the session or transactions. Aspect-oriented programming allows us to separate these cross-cutting concerns, such as session and transaction management, from our true business logic. More information about aspect-oriented programming can be found on Wikipedia at `http://en.wikipedia.org/wiki/Aspect-oriented_programming`.

In our `main` method, we have two conversations. The first begins when we save our new instance of the movie Hackers with a call to `SaveMovie`. The `SaveMovie` method is wrapped in a transaction. This transaction is automatically committed at the end of the method when the conversation is implicitly paused. However, because CpBT uses `FlushMode.Never`, the movie was only associated with the session, not written to the database. This transaction is only used to meet NHibernate's requirement regarding transaction usage. It does not persist the unit of work. When we call the `SaveAll` method, the conversation is resumed and another transaction is started. Because this method is decorated with `EndMode.End`, when the method ends, CpBT explicitly calls `session.Flush()`. The unit of work containing the insert of our new Hackers movie is persisted to the database, and finally the transaction is committed.

Because our current conversation just ended, the next conversation begins with the call to `GetMovie`. A new session and transaction are started, and the Hackers movie is fetched from the database using the movie's ID. When `GetMovie` ends, the transaction is committed without persisting our (currently empty) unit of work. We then change the movie's description to "Greatest Movie Ever". However, we quickly change our minds and call `CancelAll`. When we call `CancelAll`, we abort the session, abandoning our changes to the movie's description.

There's more...

When relying on `FlushMode.Never` and explicit flushing of the session as we are with CpBT, choose an identity generator that does not require data to be inserted in the database in order for a persistent object identifier (POID) to be generated. The POID generator `identity` on all RDBMS, as well as native when running on Microsoft SQL Server, will cause your data to be flushed early in the conversation in order to generate an ID value, breaking the unit of work. If you were to abort this conversation, those database changes would not be undone.

uNhAddIns also includes CpBT implementations for the Spring framework, and the PostSharp tool, or with a solid understanding of aspect oriented programming, you can write your own.

See also

▶ *Setting up session per presenter*

▶ *Using the Burrows framework*

Using session.Merge

`session.Merge` is perhaps one of the most misunderstood features in NHibernate. In this recipe, I'll show you how to use `session.Merge` to associate a dirty, detached entity with a new session. This is particularly handy when recovering from `StaleObjectStateException`s.

Getting ready

Using our `Eg.Core` model from *Chapter 1* and the *Configuring NHibernate with App.config* recipe from *Chapter 2*, set up a console application.

How to do it...

1. Add the following code to your `Main` method:

```
var book = CreateAndSaveBook(sessionFactory);
book.Name = "Dormice in Action";
book.Description = "Hibernation of the Hazel Dormouse";
book.UnitPrice = 0.83M;
book.ISBN = "0123";

using (var session = sessionFactory.OpenSession())
{
  using (var tx = session.BeginTransaction())
  {
    var mergedBook = (Book) session.Merge(book);
    tx.Commit();

    // Returns false
    ReferenceEquals(book, mergedBook);

  }
}
```

2. Add the `CreateAndSaveBook` method:

```
private static Book CreateAndSaveBook(
  ISessionFactory sessionFactory)
{
  var book = new Book()
  {
    Name = "NHibernate 3.0 Cookbook",
    Description = "Pure Awesome.",
    UnitPrice = 50.0M,
    ISBN = "3043",
```

```
        Author = "Jason Dentler",
    };

    using (var session = sessionFactory.OpenSession())
    {
      using (var tx = session.BeginTransaction())
      {
        session.Save(book);
        tx.Commit();
        session.Evict(book);
      }
    }

    return book;
}
```

How it works...

In `CreateAndSaveBook`, we create a book and save it to the database. We commit our transaction, evict the book from session, close the session, and return the book. This sets up our problem. We now have an entity without a session. Changes to this entity are not being tracked. It's just a plain ordinary book object.

We continue to change the book object, and now we want to save those changes. NHibernate doesn't know what we've done to this book. It could have been passed through other layers or tiers of a large application. We don't know with which session it's associated, if any. We may not even know if the book exists in the database.

`Session.Merge` handles all of this uncertainty for us. If the current session has a book with this ID, data from our book is copied on to the persistent book object in the session, and the persistent book object is returned.

If the current session doesn't have a book with this ID, NHibernate loads it from the database. The changes are copied on to the persistent book object that was just loaded in to the session. The persistent book object is returned.

If NHibernate didn't find a book with that ID in the database, it copies data from our book object on to a new persistent book associated with the session, and returns the new persistent book object.

The end result of `session.Merge` is the same. The book it returns is not the same instance we passed in, but it contains all of our changes and is associated with the current session. When we commit our transaction, those changes are written to the database.

The book we passed in is not associated with the current session.

▶ *Using session.Refresh*

Using session.Refresh

Especially in desktop applications, it may be necessary to reload an entity to reflect recent changes made in a different session. In this recipe, we'll use `session.Refresh` to refresh an entity's data as it is being manipulated by two sessions.

Getting ready

Following *Configuring NHibernate with App.config* from *Chapter 2*, setup a console application for NHibernate with our `Eg.Core` model from *Chapter 1*.

How to do it...

1. Add the following code to your `Main` method.

```
var sessionA = sessionFactory.OpenSession();
var sessionB = sessionFactory.OpenSession();

Guid productId;
Product productA;
Product productB;

productA = new Product()
{
  Name = "Lawn Chair",
  Description = "Lime Green, Comfortable",
  UnitPrice = 10.00M
};

using (var tx = sessionA.BeginTransaction())
{
  Console.WriteLine("Saving product.");
  productId = (Guid) sessionA.Save(productA);
  tx.Commit();
}

using (var tx = sessionB.BeginTransaction())
{
  Console.WriteLine("Changing price.");
  productB = sessionB.Get<Product>(productId);
```

```csharp
      productB.UnitPrice = 15.00M;
      tx.Commit();
   }

   using (var tx = sessionA.BeginTransaction())
   {
      Console.WriteLine("Price was {0:c}",
        productA.UnitPrice);

      sessionA.Refresh(productA);

      Console.WriteLine("Price is {0:c}",
        productA.UnitPrice);
      tx.Commit();
   }
   sessionA.Close();
   sessionB.Close();

   Console.ReadKey();
```

2. Run your application. You will see the following output:

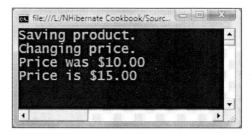

How it works...

In this contrived example, we open two sessions and manipulate two instances of the same entity. In session A, we save a newly created product – a **$10** lime green lawn chair. Then in session B, we get the very same lawn chair. We now have two instances of the same entity. One is associated with session A and the other with session B.

We change the price of session B's lawn chair to **$15**. Notice that we don't call any method to save or update the database. Because session B loaded the lawn chair, it is tracking the changes and will automatically update the database when the session is flushed. This happens automatically when we commit the transaction. This is called **automatic dirty checking**. Session A's instance of lawn chair is still priced at **$10**.

When we call sessionA.Refresh, NHibernate will update session A's lawn chair with fresh data from the database. Now session A's lawn chair shows the new **$15** price.

There's more...

`session.Refresh` is especially important in desktop applications, where we may have several sessions running simultaneously to handle multiple databound forms, and we want our saved changes on one form to be reflected immediately on another form displaying the same entity.

In this scenario, you will most likely set up some sort of message publishing between forms so that saving an entity on one form broadcasts an "I saved this entity" message to other forms displaying the same entity. When a form receives such a message, it calls `session.Refresh` to get the new data.

See also

▸ *Setting up session per presenter*

Using stateless sessions

When processing large amounts of data, you can usually improve performance by using an API that's closer to the "bare metal", often times trading off some higher-level features in the process. In NHibernate, this high performance, low-level API is the stateless session.

In this recipe, we'll use a stateless session to update our movie prices.

Getting ready

Just as before, follow *Configuring NHibernate with App.config* from *Chapter 2* to set up a console application with NHibernate and our `Eg.Core` model.

How to do it...

1. To create some data with which to work, add the following code to your `Main` method:

```
using (var session = sessionFactory.OpenStatelessSession())
{
  using (var tx = session.BeginTransaction())
  {
    for (int i = 0; i < 1000; i++)
    session.Insert(new Movie()
    {
      Name = "Movie " + i.ToString(),
      Description = "A great movie!",
      UnitPrice = 14.95M,
```

```
            Director = "Johnny Smith"
        });
        tx.Commit();
    }
}
```

2. Next, let's update our movie prices. Add the following code to the `Main` method:

```
using (var session = sessionFactory.OpenStatelessSession())
{
    using (var tx = session.BeginTransaction())
    {
    var movies = GetMovies(session);
    foreach (var movie in movies)
    {
        UpdateMoviePrice(movie);
        session.Update(movie);
    }
    tx.Commit();
    }
}
```

3. Add the `GetMovies` method:

```
static IEnumerable<Movie> GetMovies(IStatelessSession session)
{
    return session.CreateQuery("from Movie")
    .List<Movie>();
}
```

4. Finally, add our `UpdateMoviePrice` method:

```
static Random rnd = new Random();

static void UpdateMoviePrice(Movie movie)
{
    // Random price between $9.95 and $24.95
    movie.UnitPrice = (decimal) rnd.Next(10, 26) - 0.05M;
}
```

How it works...

Using a stateless session, we create 1000 movies. Stateless sessions don't implement **transactional write-behind**, meaning that the SQL statements are not delayed until we commit the transaction. However, because we have batching turned on, they don't happen immediately either. 100 insert statements are queued up at a time and sent all together. If we turned batching off, these would be sent one at a time immediately with each call to `session.Insert`.

Next, we fetch all of our movies from the database with a query. These movies are detached; they are not associated with a session. Entities can't be associated with stateless sessions. This is the case whether we load our entities with a query or the `Get` method.

Because stateless sessions don't implement **automatic dirty checking**, we have to call `session.Update` to save our changes to each movie.

There's more...

A stateless session is essentially a stripped-down version of a standard NHibernate session. It doesn't use a first level cache or perform automatic dirty checking, and it doesn't support lazy loading. In fact, it doesn't even keep references to entities, which helps avoid memory leaks when processing thousands of entities. Cascading is ignored. You must explicitly insert, update, or delete each entity one at a time. Stateless sessions also bypass the second-level cache, event listeners, interceptors, and even the NHibernate.SQL log4net logger.

Despite these limitations, stateless sessions are very useful in high performance batch processing situations where you need to work with real objects. When you can work with the raw data, there are usually better alternatives like plain old SQL, HQL bulk actions, SqlBulkCopy, or ETL tools. For the plain old SQL route, simple access the ADO.NET `connection` object from `session.Connection` and write your ADO.NET code as you normally would.

Using dictionaries as entities

A little-known feature of NHibernate is `EntityMode.Map`. In this recipe, I'll show you how we can use this feature to persist entities without classes.

Getting ready

Set up a new console project for NHibernate by following these steps:

1. Create a new console project.
2. Add references to `NHibernate.dll` and `NHibernate.ByteCode.Castle.dll`.

3. Add the following code to your main function:

```
var nhConfig = new Configuration().Configure();
var sessionFactory = nhConfig.BuildSessionFactory();
```

4. Add an `App.config` file to your project.

5. Inside the `configuration` element, declare a `hibernate-configuration` section, as shown:

```
<configSections>
  <section name="hibernate-configuration"
           type="NHibernate.Cfg.ConfigurationSectionHandler,
NHibernate"/>
</configSections>
```

6. Inside the `configuration` element, add a connection string named `db` as shown:

```
<connectionStrings>
    <add name="db" connectionString="Server=.\SQLExpress;
Database=NHCookbook; Trusted_Connection=SSPI"/>
  </connectionStrings>
```

7. Add the `hibernate-configuration` section with the following configuration:

```
<hibernate-configuration
xmlns="urn:nhibernate-configuration-2.2">
<session-factory>

  <property name="proxyfactory.factory_class">
  NHibernate.ByteCode.Castle.ProxyFactoryFactory,
  NHibernate.ByteCode.Castle
  </property>

  <property name="dialect">
  NHibernate.Dialect.MsSql2008Dialect,
  NHibernate
  </property>

  <property name="connection.connection_string_name">
  db
  </property>

  <property name="adonet.batch_size">
  100
  </property>

  <mapping assembly="yourAssemblyHere"/>

</session-factory>
</hibernate-configuration>
```

8. Set the mapping assembly value to the name of your project.

How to do it...

1. In your `hibernate-configuration session-factory` element, add a `default_entity_mode` property with the value `dynamic-map`.

2. Create a new `Product.hbm.xml` mapping file with this mapping:

```xml
<?xml version="1.0" encoding="utf-8" ?>
<hibernate-mapping xmlns="urn:nhibernate-mapping-2.2">
  <class entity-name="Product"
         discriminator-value="Eg.Core.Product">
    <id name="Id" type="Guid">
      <generator class="guid.comb" />
    </id>
    <discriminator column="ProductType" type="String" />
    <natural-id mutable="true">
      <property name="Name" not-null="true"
                type="String" />
    </natural-id>
    <version name="Version" type="Int32"/>
    <property name="Description" type="String" />
    <property name="UnitPrice" not-null="true"
              type="Currency" />
  </class>
</hibernate-mapping>
```

3. Again, create a mapping file named `Movie.hbm.xml` with the following mapping:

```xml
<?xml version="1.0" encoding="utf-8" ?>
<hibernate-mapping xmlns="urn:nhibernate-mapping-2.2">
  <subclass entity-name="Movie" extends="Product"
            discriminator-value="Eg.Core.Movie">
    <property name="Director" type="String" />
    <list name="Actors" cascade="all-delete-orphan">
      <key column="MovieId" />
      <index column="ActorIndex" />
      <one-to-many entity-name="ActorRole"/>
    </list>
  </subclass>
</hibernate-mapping>
```

4. Finally, create a mapping file named `ActorRole.hbm.xml` with the following mapping:

```xml
<?xml version="1.0" encoding="utf-8" ?>
<hibernate-mapping xmlns="urn:nhibernate-mapping-2.2">
  <class entity-name="ActorRole">
```

```
        <id name="Id" type="Guid">
          <generator class="guid.comb" />
        </id>
        <version name="Version" type="Int32" />
        <property name="Actor" type="String"
                   not-null="true" />
        <property name="Role" type="String"
                   not-null="true" />
     </class>
</hibernate-mapping>
```

5. Don't forget to set your mapping files as embedded resources.

6. In `main`, after building the session factory, create a movie object as a dictionary using the following code:

```
var movieActors = new List<Dictionary<string, object>>()
{
   new Dictionary<string, object>() {
   {"Actor","Keanu Reeves"},
   {"Role","Neo"}
   },
   new Dictionary<string, object>() {
   {"Actor", "Carrie-Ann Moss"},
   {"Role", "Trinity"}
   }
};

var movie = new Dictionary<string, object>()
{
   {"Name", "The Matrix"},
   {"Description", "Sci-Fi Action film"},
   {"UnitPrice", 18.99M},
   {"Director", "Wachowski Brothers"},
   {"Actors", movieActors}
};
```

7. After building the movie dictionary, save it using the following code:

```
using (var session = sessionFactory.OpenSession())
{
   using (var tx = session.BeginTransaction())
   {
   session.Save("Movie", movie);
   tx.Commit();
   }
}
```

8. Build and run your application.

9. Check your database's `Product` and `ActorRole` tables.

How it works...

`EntityMode.Map` allows us to define our entities as dictionaries instead of statically typed objects. There are three key pieces to this approach.

First, instead of creating sessions using the default `EntityMode.Poco` where NHibernate expects us to interact with it using plain old class objects, we've told NHibernate to use `EntityMode.Map` by setting `default_entity_mode` to `dynamic-map`. Remember from *Chapter 1* that, because of NHibernate's Java roots, NHibernate uses the term map in place of dictionary.

Next, we've made some slight changes to our mappings. First, you'll notice that we've set an `entity-name` instead of a `class name`. This allows us to specify an entity by name, instead of allowing NHibernate to decide based on the type of object we pass in. Next, you'll notice we specify types for all of our properties. We don't have classes that NHibernate can reflect to guess our data types. We have to tell it. Finally, we specify discriminator values. You'll remember from *Chapter 2* that the default discriminator value is the type's `FullName`. The default discriminator is actually the entity-name, which defaults to the type's `FullName`. In this case, we don't have a type, and if we used our entity-names, the data wouldn't match our normal mappings. We override the values simply so the data will match perfectly with the data from our other recipes.

Finally, we interact with the session using dictionaries (maps) and entity-name strings instead of objects with types.

There's more...

While this example may seem a bit academic, with the release of the Dynamic Language Runtime and the new `dynamic` feature of C# 4, this type of scenario will undoubtedly prove useful in bridging the gap between NHibernate and the dynamic language world.

Partially dynamic

It's rarely desirable to use `EntityMode.Map` throughout your application, as shown in this recipe. Instead, you may want to use it only in a specific case, where you would rather not create matching classes. In this scenario, we would not set the `default_entity_mode` property, and would instead open a child session in map mode. The code to accomplish this is as follows:

```
using (var pocoSession = sessionFactory.OpenSession())
{
  using (var childSession =
```

```
    pocoSession.GetSession(EntityMode.Map))
    {
      // Do something here
    }
}
```

Using NHibernate with TransactionScope

Reliable integration with other systems is a common business requirement. When these systems report error conditions, it's necessary to roll back not only the local database work, but perhaps the work of multiple transactional resources. In this recipe, I'll show you how to use Microsoft's TransactionScope and NHibernate to achieve this goal.

Getting ready

Create a new console application project.

Add references to the `Eg.Core` project in *Chapter 1*, `NHibernate.dll`, and `NHibernate.ByteCode.Castle.dll`.

Get the console application ready by following the *Configuring NHibernate with App.config* and *Configuring log4net* recipes in *Chapter 2*.

How to do it...

1. Add a reference to `System.Transaction`.
2. Add a public interface named `IReceiveProductUpdates` with the following three methods:
    ```
    void Add(Product product);
    void Update(Product product);
    void Remove(Product product);
    ```
3. Add a public class named `WarehouseFacade` with this code:
    ```
    public class WarehouseFacade : IReceiveProductUpdates
    {
      public void Add(Product product)
      {
        Console.WriteLine("Adding {0} to warehouse system.",
                  product.Name);
      }

      public void Update(Product product)
      {
    ```

```
    Console.WriteLine("Updating {0} in warehouse system.",
                      product.Name);
  }

  public void Remove(Product product)
  {
    Console.WriteLine("Removing {0} from warehouse system.",
                      product.Name);
    var message = string.Format(
      "Warehouse still has inventory of {0}.",
      product.Name);
    throw new ApplicationException(message);
  }

}
```

4. Add a public class named `ProductCatalog` with this code:

```
public class ProductCatalog : IReceiveProductUpdates
{
  private readonly ISessionFactory _sessionFactory;

  public ProductCatalog(ISessionFactory sessionFactory)
  {
    _sessionFactory = sessionFactory;
  }

  public void Add(Product product)
  {
    Console.WriteLine("Adding {0} to product catalog.",
                      product.Name);
    using (var session = _sessionFactory.OpenSession())
    using (var tx = session.BeginTransaction())
    {
      session.Save(product);
      tx.Commit();
    }
  }

  public void Update(Product product)
  {
    Console.WriteLine("Updating {0} in product catalog.",
                      product.Name);
    using (var session = _sessionFactory.OpenSession())
    using (var tx = session.BeginTransaction())
```

```
        {
          session.Update(product);
          tx.Commit();
        }
      }

      public void Remove(Product product)
      {
        Console.WriteLine("Removing {0} from product catalog.",
                          product.Name);
        using (var session = _sessionFactory.OpenSession())
        using (var tx = session.BeginTransaction())
        {
          session.Delete(product);
          tx.Commit();
        }
      }

    }
```

5. Update the `Program` class with the following code:

```
class Program
{

  static void Main(string[] args)
  {
    var nhConfig = new Configuration()
      .Configure();
    var sessionFactory = nhConfig
      .BuildSessionFactory();

    var catalog = new ProductCatalog(sessionFactory);
    var warehouse = new WarehouseFacade();

    var p = new Program(catalog, warehouse);

    var sprockets = new Product()
                      {
                          Name = "Sprockets",
                          Description = "12 pack, metal",
                          UnitPrice = 14.99M
                      };

    p.AddProduct(sprockets);

    sprockets.UnitPrice = 9.99M;
```

```
    p.UpdateProduct(sprockets);

    p.RemoveProduct(sprockets);

    Console.WriteLine("Press any key.");

    Console.ReadKey();

}

private readonly IReceiveProductUpdates[] _services;

public Program(params IReceiveProductUpdates[] services)
{
  _services = services;
}

private void AddProduct(Product newProduct)
{
  Console.WriteLine("Adding {0}.", newProduct.Name);
  try
  {
    using (var scope = new TransactionScope())
    {
      foreach (var service in _services)
        service.Add(newProduct);
      scope.Complete();
    }
  }
  catch (Exception ex)
  {
    Console.WriteLine("Product could not be added.");
    Console.WriteLine(ex.Message);
  }
}

private void UpdateProduct(Product changedProduct)
{
  Console.WriteLine("Updating {0}.",
                    changedProduct.Name);
  try
  {
    using (var scope = new TransactionScope())
    {
      foreach (var service in _services)
        service.Update(changedProduct);
```

```
          scope.Complete();
        }
      }
      catch (Exception ex)
      {
        Console.WriteLine("Product could not be updated.");
        Console.WriteLine(ex.Message);
      }
    }

    private void RemoveProduct(Product oldProduct)
    {
      Console.WriteLine("Removing {0}.",
                        oldProduct.Name);
      try
      {
        using (var scope = new TransactionScope())
        {
          foreach (var service in _services)
            service.Remove(oldProduct);
          scope.Complete();
        }
      }
      catch (Exception ex)
      {
        Console.WriteLine("Product could not be removed.");
        Console.WriteLine(ex.Message);
      }
    }

}
```

6. Build and run your application. You should see this output:

```
file:///L:/NHibernate Cookbook/Source/3 Sessions and Transactions/3.10/TxScope/bin/De...
Adding Sprockets.
Adding Sprockets to product catalog.
Adding Sprockets to warehouse system.
Updating Sprockets.
Updating Sprockets in product catalog.
Updating Sprockets in warehouse system.
Removing Sprockets.
Removing Sprockets from product catalog.
Removing Sprockets from warehouse system.
Product could not be removed.
Warehouse still has inventory of Sprockets.
Press any key.
```

7. Check the `NHCookbook` database. You should find a `Product` row for Sprockets with a unit price of $9.99.

How it works...

In this recipe, we work with two services that receive product updates. The first, a product catalog, uses NHibernate to store product data. The second, a small facade, is not as well-defined. It could use a number of different technologies to integrate our application with the larger warehouse system it represents.

Our services allow us to add, update, and remove products in these two systems. By wrapping these changes in a `TransactionScope`, we gain the ability to roll back the product catalog changes if the warehouse system fails, maintaining a consistent state.

Remember that NHibernate requires an NHibernate transaction when interacting with the database. `TransactionScope` is not a substitute. As illustrated in the next image, the `TransactionScope` should completely surround both the session and NHibernate transaction. The call to `TransactionScope.Complete()` should occur after the session has been disposed. Any other order will most likely lead to nasty, production crashing bugs like connection leaks.

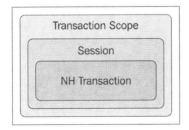

When we attempt to remove a product, our `WarehouseFacade` throws an exception, and things get a little strange. We committed the NHibernate transaction, so why didn't our delete happen? It did, but it was rolled back by the `TransactionScope`. When we started our NHibernate transaction, NHibernate detected the ambient transaction created by the `TransactionScope` and enlisted. The underlying connection and database transaction were held until the `TransactionScope` committed, or in this case, rolled back.

See also

- ▶ *Creating a session ASP.NET MVC action filter*
- ▶ *Creating a transaction ASP.NET MVC action filter*

4
Queries

In this chapter, we will cover the following topics:

- ▶ Using CriteriaQueries
- ▶ Using QueryOver
- ▶ Using QueryOver projections and aggregates
- ▶ Using MultiCriteria
- ▶ Using the Hibernate Query Language
- ▶ Using MultiQuery
- ▶ Using Named Queries
- ▶ Using Futures
- ▶ Eager loading child collections
- ▶ Using LINQ to NHibernate
- ▶ Using Detached Queries
- ▶ Using HQL for bulk data changes

Introduction

All but the last two recipes in this chapter begin with the following common steps. In addition to the normal process of mapping our model and configuring log4net and NHibernate, this also takes care of the necessary but repetitive plumbing code.

1. Complete the `Eg.Core` model and mapping project from *Chapter 1*.
2. Add a new console application to your solution.
3. Add an `App.config` file.

4. In `App.config`, configure NHibernate and log4net following the *Configuring NHibenate with App.config* and *Configuring NHibernate Logging* recipes in *Chapter 2*.

5. Create a new class called `ExampleDataCreator` with the following code:

```
public class ExampleDataCreator
{
  private readonly ISessionFactory _sessionFactory;

  public ExampleDataCreator(
    ISessionFactory sessionFactory)
  {
    if (sessionFactory == null)
      throw new ArgumentNullException("sessionFactory");
    _sessionFactory = sessionFactory;
  }

  public void SetUpDatabase()
  {
    using (var session = _sessionFactory.OpenSession())
    using (var tx = session.BeginTransaction())
    {
      ClearDatabase(session);
      CreateMovies(session);
      CreateBook(session);
      tx.Commit();
    }
  }

  private static void ClearDatabase(ISession session)
  {
    session
      .CreateQuery("delete from ActorRole")
      .ExecuteUpdate();

    session
      .CreateQuery("delete from Product")
      .ExecuteUpdate();
  }

  private static void CreateMovies(ISession session)
  {
    session.Save(
      new Movie()
        {
```

```
                Name = "Raiders of the Lost Ark",
                Description = "Awesome",
                UnitPrice = 9.59M,
                Director = "Steven Spielberg",
                Actors = new List<ActorRole>()
                            {
                                new ActorRole()
                                  {
                                    Actor = "Harrison Ford",
                                    Role = "Indiana Jones"
                                  }
                            }
            });

    session.Save(
      new Movie()
        {
          Name = "The Bucket List",
          Description = "Good",
          UnitPrice = 15M,
          Director = "Rob Reiner",
          Actors = new List<ActorRole>()
                      {
                          new ActorRole()
                            {
                              Actor = "Jack Nicholson",
                              Role = "Edward Cole"
                            },
                          new ActorRole()
                            {
                              Actor = "Morgan Freeman",
                              Role = "Carter Chambers"
                            }
                      }
            });
}
private static void CreateBook(ISession session)
{
  session.Save(
    new Book()
        {
```

```
            Name = "NHibernate 3.0 Cookbook",
            Description = "NHibernate examples",
            UnitPrice = 50M,
            Author = "Jason Dentler",
            ISBN = "978-1-849513-04-3"
          });
    }

}
```

6. Create another class called `NameAndPrice` with the following code:

```
public class NameAndPrice
{
  public NameAndPrice()
  {
  }
  public NameAndPrice(string name, decimal price)
  {
    Name = name;
    Price = price;
  }

  public string Name { get; set; }
  public decimal Price { get; set; }
}
```

7. Create a new class called `Queries` with this code:

```
public class Queries
{
  private readonly ISession _session;
  public Queries(ISession session)
  {
    if (session == null)
      throw new ArgumentNullException("session");
    _session = session;
  }
}
```

8. In `Program.cs`, add the following methods to the `Program` class:

```
static void RunQueries(ISession session)
{
```

```
}

static void Show(string heading,
           IEnumerable<Movie> movies)
{
  Console.WriteLine(heading);
  foreach (var m in movies)
    ShowMovie(m);
  Console.WriteLine();
}

static void Show(string heading, Book book)
{
  Console.WriteLine(heading);
  ShowBook(book);
  Console.WriteLine();
}

static void Show(string heading,
            IEnumerable<Product> products)
{
  Console.WriteLine(heading);
  foreach (var p in products)
  {
    if (p is Movie)
    {
      ShowMovie((Movie)p);
    }
    else if (p is Book)
    {
      ShowBook((Book)p);
    }
    else
      ShowProduct(p);
  }
  Console.WriteLine();
}

static void Show(string heading,
            decimal moneyValue)
{
  Console.WriteLine(heading);
  Console.WriteLine("{0:c}", moneyValue);
```

```
    Console.WriteLine();
  }

  static void Show(string heading,
                   IEnumerable<NameAndPrice> results)
  {
    Console.WriteLine(heading);
    foreach (var item in results)
      ShowNameAndPrice(item);
    Console.WriteLine();
  }

  static void ShowNameAndPrice(NameAndPrice item)
  {
    Console.WriteLine("{0:c} {1}",
                      item.Price, item.Name);
  }

  static void ShowProduct(Product p)
  {
    Console.WriteLine("{0:c} {1}",
                      p.UnitPrice, p.Name);
  }

  static void ShowBook(Book b)
  {
    Console.WriteLine("{0:c} {1} (ISBN {2})",
      b.UnitPrice, b.Name, b.ISBN);
  }

  static void ShowMovie(Movie movie)
  {
    var star = movie.Actors
      .Select(actorRole => actorRole.Actor)
      .FirstOrDefault();

    Console.WriteLine("{0:c} {1} starring {2}",
      movie.UnitPrice, movie.Name, star ?? "nobody");
  }
```

9. Add the following code in the `Main` method:

```
log4net.Config.XmlConfigurator.Configure();

var nhConfig = new Configuration().Configure();
var sessionFactory = nhConfig.BuildSessionFactory();
```

```
new ExampleDataCreator(sessionFactory)
  .SetUpDatabase();

using (var session = sessionFactory.OpenSession())
using (var tx = session.BeginTransaction())
{
  RunQueries(session);
  tx.Commit();
}

Console.WriteLine("Press any key");
Console.ReadKey();
```

The SQL queries shown in this chapter, and in fact, throughout the book, are specific to the Microsoft SQL Server 2008 dialect. If you use a different dialect and RDBMS, the SQL queries resulting from these examples may be slightly different.

Using Criteria Queries

In the last chapter, we fetched our entities by their ID. In this recipe, I'll show you a few basic criteria queries to fetch entities by other properties.

How to do it...

1. Complete the setup steps in the introduction at the beginning of this chapter.

2. In the `Queries` class, add the following method:

```
public IEnumerable<Movie> GetMoviesDirectedBy(string directorName)
{
  return _session.CreateCriteria<Movie>()
    .Add(Restrictions.Eq("Director", directorName))
    .List<Movie>();
}
```

3. In the `Queries` class, add the following method to query for movies by actor name:

```
public IEnumerable<Movie> GetMoviesWith(string actorName)
{
  return _session.CreateCriteria<Movie>()
    .CreateCriteria("Actors", JoinType.InnerJoin)
    .Add(Restrictions.Eq("Actor", actorName))
    .List<Movie>();
}
```

4. To query for a book by its ISBN, add the following method:

```
public Book GetBookByISBN(string isbn)
{
  return _session.CreateCriteria<Book>()
    .Add(Restrictions.Eq("ISBN", isbn))
    .UniqueResult<Book>();
}
```

5. Add the following method to find all the products in a price range:

```
public IEnumerable<Product> GetProductByPrice(
  decimal minPrice,
  decimal maxPrice)
{
  return _session.CreateCriteria<Product>()
    .Add(Restrictions.And(
      Restrictions.Ge("UnitPrice", minPrice),
      Restrictions.Le("UnitPrice", maxPrice)
          ))
    .AddOrder(Order.Asc("UnitPrice"))
    .List<Product>();
}
```

6. In `Program.cs`, use the following code for the `RunQueries` method:

```
static void RunQueries(ISession session)
{
  var queries = new Queries(session);

  Show("Movies directed by Spielberg:",
    queries.GetMoviesDirectedBy(
    "Steven Spielberg"));

  Show("Movies with Morgan Freeman:",
    queries.GetMoviesWith(
    "Morgan Freeman"));

  Show("This book:",
    queries.GetBookByISBN(
    "978-1-849513-04-3"));

  Show("Cheap products:",
    queries.GetProductByPrice(0M, 15M));
}
```

7. Build and run your application. You should see the following output:

```
file:///L:/NHibernate Cookbook/Source/4 Queries/4.01 ICriteria/CriteriaExample/bin/Debug/CriteriaExample.EXE
Movies directed by Spielberg:
$9.59 Raiders of the Lost Ark starring Harrison Ford

Movies with Morgan Freeman:
$15.00 The Bucket List starring Jack Nicholson

This book:
$50.00 NHibernate 3.0 Cookbook (ISBN 978-1-849513-04-3

Cheap products:
$9.59 Raiders of the Lost Ark starring Harrison Ford
$15.00 The Bucket List starring Jack Nicholson

Quality products:
$15.00 The Bucket List starring Jack Nicholson
$50.00 NHibernate 3.0 Cookbook (ISBN 978-1-849513-04-3

Press any key
```

How it works...

Let's work through each of these four queries individually.

▶ GetMoviesDirectedBy query

```
_session.CreateCriteria<Movie>()
        .Add(Restrictions.Eq("Director", directorName))
        .List<Movie>();
```

In the above code, we use `session.CreateCriteria` to get an `ICriteria` object. Our generic parameter, `Movie`, tells NHibernate that we're going to query on movies. In the second line, we restrict the movies to only those directed by *Steven Spielberg*. Finally, we call the `List` method, which executes the query and returns our *Steven Spielberg* movies. Because of the generic parameter `Movie`, NHibernate returns a strongly typed `IList<Movie>` instead of an `IList`.

In Microsoft SQL Server, this results in the following SQL query:

```
SELECT    this_.Id          as Id1_0_,
          this_.Name        as Name1_0_,
          this_.Description as Descript4_1_0_,
          this_.UnitPrice   as UnitPrice1_0_,
          this_.Director    as Director1_0_
FROM      Product this_
WHERE     this_.ProductType = 'Eg.Core.Movie'
          AND this_.Director = 'Steven Spielberg' /* @p0 */
```

▸ GetMoviesWith query

```
_session.CreateCriteria<Movie>()
        .CreateCriteria("Actors", JoinType.InnerJoin)
        .Add(Restrictions.Eq("Actor", actorName))
        .List<Movie>();
```

We are again querying movies, but in this example, we are querying based on a child collection. We want all of *Morgan Freeman's* movies. In terms of our model, we want to return all of the `Movies` with an associated `ActorRole` object where the `Actor` property equals the string `'Morgan Freeman'`.

The second line sets up an inner join between `Movies` and `ActorRoles` based on the contents of a `Movie's Actors` collection. Remember from SQL that an inner join only returns the rows with a match. `CreateCriteria` also changes the context of the query from `Movie` to `ActorRole`. This allows us to filter our `ActorRoles` further on the third line.

On the third line, we simply filter the `ActorRole` objects down to only *Morgan Freeman's* roles. Because of the inner join, this also filters the `Movies`. Finally, we execute the query and get the results with a call to `List<Movie>`.

Here is the resulting SQL query in Microsoft SQL Server:

```
SELECT this_.Id            as Id1_1_,
       this_.Version       as Version1_1_,
       this_.Name          as Name1_1_,
       this_.Description    as Descript5_1_1_,
       this_.UnitPrice      as UnitPrice1_1_,
       this_.Director       as Director1_1_,
       actorrole1_.Id       as Id0_0_,
       actorrole1_.Version  as Version0_0_,
       actorrole1_.Actor    as Actor0_0_,
       actorrole1_.Role     as Role0_0_
FROM   Product this_
       inner join ActorRole actorrole1_
         on this_.Id = actorrole1_.MovieId
WHERE  this_.ProductType = 'Eg.Core.Movie'
       AND actorrole1_.Actor = 'Morgan Freeman' /* @p0 */
```

▸ GetBookByISBN query

```
_session.CreateCriteria<Book>()
        .Add(Restrictions.Eq("ISBN", isbn))
        .UniqueResult<Book>();
```

In this criteria query, we're searching for a particular book by its ISBN. Because we use `UniqueResult<Book>` instead of `List<Book>`, NHibernate returns a single `Book` object, or null if it's not found. This query assumes ISBN is unique.

We get this simple SQL query:

```
SELECT  this_.Id           as Id1_0_,
        this_.Name         as Name1_0_,
        this_.Description as Descript4_1_0_,
        this_.UnitPrice    as UnitPrice1_0_,
        this_.Author       as Author1_0_,
        this_.ISBN         as ISBN1_0_
FROM    Product this_
WHERE   this_.ProductType = 'Eg.Core.Book'
        AND this_.ISBN = '3043' /* @p0 */
```

▸ GetProductByPrice query

```
_session.CreateCriteria<Product>()
        .Add(Restrictions.And(
          Restrictions.Ge("UnitPrice", minPrice),
          Restrictions.Le("UnitPrice", maxPrice)
              ))
        .AddOrder(Order.Asc("UnitPrice"))
        .List<Product>()
```

With this criteria query, we combine a *greater than or equal to* operation and a *less than or equal to* operation using an `And` operation to return products priced between two values. The `And` restriction takes two child restrictions as parameters.

We could also use the `Between` restriction to create an equivalent criteria query like this:

```
.Add(Restrictions.Between("UnitPrice", minPrice, maxPrice))
```

We use the `AddOrder` method to sort our product results by ascending unit price.

Here's the resulting SQL query in Microsoft SQL Server:

```
SELECT  this_.Id           as Id1_0_,
        this_.Name         as Name1_0_,
        this_.Description as Descript4_1_0_,
        this_.UnitPrice    as UnitPrice1_0_,
        this_.Director     as Director1_0_,
        this_.Author       as Author1_0_,
        this_.ISBN         as ISBN1_0_,
        this_.ProductType as ProductT2_1_0_
```

```
FROM       Product this_
WHERE      (this_.UnitPrice >= 0 /* @p0 */
            and this_.UnitPrice <= 15 /* @p1 */)
ORDER BY this_.UnitPrice asc
```

There's more...

The criteria API is intended for dynamically built queries, such as the advanced search feature we see on many retail websites, where the user may choose any number of filter and sort criteria. However, these queries must be parsed and compiled on the fly.

For relatively static queries with a set of well-known parameters, it is preferable to use named HQL queries, as these are precompiled when we build the session factory.

The criteria API suffers from the **magic strings** problem, where strings refer to properties and classes in our application. With strongly typed APIs, we can easily change a property name using the refactoring tools of Visual Studio or ReSharper. With the criteria API, when we change a property name in our model, we have to find and update every criteria query that uses the property. As we will see in the next recipe, the new QueryOver API helps solve this problem.

See also

- ▶ *Using QueryOver*
- ▶ *Using QueryOver projections and aggregates*
- ▶ *Using MultiCriteria*
- ▶ *Using Named Queries*
- ▶ *Using Detached Queries*

Using QueryOver

NHibernate 3.0 has added a new fluent syntax to criteria queries. Although it's not an actual LINQ provider, it does bring the familiar lambda syntax to criteria queries, eliminating the magic strings problem. In this recipe, I'll show you the new QueryOver syntax for the criteria queries from our last recipe.

How to do it...

1. Complete the setup steps in the introduction at the beginning of this chapter.
2. In the `Queries` class, add the following method:

   ```
   public IEnumerable<Movie> GetMoviesDirectedBy(string directorName)
   ```

```
{
   return _session.QueryOver<Movie>()
      .Where(m => m.Director == directorName)
      .List();
}
```

3. In the `Queries` class, add the following method to query for movies by actor's name:

```
public IEnumerable<Movie> GetMoviesWith(string actorName)
{
   return _session.QueryOver<Movie>()
      .OrderBy(m => m.UnitPrice).Asc
      .Inner.JoinQueryOver<ActorRole>(m => m.Actors)
      .Where(a => a.Actor == actorName)
      .List();
}
```

4. So we can query for a book by its ISBN by adding the following method:

```
public Book GetBookByISBN(string isbn)
{
   return _session.QueryOver<Book>()
      .Where(b => b.ISBN == isbn)
      .SingleOrDefault();
}
```

5. Add the following method to find all the products in a price range:

```
public IEnumerable<Product> GetProductByPrice(
   decimal minPrice,
   decimal maxPrice)
{
   return _session.QueryOver<Product>()
      .Where(p => p.UnitPrice >= minPrice
                  && p.UnitPrice <= maxPrice)
      .OrderBy(p => p.UnitPrice).Asc
      .List();
}
```

6. In `Program.cs`, use the following code for the `RunQueries` method:

```
static void RunQueries(ISession session)
{
   var queries = new Queries(session);

   Show("Movies directed by Spielberg:",
      queries.GetMoviesDirectedBy(
      "Steven Spielberg"));
```

```
Show("Movies with Morgan Freeman:",
  queries.GetMoviesWith(
  "Morgan Freeman"));

Show("This book:",
  queries.GetBookByISBN(
  "978-1-849513-04-3"));

Show("Cheap products:",
  queries.GetProductByPrice(0M, 15M));
}
```

7. Build and run your application. You should see the following screenshot:

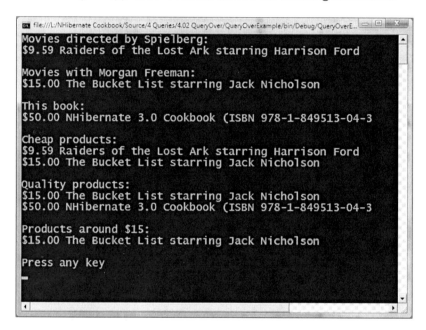

How it works...

In the previous code, we've implemented the queries from the last recipe using NHibernate's new QueryOver syntax. Using this syntax, most restrictions can be represented using the `Where` method, which takes a lambda expression as input. For example, to filter our movies on director name, we use `.Where(m => m.Director == directorName)`. In many cases, we can combine multiple restrictions in a single `Where`. To get products within a particular price range, we could write this:

```
.Where(p => p.UnitPrice >= minPrice)
.And(p => p.UnitPrice <= maxPrice)
```

We could also combine it into one `Where`, like this:

```
.Where(p => p.UnitPrice >= minPrice && p.UnitPrice <= maxPrice)
```

Some restrictions, such as `Between`, don't have equivalent lambda expressions. For these operations, we begin with `WhereRestrictionOn` to specify the property we'll use. Then, we follow it with a call to the restriction's method. For example, we could write this same price range filter using Criteria's `Between` restriction:

```
.WhereRestrictionOn(p => p.UnitPrice)
.IsBetween(minPrice).And(maxPrice)
```

To create a join, we use `JoinQueryOver`, like this:

```
.Inner.JoinQueryOver<ActorRole>(m => m.Actors)
```

In QueryOver, `UniqueResult` is replaced with the LINQ-like `SingleOrDefault`.

There's more...

QueryOver is a new API on top of NHibernate's existing criteria queries. Should we need to use the criteria API directly, we can get to the criteria query inside through QueryOver's `UnderlyingCriteria` property.

See also

- ▶ *Using QueryOver projections and aggregates*
- ▶ *Using Criteria Queries*
- ▶ *MultiCriteria*
- ▶ *Named Queries*
- ▶ *Detached Queries*

Using QueryOver projections and aggregates

In some cases, we only need specific properties of an entity. In other cases, we may need the results of an aggregate function, such as average or count. In this recipe, I'll show you how to write QueryOver queries with projections and aggregates.

How to do it...

1. Complete the setup steps in the introduction at the beginning of this chapter.

2. Add the following method to the `Queries` class.

```
public IEnumerable<NameAndPrice> GetMoviePriceList()
{
  return _session.QueryOver<Movie>()
    .Select(m => m.Name, m => m.UnitPrice)
    .List<object[]>()
    .Select(props =>
      new NameAndPrice()
      {
        Name = (string)props[0],
        Price = (decimal)props[1]
      });
}
```

3. Add the following method to `Queries` to fetch a simple average movie price:

```
public decimal GetAverageMoviePrice()
{
  var result = _session.QueryOver<Movie>()
    .Select(Projections.Avg<Movie>(m => m.UnitPrice))
    .SingleOrDefault<double>();
  return Convert.ToDecimal(result);
}
```

4. To get a list of directors and the average price of their movies, add the following method:

```
public IEnumerable<NameAndPrice> GetAvgDirectorPrice()
{
  return _session.QueryOver<Movie>()
    .Select(list => list
      .SelectGroup(m => m.Director)
      .SelectAvg(m => m.UnitPrice)
    )
    .List<object[]>()
    .Select(props =>
      new NameAndPrice()
      {
        Name = (string)props[0],
        Price = Convert.ToDecimal(props[1])
```

```
    });
  }
```

5. In `Program.cs`, use the following code in the `RunQueries` method:

```
static void RunQueries(ISession session)
{
  var queries = new Queries(session);

  Show("Movie Price List:",
    queries.GetMoviePriceList());

  Show("Average Movie Price:",
    queries.GetAverageMoviePrice());

  Show("Average Price by Director:",
    queries.GetAvgDirectorPrice());
}
```

6. Build and run your application. You should see the following output:

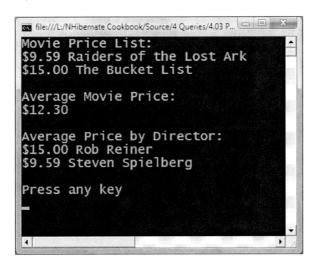

How it works...

Again, we'll discuss each query separately. The queries are as follows:

▶ GetMoviePriceList query

Here's the code we used for our movie price list query:

```
_session.QueryOver<Movie>()
.Select(m => m.Name, m => m.UnitPrice)
.List<object[]>()
```

```
.Select(props =>
  new NameAndPrice()
  {
    Name = (string)props[0],
    Price = (decimal)props[1]
  });
```

In this query, we want to return a list containing only movie names and their prices. To accomplish this, we project two properties from our `Movie` object: `Name` and `UnitPrice`. We do this using QueryOver's `Select` method. Our QueryOver ends with a call to `List`. Because we are returning the values of individual properties instead of entire `Movie` objects, our generic argument specifies that we'll return a list of object arrays. Each element in the list represents a row in our query results. The first element of each of those object arrays is the movie's `Name`. The second is the movie's `UnitPrice`.

The resulting SQL query for Microsoft SQL Server is as follows:

```
SELECT this_.Name      as y0_,
       this_.UnitPrice as y1_
FROM   Product this_
WHERE  this_.ProductType = 'Eg.Core.Movie'
```

To return a list of strongly typed objects instead of these object arrays, we use a standard LINQ to Objects `Select` from `System.Linq` to put our query results into neat `NameAndPrice` objects.

▶ GetAverageMoviePrice query

```
_session.QueryOver<Movie>()
.Select(Projections.Avg<Movie>(m => m.UnitPrice))
.SingleOrDefault<double>();
```

In the previous code, we query for the average price of all movies in the database. We call our aggregate function through `Projections.Avg`, and then project the result.

Because we have projected a single aggregate result, we execute the query and get the result with a call to `.SingleOrDefault<double>()`. We expect a `double` to be returned by the average aggregate function. However, because we're dealing with money, we'll convert it to a `decimal` before returning it to our application.

This QueryOver results in the following SQL Query:

```
SELECT avg(cast(this_.UnitPrice as DOUBLE PRECISION)) as y0_
FROM   Product this_
WHERE  this_.ProductType = 'Eg.Core.Movie'
```

▶ GetAvgDirectorPrice query

With the following code, we query for a list of movie directors and the average price of their movies.

```
_session.QueryOver<Movie>()
.Select(list => list
    .SelectGroup(m => m.Director)
    .SelectAvg(m => m.UnitPrice)
)
.List<object[]>()
.Select(props =>
    new NameAndPrice()
    {
        Name = (string)props[0],
        Price = Convert.ToDecimal(props[1])
    });
```

In this case, we will group by and project the `Director` property and project the average `UnitPrice`, using this syntax:

```
.Select(list => list
    .SelectGroup(m => m.Director)
    .SelectAvg(m => m.UnitPrice)
)
```

Just as we did in our first query, we return a list of object arrays, and then transform them into a list of `NameAndPrice` objects with LINQ to Objects.

Here is the resulting SQL query:

```
SELECT   this_.Director                              as y0_,
         avg(cast(this_.UnitPrice as DOUBLE PRECISION)) as y1_
FROM     Product this_
WHERE    this_.ProductType = 'Eg.Core.Movie'
GROUP BY this_.Director
```

See also

▶ *Using Criteria Queries*

▶ *Using QueryOver*

▶ *Using MultiCriteria*

▶ *Using Named Queries*

▶ *Using Detached Queries*

Using MultiCriteria

To display many forms and web pages, we need to run several queries. For example, it's common to display search results one page at a time. This typically requires two queries. The first counts all the available results, and the second fetches the data for only 10 or 20 results. MultiCriteria allows us to combine these two queries into a single database round trip, speeding up our application. In this recipe, I'll show you how to use MultiCriteria to fetch a paged result set of products.

How to do it...

1. Complete the setup steps in the introduction at the beginning of this chapter.

2. Add the following structure inside the `Queries` class:

```
public struct PageOf<T>
{
    public int PageCount;
    public int PageNumber;
    public IEnumerable<T> PageOfResults;
}
```

3. Add the following methods to the `Queries` class:

```
public PageOf<Product> GetPageOfProducts(
    int pageNumber,
    int pageSize)
{
    var skip = (pageNumber - 1) * pageSize;

    var countQuery = GetCountQuery();
    var resultQuery = GetPageQuery(skip, pageSize);

    var multiCrit = _session.CreateMultiCriteria()
        .Add<int>("count", countQuery)
        .Add<Product>("page", resultQuery);

    var productCount = ((IList<int>)multiCrit
        .GetResult("count")).Single();

    var products = (IList<Product>)multiCrit
        .GetResult("page");

    var pageCount = (int) Math.Ceiling(
        productCount/(double) pageSize);

    return new PageOf<Product>()
        {
```

```
                    PageCount = pageCount,
                    PageOfResults = products,
                    PageNumber = pageNumber
                };
  }

  private ICriteria GetCountQuery()
  {
    return _session.QueryOver<Product>()
      .Select(list => list
                .SelectCount(m => m.Id))
      .UnderlyingCriteria;
  }

  private ICriteria GetPageQuery(int skip, int take)
  {
    return _session.QueryOver<Product>()
      .OrderBy(m => m.UnitPrice).Asc
      .Skip(skip)
      .Take(take)
      .UnderlyingCriteria;
  }
```

4. In `Program.cs`, use the following code in the `RunQueries` method:

```
static void RunQueries(ISession session)
{
  var queries = new Queries(session);
  var result = queries.GetPageOfProducts(1, 2);
  var heading = string.Format("Page {0} of {1}",
                                  result.PageNumber,
                                  result.PageCount);
  Show(heading, result.PageOfResults);
}
```

5. Build and run your application. You should see the following output:

```
file:///L:/NHibernate Cookbook/Source/4 Queries/4.04 MultiCriteria/MultiCriteriaExample/bin/Debug/...
Page 1 of 2
$9.59 Raiders of the Lost Ark starring Harrison Ford
$15.00 The Bucket List starring Jack Nicholson

Press any key
```

How it works...

The MultiCriteria API may be used with any NHibernate-supported RDBMS. However, only Microsoft SQL Server and Oracle can combine these queries into a single round trip to the database. For all other RDBMS, this functionality is simulated. In either case, your application doesn't need to be concerned. It just works.

In this recipe, we combine two criteria queries in a single round trip to the database. Our first query counts all the products in the database. Our second query returns a page with the first two of our three products, sorted by unit price. We use QueryOver's `Skip` and `Take` to accomplish this.

There are a couple of interesting things to point out with the `MultiCriteria` syntax.

```
var multiCrit = session.CreateMultiCriteria()
    .Add<int>("count", countQuery)
    .Add<Movie>("page", resultQuery);
```

First, you'll notice that we've labeled our queries with `"count"` and `"page"`. This is not required. Instead, we could use the index of each criteria object in the `MultiCriteria` to fetch the results. It's a little more difficult to mess up names than list indices, so we'll use names.

We use generic arguments to specify the element type for our results. That is, our first query returns a list of integers and the second returns a list of movies. The `MultiCriteria` doesn't provide a method for directly returning a single entity or scalar value. Instead, we use LINQ to Object's `Single` method to fetch the first and only value from the list.

When we get the product count, both queries are immediately executed, and the results are stored in memory. When we get the page of products, the `MultiCriteria` simply returns the results of the already-executed query.

See also

- ▸ *Using QueryOver*
- ▸ *Using MultiQuery*
- ▸ *Using Futures*

Using the Hibernate Query Language

So far, we've covered various queries using NHibernate's Criteria API and its new QueryOver syntax. NHibernate provides another, more powerful query method named Hibernate Query Language, a domain-specific language that blends familiar SQL-like syntax with object-oriented thinking. In this recipe, I'll show you how to use the Hibernate Query Language to perform those same queries.

How to do it...

1. Complete the steps in the introduction at the beginning of this chapter, naming the new console application `HQLExample`.

2. Add a new mapping document named `NameAndPrice.hbm.xml` with this xml code. Don't forget to set the **Build action** to **Embedded Resource**.

```xml
<?xml version="1.0" encoding="utf-8" ?>
<hibernate-mapping xmlns="urn:nhibernate-mapping-2.2"
    assembly="HQLExample"
    namespace="HQLExample">
  <import class="NameAndPrice"/>
</hibernate-mapping>
```

3. In `App.config`, add `<mapping assembly="HQLExample"/>` below the mapping element for `Eg.Core`.

4. Add the following methods to the `Queries` class:

```csharp
public IEnumerable<Movie> GetMoviesDirectedBy(string directorName)
{
  var hql = @"from Movie m
            where m.Director = :director";
  return _session.CreateQuery(hql)
    .SetString("director", directorName)
    .List<Movie>();
}

public IEnumerable<Movie> GetMoviesWith(string actorName)
{
  var hql = @"select m
            from Movie m
            inner join m.Actors as ar
            where ar.Actor = :actorName";
  return _session.CreateQuery(hql)
    .SetString("actorName", actorName)
    .List<Movie>();
}

public Book GetBookByISBN(string isbn)
{
  var hql = @"from Book b
            where b.ISBN = :isbn";
  return _session.CreateQuery(hql)
    .SetString("isbn", isbn)
```

```
        .UniqueResult<Book>();
}

public IEnumerable<Product> GetProductByPrice(
  decimal minPrice,
  decimal maxPrice)
{
  var hql = @"from Product p
              where p.UnitPrice >= :minPrice
              and p.UnitPrice <= :maxPrice
              order by p.UnitPrice asc";

  return _session.CreateQuery(hql)
    .SetDecimal("minPrice", minPrice)
    .SetDecimal("maxPrice", maxPrice)
    .List<Product>();
}

public IEnumerable<NameAndPrice> GetMoviePriceList()
{
  var hql = @"select new NameAndPrice(
              m.Name, m.UnitPrice)
              from Movie m";
  return _session.CreateQuery(hql)
    .List<NameAndPrice>();

}

public decimal GetAverageMoviePrice()
{
  var hql = @"select Cast(avg(m.UnitPrice)
              as Currency)
              from Movie m";
  return _session.CreateQuery(hql)
    .UniqueResult<decimal>();
}

public IEnumerable<NameAndPrice> GetAvgDirectorPrice()
{
  var hql = @"select new NameAndPrice(
                m.Director,
                Cast(avg(m.UnitPrice) as Currency)
                )
                from Movie m
```

```
            group by m.Director";
    return _session.CreateQuery(hql)
        .List<NameAndPrice>();
}
```

5. In `Program.cs`, use the following code in the `RunQueries` method:

```
static void RunQueries(ISession session)
{
    var queries = new Queries(session);

    Show("Movies directed by Spielberg:",
        queries.GetMoviesDirectedBy(
        "Steven Spielberg"));

    Show("Movies with Morgan Freeman:",
        queries.GetMoviesWith(
        "Morgan Freeman"));

    Show("This book:",
        queries.GetBookByISBN(
        "978-1-849513-04-3"));

    Show("Cheap products:",
        queries.GetProductByPrice(0M, 15M));

    Show("Movie Price List:",
        queries.GetMoviePriceList());

    Show("Average Movie Price:",
        queries.GetAverageMoviePrice());

    Show("Average Price by Director:",
        queries.GetAvgDirectorPrice());
}
```

6. Build and run your application. You should see the following output:

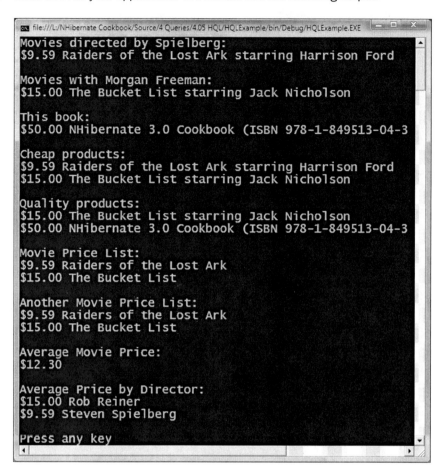

```
file:///L:/NHibernate Cookbook/Source/4 Queries/4.05 HQL/HQLExample/bin/Debug/HQLExample.EXE

Movies directed by Spielberg:
$9.59 Raiders of the Lost Ark starring Harrison Ford

Movies with Morgan Freeman:
$15.00 The Bucket List starring Jack Nicholson

This book:
$50.00 NHibernate 3.0 Cookbook (ISBN 978-1-849513-04-3

Cheap products:
$9.59 Raiders of the Lost Ark starring Harrison Ford
$15.00 The Bucket List starring Jack Nicholson

Quality products:
$15.00 The Bucket List starring Jack Nicholson
$50.00 NHibernate 3.0 Cookbook (ISBN 978-1-849513-04-3

Movie Price List:
$9.59 Raiders of the Lost Ark
$15.00 The Bucket List

Another Movie Price List:
$9.59 Raiders of the Lost Ark
$15.00 The Bucket List

Average Movie Price:
$12.30

Average Price by Director:
$15.00 Rob Reiner
$9.59 Steven Spielberg

Press any key
```

How it works...

Hibernate Query Language (HQL) syntax resembles SQL in many ways, but operates at an object level. We build all of our queries as strings. Much like DbCommands in ADO.NET, we create IQuery objects around those query strings, set the parameter values, and execute our queries with List or UniqueResult. Similar to the "at" sign (@) in Microsoft SQL Server queries, in HQL, we prepend our parameter names with a colon (:) in the query string. When we set the parameter value, we don't include the colon.

▶ GetMoviesDirectedBy query

We have this very basic HQL query:

```
from Movie m
where m.Director = :director
```

For brevity, we've aliased our movies as simply `m`. In this case, there is an implied `select m` to project our movies. We have a single parameter, `director`, which we use to filter our movies.

▶ GetMoviesWith query

```
select m
from Movie m
inner join m.Actors as ar
where ar.Actor = :actorName
```

In this query, we join from movies to their actor roles. Notice that unlike SQL, we don't need to specify `ActorRoles` or set up a comparison with an `ON` clause explicitly. NHibernate already understands the relationships between our entities. We filter those actor roles based on actor name. Just as with SQL, because we use an inner join, this filter on actor role effectively filters our movies as well.

▶ GetProductByPrice query

```
from Product p
where p.UnitPrice >= :minPrice
and p.UnitPrice <= :maxPrice
order by p.UnitPrice asc
```

In this query, we filter our `Product` based on a price range defined by the two parameters, `minPrice` and `maxPrice`. This query could also be written using HQL's `between`:

```
from Product p
where p.UnitPrice between
:minPrice and :maxPrice
order by p.UnitPrice asc
```

As with SQL, the order by clause sorts our products by unit price.

▶ GetMoviePriceList query

We have this simple query:

```
select new NameAndPrice(m.Name, m.UnitPrice)
from Movie m
```

When working with HQL, think in terms of objects and properties, not tables and columns. This query passes the `Name` and `UnitPrice` properties into this constructor of our `NameAndPrice` class:

```
public NameAndPrice(string name, decimal unitPrice)
```

Then it projects the resulting `NameAndPrice` instances. To make NHibernate aware of this class, we use the following import mapping:

```
<import class="NameAndPrice"/>
```

As an alternative, just as with criteria and QueryOver, we could simply project `Name` and `UnitPrice`, return a list of object arrays, and then use LINQ to Objects to transform those object arrays into `NameAndPrice` instances, as shown in the following code:

```
var hql = @"select m.Name, m.UnitPrice
          from Movie m";
var query = session.CreateQuery(hql);
return query.List<object[]>()
  .Select(props =>
    new NameAndPrice(
      (string)props[0],
      (decimal)props[1]));
```

In this case, we wouldn't need to import our `NameAndPrice` class.

▶ GetAverageMoviePrice query

```
select Cast(avg(m.UnitPrice) as Currency)
from Movie m
```

In this query, we use the aggregate function average. This returns a scalar value of type `double`, so we cast it back to NHibernate's `Currency` type. The equivalent .NET type is `decimal`, so we execute the query using `UniqueResult<decimal>()`.

▶ GetAvgDirectorPrice query

```
select new NameAndPrice(
    m.Director,
    Cast(avg(m.UnitPrice) as Currency)
)
from Movie m
group by m.Director
```

In this query, we group by `Director`. We then pass `Director` and our average `UnitPrice` into the constructor of `NameAndPrice`. Just as before, because `avg` returns a `double`, we'll need to `Cast` it back to `Currency` first.

There's more...

In addition to the mapped properties and collections on our entities, HQL allows you to query on two implied and special properties:

▶ The property `class` is the full name of the type of our entity. For example, to query for books, we could write the following:

```
from Product p where p.class='Eg.Core.Book'
```

- The property `id` always represents the POID of the entity, regardless of what we may name it in our entity. We can query for three books at a time with this query:

```
from Book b where b.id in (@id0, @id1, @id2)
```

See also

- *Using Criteria Queries*
- *Using QueryOver*
- *Using MultiQuery*
- *Using Named Queries*
- *Using Detached Queries*

Using MultiQuery

Just like we can combine several ICriteria and QueryOver queries into a single database round trip with MultiCriteria, we can combine several HQL queries with MultiQuery. Particularly in a production setting where the database and application are on separate machines, each round trip to the database is very expensive. Combining work in this way can greatly improve application performance. In this recipe, I'll show you how to fetch a product count and page of product results using a MultiQuery.

How to do it...

1. Complete the setup steps in the introduction at the beginning of this chapter.
2. Add the following structure inside the `Queries` class:

```
public struct PageOf<T>
{
    public int PageCount;
    public int PageNumber;
    public IEnumerable<T> PageOfResults;
}
```

3. Add the following methods to the `Queries` class:

```
public PageOf<Product> GetPageOfProducts(
    int pageNumber,
    int pageSize)
{
    var skip = (pageNumber - 1) * pageSize;

    var countQuery = GetCountQuery();
    var resultQuery = GetPageQuery(skip, pageSize);
```

```
    var multiQuery = _session.CreateMultiQuery()
      .Add<long>("count", countQuery)
      .Add<Product>("page", resultQuery);

    var productCount = ((IList<long>)multiQuery
      .GetResult("count")).Single();

    var products = (IList<Product>)multiQuery
      .GetResult("page");

    var pageCount = (int) Math.Ceiling(
      productCount/(double) pageSize);

    return new PageOf<Product>()
            {
              PageCount = pageCount,
              PageOfResults = products,
              PageNumber = pageNumber
            };
}

private IQuery GetCountQuery()
{
  var hql = @"select count(p.Id) from Product p";
  return _session.CreateQuery(hql);
}

private IQuery GetPageQuery(int skip, int take)
{
  var hql = @"from Product p order by p.UnitPrice asc";

  return _session.CreateQuery(hql)
    .SetFirstResult(skip)
    .SetMaxResults(take);
}
```

4. In `Program.cs`, use the following code in the `RunQueries` method:

```
static void RunQueries(ISession session)
{
  var queries = new Queries(session);
  var result = queries.GetPageOfProducts(1, 2);
  var heading = string.Format("Page {0} of {1}",
                              result.PageNumber,
                              result.PageCount);
  Show(heading, result.PageOfResults);
}
```

5. Build and run your application. You should see the following output:

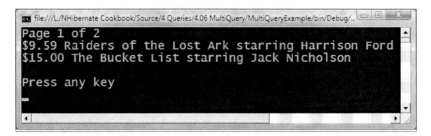

How it works...

In this recipe, we build two HQL queries. The first returns a count of all our products. It's important to note that HQL's count returns an `Int64` or `long`.

The second query returns a single page of products. We use `SetFirstResult` to determine where our results begin. For example, passing zero to `SetFirstResult` will return all the results. Passing 10 will skip the first 10 results, returning the 11th product and beyond. We combine this with `SetMaxResults` to return a single page of results. `.SetFirstResult(10).SetMaxResults(10)` will return the 11th through 20th product.

We add each of our queries to our `MultiQuery` object, specifying a label or name, and, with the generic argument, the type of list to return. Just as with `MultiCriteria`, there's no way to return a single entity or scalar value directly. In this example, our count query will return a list of `Int64s` containing one item, and our page query will return a list of `Products`. We'll use LINQ to Objects's `Single()` method to extract the actual count value.

We use the label again in our call to `GetResults` to return a specific result set. The first call to `GetResults` executes all the queries in a single batch. Each subsequent call only returns the results of an already executed query.

See also

▸ *Using MultiCritieria*

▸ *Using Named Queries*

Using Named Queries

Just as with SQL, mixing inline HQL with business logic is generally a losing battle. The code becomes unreadable, and the queries are nearly impossible to properly unit test. In this recipe, I'll show you how we can move these HQL queries out of our code, improve readability and testability, and even improve performance by parsing and pre-compiling queries.

How to do it...

1. Complete the steps in the introduction at the beginning of this chapter, naming the new console application `NamedQueryExample`.

2. Add a new mapping document named `GetBookByISBN.hbm.xml` with the following xml code. Don't forget to set the **Build action** to **Embedded Resource**.

```xml
<?xml version="1.0" encoding="utf-8" ?>
<hibernate-mapping xmlns="urn:nhibernate-mapping-2.2">
  <query name="GetBookByISBN">
    <![CDATA[
    from Book b where b.ISBN = :isbn
    ]]>
  </query>
</hibernate-mapping>
```

3. In `App.config`, add `<mapping assembly="NamedQueryExample"/>` below the mapping element for `Eg.Core`.

4. Add the following methods to the `Queries` class:

```csharp
public Book GetBookByISBN(string isbn)
{
  return _session.GetNamedQuery("GetBookByISBN")
    .SetString("isbn", isbn)
    .UniqueResult<Book>();
}
```

5. In `Program.cs`, use the following code in the `RunQueries` method:

```csharp
static void RunQueries(ISession session)
{
  var queries = new Queries(session);
  Show("This book:", queries.GetBookByISBN(
    "978-1-849513-04-3"));
}
```

6. Build and run your application. You should see the following output:

```
file:///L:/NHibernate Cookbook/Source/4 Queries/4.07 Named Queries/NamedQueryExample/bin/Debug/Nam...
This book:
$50.00 NHibernate 3.0 Cookbook (ISBN 978-1-849513-04-3)

Press any key
```

How it works...

In this recipe, we use the familiar `GetBookByISBN` query. We use `GetNamedQuery` to build a standard HQL `IQuery` object. This time, we've defined the query in a mapping document rather than in code.

This is the optimal method for querying with NHibernate in nearly every case. As with any HQL query, NHibernate will parse, compile, and verify this query against our entity mappings and model. Because it's in a mapping document, this work is done upfront when we build the session factory. If NHibernate finds any errors, it will throw an exception when we build our session factory, instead of when we execute the query. This is preferable for the same reasons that compiler errors are preferable to runtime exceptions. It provides an obvious, upfront check. In addition, this upfront parsing and compilation is cached for later use. NHibernate only has to build the necessary SQL once.

There's more...

MultiQuery provides a shortcut for adding named queries. It looks like the following code:

```
var multiQuery = session.CreateMultiQuery()
  .AddNamedQuery<int>("count", "CountAllProducts")
  .Add<Product>("page", pageQuery);
```

In this case, we use the shortcut to add our count query. In order to set the first result and maximum result count, we need to build our page query separately.

Named SQL queries

In addition to HQL, NHibernate also allows us to create named queries in SQL. This is only appropriate in advanced cases where HQL simply won't work, or where a query has been hand-optimized. The C# code for working with a SQL named query is identical to an HQL named query. This allows you to create queries in HQL and swap in a faster SQL query later without changing your application code. Only the mapping document is different. It looks like the following code:

```xml
<?xml version="1.0" encoding="utf-8" ?>
<hibernate-mapping xmlns="urn:nhibernate-mapping-2.2">
  <sql-query name="GetBookByISBN_SQL">
    <return alias="b" class="Eg.Core.Book, Eg.Core" />
    <![CDATA[
    SELECT
      b.Id AS [b.Id],
      b.Name AS [b.Name],
      b.Description AS [b.Description],
      b.UnitPrice AS [b.UnitPrice],
      b.Author AS [b.Author],
```

```
      b.ISBN as [b.ISBN]
    FROM Product b
    WHERE b.ProductType = 'Eg.Core.Book'
    AND b.ISBN = :isbn
    ]]>
    <query-param name="isbn" type="string"/>
  </sql-query>
</hibernate-mapping>
```

The return element defines the alias we use in our query results, as well as the entity to build from that data.

HQL AddIn

The free open source HQL AddIn tool from *Jose Romaniello* integrates with Visual Studio 2010 to provide IntelliSense syntax highlighting, and syntax checking when designing HQL queries.

More information is available from the project's website at
`http://hqladdin.codeplex.com/`.

See also

▶ *Using the Hibernate Query Language*

▶ *Using Detached Queries*

Using Futures

We've learned to use MultiCriteria and MultiQuery to batch our queries together. NHibernate's Futures feature provides a simpler API for batching criteria and queries. In this recipe, I'll show you how to use NHibernate's new Futures feature to return a paged product result.

How to do it...

1. Complete the setup steps in the introduction at the beginning of this chapter, naming the new console application `PagingResults`.

2. Add a new mapping document named `CountAllProducts.hbm.xml` with the following xml code. Don't forget to set the **Build action** to **Embedded Resource**.

```xml
<?xml version="1.0" encoding="utf-8" ?>
<hibernate-mapping xmlns="urn:nhibernate-mapping-2.2">
  <query name="CountAllProducts">
    <![CDATA[
    select count(p.Id) from Product p
    ]]>
  </query>
</hibernate-mapping>
```

3. Add another mapping document named `GetAllProducts.hbm.xml` and set the **Build action** to **embedded resource**. Use the following xml:

```xml
<?xml version="1.0" encoding="utf-8" ?>
<hibernate-mapping xmlns="urn:nhibernate-mapping-2.2">
  <query name="GetAllProducts">
    <![CDATA[
    from Product p order by p.UnitPrice asc
    ]]>
  </query>
</hibernate-mapping>
```

4. In `App.config`, add `<mapping assembly="PagedResults"/>` below the mapping element for `Eg.Core`.

5. Add the following structure inside the `Queries` class:

```csharp
public struct PageOf<T>
{
  public int PageCount;
  public int PageNumber;
  public IEnumerable<T> PageOfResults;
}
```

6. Add the following method to the `Queries` class:

```csharp
public PageOf<Product> GetPageOfProducts(
  int pageNumber,
  int pageSize)
{
  var skip = (pageNumber - 1) * pageSize;

  var productCount =
    _session.GetNamedQuery("CountAllProducts")
    .FutureValue<long>();

  var products =
```

```
    _session.GetNamedQuery("GetAllProducts")
    .SetFirstResult(skip)
    .SetMaxResults(pageSize)
    .Future<Product>();

var pageCount = (int) Math.Ceiling(
    productCount.Value/(double) pageSize);

return new PageOf<Product>()
        {
            PageCount = pageCount,
            PageOfResults = products,
            PageNumber = pageNumber
        };
}
```

7. In `Program.cs`, use the following code in the `RunQueries` method:

```
static void RunQueries(ISession session)
{
    var queries = new Queries(session);
    var result = queries.GetPageOfProducts(1, 2);
    var heading = string.Format("Page {0} of {1}",
                                result.PageNumber,
                                result.PageCount);
    Show(heading, result.PageOfResults);
}
```

8. Build and run your application. You should see the following output:

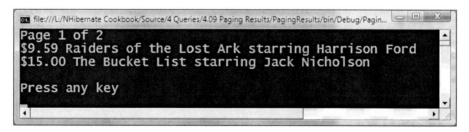

How it works...

In this recipe, we are using the simpler Futures syntax to again retrieve a count of all products, along with a page of products for display.

When we call `IQuery` or `ICriteria`'s `Future` or `FutureValue`, NHibernate returns an object representing the potential results of that query. It also queues up the query in a hidden `MultiCriteria` or `MultiQuery` inside the session.

When we call `FutureValue`, it returns an `IFutureValue<>`, representing a single entity or scalar value. For `Future`, it returns an `IEnumerable<>`. NHibernate waits until we access `Value` property of `IFutureValue<>` or enumerate the `IEnumerable`. When we do, NHibernate executes the hidden futures `MultiCriteria` and `MultiQuery` for this session.

In this specific example, both queries are executed when we use `productCount.Value` to calculate the page count. As you can see, this delayed loading is mostly transparent to the application.

There's more...

The two minor caveats when using futures are as follows:

- An attempt to load the results of a future query after the session has been closed will throw an exception.
- While the syntax is identical, ICriteria and IQuery objects are handled separately in the session. If you have an ICriteria-based future and an IQuery-based future, evaluating one will not cause the other to execute.

See also

- *Using Criteria Queries*
- *Using QueryOver*
- *Using MultiCriteria*
- *Using the Hibernate Query Language*
- *Using MultiQuery*

Eager loading child collections

Often, when we query for some set of entities, we also need to load some children of those entities. In this recipe, I'll show you how we can use NHibernate's Futures with the session cache to eager load the child collections of our query results.

How to do it...

1. Complete the setup steps in the introduction at the beginning of this chapter.
2. Add the following method to the `Queries` class:

```
public IEnumerable<Product> GetAllProducts()
{
  var products = _session.CreateQuery(
    @"from Product p
```

```
        order by p.UnitPrice asc")
    .Future<Product>();

  _session.CreateQuery(
    @"from Movie m
       left join fetch m.Actors")
    .Future<Movie>();

  return products.ToList();
}
```

3. In `Program.cs`, use the following code in the `RunQueries` method:

```
static void RunQueries(ISession session)
{
  var queries = new Queries(session);
  Show("Product List:",
        queries.GetAllProducts());
}
```

4. Build and run your application. You should see the following output:

```
file:///L:/NHibernate Cookbook/Source/4 Queries/4.10 Eager Loading Collections/EagerLoadingCollection...
Product List:
$9.59 Raiders of the Lost Ark starring Harrison Ford
$15.00 The Bucket List starring Jack Nicholson
$50.00 NHibernate 3.0 Cookbook (ISBN 978-1-849513-04-3)

Press any key
```

How it works...

In this recipe, we eagerly load the ActorRoles for our Movies to avoid a select N+1 bug. In a **select N+1** situation, with one select statement, you load some entities from the database and begin to enumerate through them. As you enumerate through them, you access some lazy loaded property or collection. This triggers a separate database query for each entity in the original query. If we iterated through 1000 entities, we would have the original query plus 1000 nearly identical queries because we triggered lazy loading, hence the name select N+1. This creates N+1 round trips to the database, which will quickly kill performance, overwork the database, and could even crash the database.

In this recipe's code, we iterate through each product in the database. For each movie, we display the name of the actor in the starring role. This would normally trigger a separate database query for each movie, a potential select N+1 problem.

Our recipe uses two Futures queries. The first simply returns all products, sorted by unit price. The second Futures query, shown next, has the secret sauce:

```
_session.CreateQuery(
  @"from Movie m
    left join fetch m.Actors")
  .Future<Movie>();
```

We query for all movies with a left outer join to actor roles. This returns all movies and their actor roles, including the movies without actor roles. The word `fetch` tells NHibernate that we want to also load the actor role entities, not just join for the purposes of filtering. So, our second Futures query loads all `Movies` and their `ActorRoles`.

You have probably noticed that we don't actually assign the resulting `IEnumerable<Movie>` to a variable and use it anywhere. That's because we don't actually care about the results of this query. Its only purpose is to sneak into the session's hidden `MultiQuery` for futures and get executed.

When we enumerate the result of the first query, both queries get executed. First, NHibernate loads up all the products, including movies, and puts those in the session cache. At this point, each movie's `Actors` collection is uninitialized. When NHibernate executes the second query, it initializes those collections as it loads the query results.

The end result is that we can output the name of the movie's star without causing another query. That data has already been loaded.

The following are the resulting SQL queries:

```
select    product0_.Id          as Id1_,
          product0_.Version     as Version1_,
          product0_.Name        as Name1_,
          product0_.Description as Descript5_1_,
          product0_.UnitPrice   as UnitPrice1_,
          product0_.Director    as Director1_,
          product0_.Author      as Author1_,
          product0_.ISBN        as ISBN1_,
          product0_.ProductType as ProductT2_1_
from      Product product0_
order by product0_.UnitPrice asc

select movie0_.Id          as Id1_0_,
       actors1_.Id         as Id0_1_,
       movie0_.Version     as Version1_0_,
       movie0_.Name        as Name1_0_,
       movie0_.Description as Descript5_1_0_,
       movie0_.UnitPrice   as UnitPrice1_0_,
       movie0_.Director    as Director1_0_,
```

```
       actors1_.Version    as Version0_1_,
       actors1_.Actor      as Actor0_1_,
       actors1_.Role       as Role0_1_,
       actors1_.MovieId     as MovieId0__,
       actors1_.Id          as Id0__,
       actors1_.ActorIndex as ActorIndex0__
from   Product movie0_
       left outer join ActorRole actors1_
         on movie0_.Id = actors1_.MovieId
where  movie0_.ProductType = 'Eg.Core.Movie'
```

There's more...

An alternative for greatly reducing the impact of a select N+1 problem is to use the batch-size property in the mapping. Suppose we had added batch-size to our movies mapping, as shown in the following code:

```xml
<?xml version="1.0" encoding="utf-8" ?>
<hibernate-mapping xmlns="urn:nhibernate-mapping-2.2"
    assembly="Eg.Core"
    namespace="Eg.Core">
  <subclass name="Movie" extends="Product">
    <property name="Director" />
    <list name="Actors" cascade="all-delete-orphan"
          batch-size="10">
      <key column="MovieId" />
      <index column="ActorIndex" />
      <one-to-many class="ActorRole"/>
    </list>
  </subclass>
</hibernate-mapping>
```

With a typical select N+1 bug, we would trigger a query on each movie. When we set batch-size to 10, this behavior changes. NHibernate needs to query for the contents of an `Actors` collection to initialize it, but it notices the batch-size setting. It finds nine other uninitialized Actors collections in the session and loads all of them at once with a single query.

If we have 10 movies, we only need two queries instead of 11. For 20 movies, we need three instead of 21 and so on. This cuts out about 90 percent of our queries.

See also

▸ *Using Futures*

▸ *Using NHibernate Profiler*

Using LINQ to NHibernate

NHibernate 3.0 includes a new LINQ provider. In this recipe, I'll show you how to execute LINQ queries with NHibernate.

How to do it...

1. Complete the steps in the introduction at the beginning of this chapter.

2. Add the following methods to the `Queries` class:

```
public IEnumerable<Movie> GetMoviesDirectedBy(
  string directorName)
{
  var query = from m in _session.Query<Movie>()
              where m.Director == directorName
              select m;
  return query.ToList();
}

public IEnumerable<Movie> GetMoviesWith(
  string actorName)
{
  var query = from m in _session.Query<Movie>()
              where m.Actors.Any(
                ar => ar.Actor == actorName)
              select m;
  return query.ToList();
}

public Book GetBookByISBN(string isbn)
{
  var query = from b in _session.Query<Book>()
              where b.ISBN == isbn
              select b;
  return query.SingleOrDefault();
}

public IEnumerable<Product> GetProductByPrice(
  decimal minPrice,
  decimal maxPrice)
{
  var query = from p in _session.Query<Product>()
              where p.UnitPrice >= minPrice &&
```

```
                    p.UnitPrice <= maxPrice
                    orderby p.UnitPrice ascending
                    select p;
    return query.ToList();
}

public IEnumerable<NameAndPrice> GetMoviePriceList()
{
    var query = from m in _session.Query<Movie>()
                select new NameAndPrice(
                    m.Name,
                    m.UnitPrice);
    return query.ToList();
}

public decimal GetAverageMoviePrice()
{
    return _session.Query<Movie>()
        .Average(m => m.UnitPrice);
}

public IEnumerable<NameAndPrice> GetAvgDirectorPrice()
{
    var query = from m in _session.Query<Movie>()
                group m by m.Director
                into g
                select new NameAndPrice(
                    g.Key,
                    g.Average(i => i.UnitPrice));
    return query.ToList();
}
```

3. In `Program.cs`, use the following code in the `RunQueries` method:

```
static void RunQueries(ISession session)
{
    var queries = new Queries(session);

    Show("Movies directed by Spielberg:",
        queries.GetMoviesDirectedBy(
        "Steven Spielberg"));

    Show("Movies with Morgan Freeman:",
        queries.GetMoviesWith(
        "Morgan Freeman"));
```

```
Show("This book:",
  queries.GetBookByISBN(
  "978-1-849513-04-3"));

Show("Cheap products:",
  queries.GetProductByPrice(0M, 15M));

Show("Movie Price List:",
  queries.GetMoviePriceList());

Show("Average Movie Price:",
  queries.GetAverageMoviePrice());

Show("Average Price by Director:",
  queries.GetAvgDirectorPrice());
}
```

4. Build and run your application. You should see the following output:

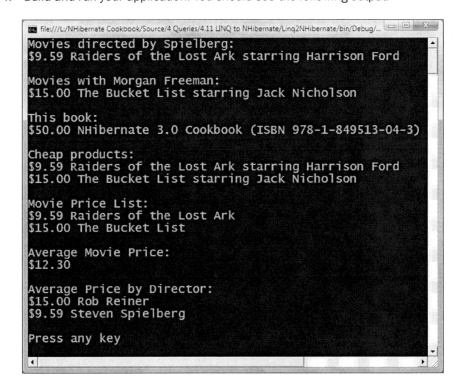

How it works...

`session.Query<>` returns an `IQueryable` for the new, fully functional NHibernate LINQ provider. This recipe uses the same well-known LINQ syntax supported by many LINQ providers. MSDN's 101 LINQ samples, found at `http://msdn.microsoft.com/en-us/vcsharp/aa336746.aspx`, provide an excellent beginner's reference to LINQ syntax.

See also

- ▸ *Named Queries*
- ▸ *Using LINQ specifications in the data access layer*

Using Detached Queries

In some cases, it may be preferable to build an HQL or criteria query object in parts of your application without access to the NHibernate session, and then execute them elsewhere with a session. In this recipe, I'll show you how to use detached queries and criteria.

Getting ready

Set up a new NHibernate console application using our `Eg.Core` model from *Chapter 1*. Configure log4net to send the NHibernate.SQL debug output to the .NET trace, just as we did in *Chapter 2*.

How to do it...

Add the following code to your `Main` method:

```
var isbn = "3043";
var query = DetachedCriteria.For<Book>()
  .Add(Restrictions.Eq("ISBN", isbn));
using (var session = sessionFactory.OpenSession())
{
  using (var tx = session.BeginTransaction())
  {
    var book = query.GetExecutableCriteria(session)
      .UniqueResult<Book>();
    tx.Commit();
  }
}
```

How it works...

In this recipe, we've used a `DetachedCriteria` object from the `NHibernate.Criterion` namespace. This allows us to set up our query without an active session. Later, inside a transaction, we call `GetExecutableCriteria` to return an `ICriteria` associated with the session. Finally, we call `UniqueResult` to return the book.

There's more...

NHibernate also provides `DetachedQuery` and `DetachedNamedQuery` in the `NHibernate.Impl` namespace for detached HQL queries. The code is given as follows:

```
var query = new DetachedNamedQuery("GetBookByISBN")
  .SetString("isbn", isbn);
var query = new DetachedQuery(hql)
  .SetString("isbn", isbn);
```

Detached criteria and queries implement the query objects pattern shown on *Martin Fowler's* website at `http://martinfowler.com/eaaCatalog/queryObject.html`.

See also

- ▶ *Using Criteria Queries*
- ▶ *Using the Hibernate Query Language*
- ▶ *Using Named Queries*

Using HQL for bulk data changes

In the previous chapter, we learned how to use NHibernate to insert, update, and delete individual entities using `ISession` methods. NHibernate also allows us to perform some bulk data changes with executable HQL. In this recipe, I'll show you how we can use HQL to update all of our books with a single statement.

Getting ready

Set up a new NHibernate console application using our `Eg.Core` model from *Chapter 1*. Configure log4net to send the NHibernate.SQL debug output to the .NET trace, just as we did in *Chapter 2*.

How to do it...

Add the following code to your `Main` method:

```
using (var session = sessionFactory.OpenSession())
{
  using (var tx = session.BeginTransaction())
  {
    var hql = @"update Book b
                set b.UnitPrice = :minPrice
                where b.UnitPrice < :minPrice";
    session.CreateQuery(hql)
      .SetDecimal("minPrice", 55M)
      .ExecuteUpdate();

    tx.Commit();
  }
}
```

How it works...

We have the following executable HQL query:

```
update Book b
set b.UnitPrice = :minPrice
where b.UnitPrice < :minPrice
```

We call `ExecuteUpdate` method of `IQuery` to run this statement. This results in the following SQL statement:

```
update Product
set    UnitPrice = 55 /* @p0 */
where  ProductType = 'Eg.Core.Book'
       and UnitPrice < 55 /* @p1 */
```

This will only affect the database. These changes will not be reflected in the state of in-memory objects, the second level cache, or anywhere else outside the database.

There's more...

We could also define this query in a mapping and load it like any other named query.

In addition to bulk updates, NHibernate also supports bulk deletes and bulk inserts. The syntax for bulk deletes is identical to bulk updates, but without `set`. Neither update nor delete support joins. Instead, use sub-queries in the where clause.

Bulk inserts

NHibernate supports bulk inserts in the following form:

```
insert into destinationEntity (id, prop1, prop2) select b.id,
b.prop1, b.prop2 from sourceEntity b where...
```

There are a few items to keep in mind when considering this solution. First, property types must match exactly. While the database may be perfectly able to convert between types such as `int` and `long`, NHibernate requires them to be the same type.

IDs are particularly limited. There are two options:

 ▶ The first option is to copy the ID from a property of the source entity. This may be the ID of the source entity, or any other property. Depending on your existing data, this is not always appropriate.

 ▶ The second option uses the entity's POID generator to create an identity for each newly inserted object. However, this only works when the ID is database-generated. This excludes nearly all of the preferred identity generators, such as `guidcomb` and `hilo`. To use the entity's ID generator, simply omit the ID column from the list of properties to be set.

See also

 ▶ *Using Named Queries*

5

Testing

In this chapter, we will cover the following topics:

- ► Using NHibernate Profiler
- ► Testing with the SQLite in-memory database
- ► Preloading data with SQLite
- ► Using the Fluent NHibernate persistence tester
- ► Using the Ghostbusters test

Introduction

Testing is a critical step in the development of any application. The recipes in this chapter are designed to ease the testing process and expose common issues.

Using NHibernate Profiler

NHibernate Profiler from Hibernating Rhinos is the number one tool for analyzing and visualizing what is happening inside your NHibernate application, and for discovering issues you may have. In this recipe, I'll show you how to get up and running with NHibernate Profiler.

Getting ready

Download NHibernate Profiler from `http://nhprof.com`, and unzip it. As it is a commercial product, you will also need a license file. You may request a 30-day trial license from the NHProf website.

Using our `Eg.Core` model from *Chapter 1*, set up a new NHibernate console application with log4net, just as we did in *Chapter 2*.

How to do it...

1. Add a reference to `HibernatingRhinos.Profiler.Appender.dll` from the NH Profiler download.

2. In the `session-factory` element of `App.config`, set the property `generate_statistics` to `true`.

3. Add the following code to your `Main` method:

```
log4net.Config.XmlConfigurator.Configure();

HibernatingRhinos.Profiler.Appender.
  NHibernate.NHibernateProfiler.Initialize();

var nhConfig = new Configuration().Configure();
var sessionFactory = nhConfig.BuildSessionFactory();

using (var session = sessionFactory.OpenSession())
{
  var books = from b in session.Query<Book>()
              where b.Author == "Jason Dentler"
              select b;

  foreach (var book in books)
    Console.WriteLine(book.Name);
}
```

4. Run `NHProf.exe` from the NH Profiler download, and activate the license.

5. Build and run your console application.

6. Check the NH Profiler. It should look like the next screenshot. Notice the gray dots indicating alerts next to the **Session #1** and **Recent Statements**.

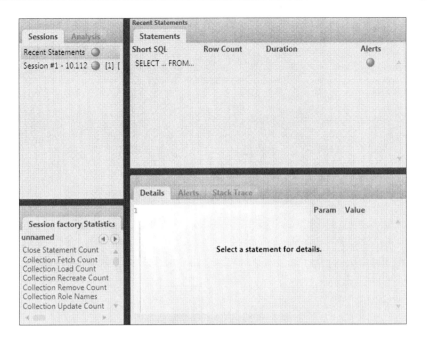

7. Select **Session #1** from the **Sessions** list at the top left pane.

8. Select the statement from the top right pane.

9. Notice the SQL statement in the following screenshot:

```
Details   Alerts   Stack Trace
 1  select book0_.Id          as Id1_,                    Param   Value
 2         book0_.Name         as Name1_,                  @p0     'Jason Dentler'
 3         book0_.Description  as Descript4_1_,
 4         book0_.UnitPrice    as UnitPrice1_,
 5         book0_.Author       as Author1_,
 6         book0_.ISBN         as ISBN1_
 7  from   Product book0_
 8  where  book0_.ProductType = 'Eg.Core.Book'
 9         and ((book0_.Author is null)
10             and ('Jason Dentler' /* @p0 */ is null)
11             or book0_.Author = 'Jason Dentler' /* @p0 */)

See the 1 row(s) resulting from this statement. EXPERIMENTAL (Alpha feature)! View the query plan for this stat
```

10. Click on **See the 1 row(s) resulting from this statement**.

11. Enter your database connection string in the field provided, and click on **OK**.

12. Close the query results window.

13. Switch to the **Alerts** tab, and notice the alert: **Use of implicit transaction is discouraged**.

14. Click on the **Read more** link for more information and suggested solutions to this particular issue.

15. Switch to the **Stack Trace** tab, as shown in the next screenshot:

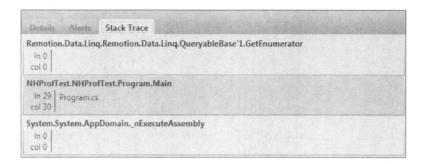

16. Double-click on the **NHProfTest.NHProfTest.Program.Main** stack frame to jump to that location inside Visual Studio.

17. Using the following code, wrap the `foreach` loop in a transaction and commit the transaction:

```
using (var tx = session.BeginTransaction())
{
    foreach (var book in books)
        Console.WriteLine(book.Name);
    tx.Commit();
}
```

18. In NH Profiler, right-click on **Sessions** on the top left pane, and select **Clear All Sessions**.

19. Build and run your application.

20. Check NH Profiler for alerts.

How it works...

NHibernate Profiler uses a custom log4net appender to capture data about NHibernate activities inside your application and transmit that data to the NH Profiler application.

As we learned in *Chapter 2*, setting `generate_statistics` allows NHibernate to capture many key data points. These statistics are displayed in the lower, left-hand side of the pane of NHibernate Profiler.

We initialize NHibernate profiler with a call to `NHibernateProfiler.Initialize()`. For best results, do this when your application begins, just after you have configured log4net.

There's more...

NHibernate profiler also supports offline and remote profiling, as well as command-line options for use with build scripts and continuous integration systems.

In addition to NHibernate warnings and errors, NH Profiler alerts us to 12 common misuses of NHibernate, which are as follows:

- Transaction disposed without explicit rollback or commit: If no action is taken, transactions will rollback when disposed. However, this often indicates a missing commit rather than a desire to rollback the transaction.

- Using a single session on multiple threads is likely a bug: A Session should only be used by one thread at a time. Sharing a session across threads is usually a bug, not an explicit design choice with proper locking.

- Use of implicit transaction is discouraged: As we have seen in *Chapter 3*, nearly all session activity should happen inside an NHibernate transaction.

- Excessive number of rows: In nearly all cases, this indicates a poorly designed query or bug.

- Large number of individual writes: This indicates a failure to batch writes, either because `adonet.batch_size` is not set, or possibly because an Identity-type POID generator is used, which effectively disables batching.

- Select N+1: This alert indicates a particular type of anti-pattern where, typically, we load and enumerate a list of parent objects, lazy-loading their children as we move through the list. Instead, we should eagerly fetch those children before enumerating the list.

- Superfluous updates, use `inverse="true"`: NH Profiler detected an unnecessary update statement from a bi-directional one-to-many relationship. Use `inverse="true"` on the many side (list, bag, set, and others) of the relationship to avoid this.

- Too many cache calls per session: This alert is targeted particularly at applications using a distributed (remote) second-level cache. By design, NHibernate does not batch calls to the cache, which can easily lead to hundreds of slow remote calls. It can also indicate an over reliance on the second-level cache, whether remote or local.

- Too many database calls per session: This usually indicates a misuse of the database, such as querying inside a loop, a select N+1 bug, or an excessive number of writes.

- Too many joins: A query contains a large number of joins. When executed in a batch, multiple simple queries with only a few joins often perform better than a complex query with many joins. This alert can also indicate unexpected Cartesian products.

- ▸ Unbounded result set: NH Profiler detected a query without a row limit. When the application is moved to production, these queries may return huge result sets, leading to catastrophic performance issues. As insurance against these issues, set a reasonable maximum on the rows returned by each query.

- ▸ Different parameter sizes result in inefficient query plan cache usage: NH Profiler detected two identical queries with different parameter sizes. Each of these queries will create a query plan. This problem grows exponentially with the size and number of parameters used. Setting `prepare_sql` to `true` allows NHibernate to generate queries with consistent parameter sizes.

See also

- ▸ *Configuring NHibernate with App.config*
- ▸ *Configuring log4net logging*

Fast testing with SQLite in-memory database

Running a full range of tests for a large NHibernate application can take some time. In this recipe, I will show you how to use SQLite's in-memory database to speed up this process.

 This is not meant to replace running integration tests against the real RDBMS before moving to production. Rather, it is a smoke test to provide feedback to developers quickly before running the slower integration tests.

Getting ready

1. Download and install NUnit from `http://nunit.org`.

2. Download and install SQLite from `http://sqlite.phxsoftware.com`.

 Note: This recipe will work with other test frameworks such as MSTest, MbUnit, and xUnit. Just replace the NUnit-specific attributes with those for your preferred framework.

How to do it...

1. Create a new, empty class library project.

2. Add references to our `Eg.Core` model from *Chapter 1*, as well as `nunit. framework`, `System.Data.Sqlite`, `log4net`, `NHibernate` and `NHibernate. ByteCode.Castle`.

`System.Data.Sqlite` has 32-bit and 64-bit versions. Use the appropriate file for your operating system and target platform.

3. Add an application configuration file with NHibernate and log4net configuration sections just as we did in *Chapter 2*.

4. Change the log4net configuration to use a `ConsoleAppender`.

5. Add a new, static class named `NHConfigurator` with the following code:

```
private const string CONN_STR =
   "Data Source=:memory:;Version=3;New=True;";

private static readonly Configuration _configuration;
private static readonly ISessionFactory _sessionFactory;

static NHConfigurator()
{

  _configuration = new Configuration().Configure()
    .DataBaseIntegration(db =>
    {
      db.Dialect<SQLiteDialect>();
      db.Driver<SQLite20Driver>();
      db.ConnectionProvider<TestConnectionProvider>();
      db.ConnectionString = CONN_STR;
    })
    .SetProperty(Environment.CurrentSessionContextClass,
      "thread_static");

  var props = _configuration.Properties;
  if (props.ContainsKey(Environment.ConnectionStringName))
    props.Remove(Environment.ConnectionStringName);

  _sessionFactory = _configuration.BuildSessionFactory();
}

public static Configuration Configuration
{
  get
  {
    return _configuration;
  }
}
```

```csharp
public static ISessionFactory SessionFactory
{
  get
  {
    return _sessionFactory;
  }
}
```

6. Add a new, abstract class named `BaseFixture` using the following code:

```csharp
protected static ILog log = new Func<ILog>(() =>
{
  log4net.Config.XmlConfigurator.Configure();
  return LogManager.GetLogger(typeof(BaseFixture));
}).Invoke();

protected virtual void OnFixtureSetup() { }
protected virtual void OnFixtureTeardown() { }
protected virtual void OnSetup() { }
protected virtual void OnTeardown() { }

[TestFixtureSetUp]
public void FixtureSetup()
{
  OnFixtureSetup();
}

[TestFixtureTearDown]
public void FixtureTeardown()
{
  OnFixtureTeardown();
}

[SetUp]
public void Setup()
{
  OnSetup();
}

[TearDown]
public void Teardown()
{
  OnTeardown();
}
```

7. Add a new, abstract class named `NHibernateFixture`, inherited from `BaseFixture`, with the following code:

```
protected ISessionFactory SessionFactory
{
  get
  {
    return NHConfigurator.SessionFactory;
  }
}

protected ISession Session
{
  get
  {
    return SessionFactory.GetCurrentSession();
  }
}

protected override void OnSetup()
{
  SetupNHibernateSession();
  base.OnSetup();
}

protected override void OnTeardown()
{
  TearDownNHibernateSession();
  base.OnTeardown();
}

protected void SetupNHibernateSession()
{
  TestConnectionProvider.CloseDatabase();
  SetupContextualSession();
  BuildSchema();
}

protected void TearDownNHibernateSession()
{
  TearDownContextualSession();
  TestConnectionProvider.CloseDatabase();
}

private void SetupContextualSession()
```

```
  {
    var session = SessionFactory.OpenSession();
    CurrentSessionContext.Bind(session);
  }

  private void TearDownContextualSession()
  {
    var sessionFactory = NHConfigurator.SessionFactory;
    var session = CurrentSessionContext.Unbind(sessionFactory);
    session.Close();
  }

  private void BuildSchema()
  {
    var cfg = NHConfigurator.Configuration;
    var schemaExport = new SchemaExport(cfg);
    schemaExport.Create(false, true);
  }
```

8. Add a new class named `PersistenceTests`, inherited from `NHibernateFixture`.

9. Decorate the `PersistenceTests` class with NUnit's `TestFixture` attribute.

10. Add the following test method to `PersistenceTests`:

```
[Test]
public void Movie_cascades_save_to_ActorRole()
{

  Guid movieId;
  Movie movie = new Movie()
  {
    Name = "Mars Attacks",
    Description = "Sci-Fi Parody",
    Director = "Tim Burton",
    UnitPrice = 12M,
    Actors = new List<ActorRole>()
      {
        new ActorRole() {
          Actor = "Jack Nicholson",
          Role = "President James Dale"
        }
      }
  };

  using (var session = SessionFactory.OpenSession())
```

```
      using (var tx = session.BeginTransaction())
      {
        movieId = (Guid)session.Save(movie);
        tx.Commit();
      }

      using (var session = SessionFactory.OpenSession())
      using (var tx = session.BeginTransaction())
      {
        movie = session.Get<Movie>(movieId);
        tx.Commit();
      }

      Assert.That(movie.Actors.Count == 1);
  }
```

11. Build the project.
12. Start NUnit.
13. Select **File | Open Project**.
14. Select the project's compiled assembly from the `bin\Debug` folder.
15. Click on **Run**.

How it works...

`NHConfigurator` loads an NHibernate configuration from the `App.config`, then overwrites the dialect, driver, connection provider, and connection string properties to use SQLite instead. It also uses the thread static session context to provide sessions to code that may rely on NHibernate contextual sessions. Finally, we remove the `connection.connection_string_name` property, as we have provided a connection string value.

The magic of SQLite happens in our custom `TestConnectionProvider` class. Typically, a connection provider will return a new connection from each call to `GetConnection()`, and close the connection when `CloseConnection()` is called. However, each SQLite in-memory database only supports a single connection. That is, each new connection creates and connects to its own in-memory database. When the connection is closed, the database is lost. When each test begins, we close any lingering connections. This ensures we will get a fresh, empty database. When NHibernate first calls `GetConnection()`, we open a new connection. We return this same connection for each subsequent call. We ignore any calls to `CloseConnection()`. Finally, when the test is completed, we dispose the database connection, effectively disposing the in-memory database with it.

This provides a perfectly clean database for each test, ensuring that remnants of a previous test cannot contaminate the current test, possibly altering the results.

In `BaseFixture`, we configure log4net and set up some virtual methods that can be overridden in inherited classes.

In `NHibernateFixture`, we override `OnSetup`, which runs just before each test. For code that may use contextual sessions, we open a session and bind it to the context. We also create our database tables with NHibernate's schema export. This, of course, opens a database connection, establishing our in-memory database.

We override `OnTeardown`, which runs after each test, to unbind the session from the session context, close the session, and finally close the database connection. When the connection is closed, the database is erased from memory.

The test uses the session from the `NHibernateFixture` to save a movie with an associated `ActorRole`. We use two separate sessions to save, and then fetch the movie to ensure that when we fetch the movie, we load it from the database rather than just returning the instance from the first level cache. This gives us a true tests of what we have persisted in the database. Once we've fetched the movie back from the database, we make sure it still has an `ActorRole`. This test ensures that when we save a movie, the save cascades down to `ActorRoles` in the `Actors` list as well.

There's more...

While SQLite in-memory databases are fast, the SQLite engine has several limitations. For example, foreign key constraints are not enforced. Its speed makes it great for providing quick test feedback, but because of the limitations, before deploying the application, it is best to run all tests against the production database engine. There are a few approaches to testing with a real RDBMS, each with significant issues, which are as follows:

- Drop and recreate the database between each test. This is extremely slow for enterprise-level databases. A full set of integration tests may take hours to run, but this is the least intrusive option.

- Roll back every transaction to prevent changes to the database. This is very limiting. For instance, even our simple Persistence test would require some significant changes to work in this way. This may require you to change business logic to suit a testing limitation.

- Clean up on a test-by-test basis. For instance, for every insert, perform a delete. This is a manual, labor-intensive, error-prone process.

See also

- *Preloading data with SQLite*
- *Using the Fluent NHibernate Persistence tester*
- *Using the Ghostbusters test*

Preloading data with SQLite

It is often desirable to preload the database with test data before running tests. In this recipe, I will show you how to quickly load the in-memory database with data from a SQLite file database.

Getting ready

Complete the previous recipe, *Fast testing with SQLite in-memory database.*

Create a SQLite file database with identical schema, containing test data. This can be accomplished in a number of ways. Perhaps the easiest is to export an in-memory database using `SQLiteLoader.ExportData` from this recipe.

How to do it...

1. Add a new class named `SQLiteLoader` using the following code:

```
private static ILog log = LogManager.GetLogger(typeof(SQLiteLoad
er));

private const string ATTACHED_DB = "asdfgaqwernb";

public void ImportData(
  SQLiteConnection conn,
  string sourceDataFile)
{

  var tables = GetTableNames(conn);
  AttachDatabase(conn, sourceDataFile);

  foreach (var table in tables)
  {
    var sourceTable = string.Format("{0}.{1}",
      ATTACHED_DB, table);

    CopyTableData(conn, sourceTable, table);
  }

  DetachDatabase(conn);
}
public void ExportData(
  SQLiteConnection conn,
  string destinationDataFile)
{
  var tables = GetTableNames(conn);
```

```
    AttachDatabase(conn, destinationDataFile);
    foreach (var table in tables)
    {
      var destTable = string.Format("{0}.{1}",
        ATTACHED_DB, table);
      CopyTableData(conn, table, destTable);
    }
    DetachDatabase(conn);
  }

  private IEnumerable<string> GetTableNames(
    SQLiteConnection conn)
  {
    string tables = SQLiteMetaDataCollectionNames.Tables;
    DataTable dt = conn.GetSchema(tables);
    return from DataRow R in dt.Rows
           select (string)R["TABLE_NAME"];
  }

  private void AttachDatabase(
    SQLiteConnection conn,
    string sourceDataFile)
  {
    SQLiteCommand cmd = new SQLiteCommand(conn);
    cmd.CommandText = String.Format("ATTACH '{0}' AS {1}",
      sourceDataFile, ATTACHED_DB);
    log.Debug(cmd.CommandText);
    cmd.ExecuteNonQuery();
  }

  private void CopyTableData(
    SQLiteConnection conn,
    string source,
    string destination)
  {
    SQLiteCommand cmd = new SQLiteCommand(conn);
    cmd.CommandText = string.Format(
      "INSERT INTO {0} SELECT * FROM {1}",
    destination, source);
  log.Debug(cmd.CommandText);
  cmd.ExecuteNonQuery();
}
```

```
private void DetachDatabase(SQLiteConnection conn)
{
   SQLiteCommand cmd = new SQLiteCommand(conn);
   cmd.CommandText = string.Format(«DETACH {0}», ATTACHED_DB);
   log.Debug(cmd.CommandText);
   cmd.ExecuteNonQuery();
   }
```

2. Add a new abstract class named `DataDependentFixture`, inherited from `NHibernateFixture`, using the following code:

```
protected abstract string GetSQLiteFilename();

protected override void OnSetup()
{
   base.OnSetup();
   var conn = (SQLiteConnection) Session.Connection;
   new SQLiteLoader().ImportData(conn, GetSQLiteFilename());
}
```

3. Add a new class named `QueryTests`, inherited from `DataDependentFixture`.

4. In `QueryTests`, override `GetSQLiteFilename()` to return the path to your SQLite file.

5. Add the following test to `QueryTests`:

```
[Test]
public void Director_query_should_return_one_movie()
{
   var query = Session.QueryOver<Movie>()
      .Where(m => m.Director == "Tim Burton");

   using (var tx = Session.BeginTransaction())
   {
      var movies = query.List<Movie>();
      Assert.That(movies.Count == 1);
      tx.Commit();
   }
}
```

6. Decorate `QueryTests` with NUnit's `TestFixture` attribute.

7. Build the project.

8. Run the NUnit tests.

How it works...

In the `QueryTests` fixture, `GetSQLiteFilename()` returns the path of the SQLite file containing our test data. `DataDependentFixture` passes this file path and our connection to the SQLite in-memory database over to `SQLiteLoader.ImportData()`.

We call `SQLiteConnection.GetSchema()` to create a list of table names in the database.

Next, we attach the file database to the in-memory database using the command `ATTACH 'filePath' AS schemaName` where `filePath` is the path to the file database and `schemaName` is a string constant. This allows us to reference the tables in the file database from the memory database. For example, if our file database has a table named `tblTestData`, and we use the string `asdf` for `schemaName`, we can execute `SELECT * FROM asdf.tblTestData`.

We loop through each table, executing the statement `INSERT INTO tableName SELECT * FROM schemaName.tableName`. This command quickly copies all the data from a table in the file database to an identical table in the memory database. Because SQLite doesn't enforce foreign key constraints, we do not need to be concerned with the order we use to copy this data.

Finally, we detach the file database using the command `DETACH schemaName`.

There's more...

We can use `SQLiteLoader.ExportData` to move data from the SQLite in-memory database to a file database. Also, each test fixture can use test data from a different file database.

See also

- ▸ *Fast testing with SQLite in-memory*
- ▸ *Using the Ghostbusters test*

Using the Fluent NHibernate Persistence Tester

Mappings are a critical part of any NHibernate application. In this recipe, I'll show you how to test those mappings using Fluent NHibernate's Persistence tester.

Getting ready

Complete the *Fast testing with SQLite in-Memory database* recipe mentioned previously in this chapter.

How to do it...

1. Add a reference to `FluentNHibernate`.

2. In `PersistenceTests.cs`, add the following using statement:

   ```
   using FluentNHibernate.Testing;
   ```

3. Add the following three tests to the `PersistenceTests` fixture:

   ```
   [Test]
   public void Product_persistence_test()
   {
     new PersistenceSpecification<Product>(Session)
       .CheckProperty(p => p.Name, "Product Name")
       .CheckProperty(p => p.Description, "Product Description")
       .CheckProperty(p => p.UnitPrice, 300.85M)
       .VerifyTheMappings();
   }

   [Test]
   public void ActorRole_persistence_test()
   {
     new PersistenceSpecification<ActorRole>(Session)
      .CheckProperty(p => p.Actor, "Actor Name")
      .CheckProperty(p => p.Role, "Role")
      .VerifyTheMappings();
   }

   [Test]
   public void Movie_persistence_test()
   {
     new PersistenceSpecification<Movie>(Session)
      .CheckProperty(p => p.Name, "Movie Name")
      .CheckProperty(p => p.Description, "Movie Description")
      .CheckProperty(p => p.UnitPrice, 25M)
      .CheckProperty(p => p.Director, "Director Name")
      .CheckList(p => p.Actors, new List<ActorRole>()
      {
        new ActorRole() { Actor = "Actor Name", Role = "Role" }
      })
      .VerifyTheMappings();
   }
   ```

4. Run these tests with NUnit.

How it works...

The Persistence tester in Fluent NHibernate can be used with any mapping method. It performs the following four steps:

1. Create a new instance of the entity (`Product`, `ActorRole`, `Movie`) using the values provided.

2. Save the entity to the database.

3. Get the entity from the database.

4. Verify that the fetched instance matches the original.

At a minimum, each entity type should have a simple Persistence test, such as the one shown previously. More information about the Fluent NHibernate Persistence tester can be found on their wiki at `http://wiki.fluentnhibernate.org/Persistence_specification_testing`.

See also

▸ *Testing with the SQLite in-memory database*

▸ *Using the Ghostbusters test*

Using the Ghostbusters test

As part of **automatic dirty checking**, NHibernate compares the original state of an entity to its current state. An otherwise unchanged entity may be updated unnecessarily because a type conversion caused this comparison to fail. In this recipe, I will show you how to detect these "ghost update" issues with the Ghostbusters test.

Getting ready

Complete the recipe *Fast testing with SQLite in-memory database*.

How to do it...

1. Add a new class named `Ghostbusters` using the following code:

```
private static readonly ILog log =
  LogManager.GetLogger(typeof(Ghostbusters));

private readonly Configuration _configuration;
private readonly ISessionFactory _sessionFactory;
private readonly Action<string> _failCallback;
private readonly Action<string> _inconclusiveCallback;
```

```csharp
public Ghostbusters(Configuration configuration,
ISessionFactory sessionFactory,
Action<string> failCallback,
Action<string> inconclusiveCallback)
{
  _configuration = configuration;
  _sessionFactory = sessionFactory;
  _failCallback = failCallback;
  _inconclusiveCallback = inconclusiveCallback;
}
public void Test()
{
  var mappedEntityNames = _configuration.ClassMappings
  .Select(mapping => mapping.EntityName);

  foreach (string entityName in mappedEntityNames)
    Test(entityName);
}
public void Test<TEntity>()
{
  Test(typeof(TEntity).FullName);
}
public void Test(string entityName)
{
  object id = FindEntityId(entityName);
  if (id == null)
  {
    var msg = string.Format(
     "No instances of {0} in database.",
      entityName);
    _inconclusiveCallback.Invoke(msg);
    return;
  }
  log.DebugFormat("Testing entity {0} with id {1}",
    entityName, id);
  Test(entityName, id);
}
public void Test(string entityName, object id)
{
```

```
    var ghosts = new List<String>();
    var interceptor = new GhostInterceptor(ghosts);

    using (var session = _sessionFactory.OpenSession(interceptor))
    using (var tx = session.BeginTransaction())
    {
      session.Get(entityName, id);
      session.Flush();
      tx.Rollback();
    }

    if (ghosts.Any())
      _failCallback.Invoke(string.Join("\n", ghosts.ToArray()));
}

private object FindEntityId(string entityName)
{
  object id;
  using (var session = _sessionFactory.OpenSession())
  {
    var idQueryString = string.Format(
      "SELECT e.id FROM {0} e",
      entityName);

    var idQuery = session.CreateQuery(idQueryString)
    .SetMaxResults(1);

    using (var tx = session.BeginTransaction())
    {
      id = idQuery.UniqueResult();
      tx.Commit();
    }
  }
  return id;
}
```

2. Add another class named GhostInterceptor using the following code:

```
private static readonly ILog log =
  LogManager.GetLogger(typeof(GhostInterceptor));

private readonly IList<string> _ghosts;
private ISession _session;

public GhostInterceptor(IList<string> ghosts)
{
  _ghosts = ghosts;
```

```
}

public override void SetSession(ISession session)
{
  _session = session;
}

public override bool OnFlushDirty(
object entity, object id, object[] currentState,
object[] previousState, string[] propertyNames, IType[] types)
{
  var msg = string.Format("Flush Dirty {0}",
    entity.GetType().FullName);
  log.Error(msg);
  _ghosts.Add(msg);
  ListDirtyProperties(entity);
  return false;
}

public override bool OnSave(
object entity, object id, object[] state,
string[] propertyNames, IType[] types)
{
  var msg = string.Format("Save {0}",
    entity.GetType().FullName);
  log.Error(msg);
  _ghosts.Add(msg);
  return false;
}

public override void OnDelete(
object entity, object id, object[] state,
string[] propertyNames, IType[] types)
{
  var msg = string.Format("Delete {0}",
    entity.GetType().FullName);
  log.Error(msg);
  _ghosts.Add(msg);
}

private void ListDirtyProperties(object entity)
{
  string className =
    NHibernateProxyHelper.GuessClass(entity).FullName;
```

```
      var sessionImpl = _session.GetSessionImplementation();
      var persister =
        sessionImpl.Factory.GetEntityPersister(className);
      var oldEntry =
        sessionImpl.PersistenceContext.GetEntry(entity);
      if ((oldEntry == null) && (entity is INHibernateProxy))
      {
        var proxy = entity as INHibernateProxy;
        object obj =
          sessionImpl.PersistenceContext.Unproxy(proxy);

        oldEntry = sessionImpl.PersistenceContext.GetEntry(obj);
      }
      object[] oldState = oldEntry.LoadedState;
      object[] currentState = persister.GetPropertyValues(entity,
        sessionImpl.EntityMode);
      int[] dirtyProperties = persister.FindDirty(currentState,
        oldState, entity, sessionImpl);
      foreach (int index in dirtyProperties)
      {
        var msg = string.Format(
          "Dirty property {0}.{1} was {2}, is {3}.",
          className,
          persister.PropertyNames[index],
          oldState[index] ?? "null",
          currentState[index] ?? "null");
        log.Error(msg);
        _ghosts.Add(msg);
      }
    }
```

3. Add the following test to the `PersistenceTests` fixture:

```
[Test]
public void GhostbustersTest()
{
  using (var tx = Session.BeginTransaction())
  {
    Session.Save(new Movie()
```

```
    {
      Name = "Ghostbusters",
      Description = "Science Fiction Comedy",
      Director = "Ivan Reitman",
      UnitPrice = 7.97M,
      Actors = new List<ActorRole>()
      {
        new ActorRole()
        {
          Actor = "Bill Murray",
          Role = "Dr. Peter Venkman"
        }
      }
    });

    Session.Save(new Book()
    {
      Name = "Who You Gonna Call?",
      Description = "The Real Ghostbusters comic series",
      UnitPrice = 30.00M,
      Author = "Dan Abnett",
      ISBN = "1-84576-141-3"
    });

    tx.Commit();
  }
  new Ghostbusters(
    NHConfigurator.Configuration,
    NHConfigurator.SessionFactory,
    new Action<string>(msg => Assert.Fail(msg)),
    new Action<string>(msg => Assert.Inconclusive(msg))
  ).Test();
}
```

4. Run the tests with NUnit.

How it works...

The Ghostbusters test finds issues where a session's automatic dirty checking determines that an entity is dirty (has unsaved changes) when, in fact, no changes were made. This can happen for a few reasons, but it commonly occurs when a database field that allows nulls is mapped to a non-nullable property such as integer or `DateTime`, or when an `enum` property is mapped with `type="int"`. For example, when a null value is loaded in to an integer property, the value is automatically converted to integer's default value, zero. When the session is flushed, automatic dirty checking will see that the value is no longer null and update the database value to zero. This is referred to as a "ghost" update.

At the heart of our Ghostbusters test, we have the `GhostInterceptor`. An interceptor allows an application to intercept session events before any database action occurs. This interceptor can be set globally on the NHibernate configuration or passed as a parameter to `sessionFactory.OpenSession` as we've done in this recipe.

When we flush a session containing a dirty entity, the interceptor's `OnFlushDirty` method is called. `GhostInterceptor` compares the current values of the dirty entity's properties to their original values and reports these back to our Ghostbusters class. Similarly, we also intercept `Save` and `Delete` events, though these are much less common.

Our `Ghostbusters` class coordinates the testing. For example, we can call `Test(entityName,id)` to test using a particular instance of an entity. If we strip this test down to its core, we end up with this:

```
session.Get(entityName, id);
session.Flush();
tx.Rollback();
```

Notice that we simply get an entity from the database and immediately flush the session. This runs automatic dirty checking on a single unchanged entity. Any database changes resulting from this `Flush()` are ghosts.

If we call `Test(entityName)` or `Test<Entity>()`, `Ghostbusters` will first query the database for an ID for the entity, then run the test. For a test on our `Movie` entity, this ID query would be:

```
SELECT e.id FROM Eg.Core.Movie e
```

This lowercase `id` property has special meaning in HQL. In HQL, lowercase `id` always refers to the entity's POID. In our model, it happens to be named `Id`, but we could have just as easily named it "*Bob.*"

Finally, if we simply call the `Test()` method, `Ghostbusters` will test one instance of each mapped entity. This is the method we use in our tests.

This Ghostbusters test has somewhat limited value in automated tests as we've done here. It really shines when testing migrated or updated production data.

See also

▶   *Using the Hibernate Query Language*

6

Data Access Layer

In this chapter, we will cover the following topics:

- ▶ Transaction Auto-wrapping for the data access layer
- ▶ Setting up an NHibernate repository
- ▶ Using Named Queries in the data access layer
- ▶ Using ICriteria in the data access layer
- ▶ Using Paged Queries in the data access layer
- ▶ Using LINQ specifications in the data access layer

Introduction

There are two styles of data access layer common in today's applications. The first recipe shows the beginnings of a typical data access object. The remaining recipes show how to set up a repository-based data access layer with NHibernate's various APIs.

Transaction Auto-wrapping for the data access layer

In this recipe, I'll show you how we can set up the data access layer to wrap all data access in NHibernate transactions automatically.

Getting ready

Complete the Eg.Core model and mappings from *Chapter 1*.

How to do it...

1. Create a new class library named `Eg.Core.Data`.

2. Add a reference to `NHibernate.dll` and the `Eg.Core` project.

3. Add the following two DAO classes:

```
public class DataAccessObject<T, TId>
  where T : Entity<TId>
{

  private readonly ISessionFactory _sessionFactory;

  private ISession session
  {
    get
    {
      return _sessionFactory.GetCurrentSession();
    }
  }

  public DataAccessObject(ISessionFactory sessionFactory)
  {
    _sessionFactory = sessionFactory;
  }

  public T Get(TId id)
  {
    return Transact(() => session.Get<T>(id));
  }

  public T Load(TId id)
  {
    return Transact(() => session.Load<T>(id));
  }

  public void Save(T entity)
  {
    Transact(() => session.SaveOrUpdate(entity));
  }

  public void Delete(T entity)
  {
    Transact(() => session.Delete(entity));
  }

  private TResult Transact<TResult>(Func<TResult> func)
```

```
  {
    if (!session.Transaction.IsActive)
    {
      // Wrap in transaction
      TResult result;
      using (var tx = session.BeginTransaction())
      {
        result = func.Invoke();
        tx.Commit();
      }
      return result;
    }
    // Don't wrap;
    return func.Invoke();
  }
  private void Transact(Action action)
  {
    Transact<bool>(() =>
    {
      action.Invoke();
      return false;
    });
  }
}
public class DataAccessObject<T>
  : DataAccessObject<T, Guid>
  where T : Entity
{
}
```

How it works...

NHibernate requires that all data access occurs inside an NHibernate transaction. As we saw with the _Transaction action filter_ recipe in _Chapter 4_, this can be easily accomplished with AOP.

 Remember, the ambient transaction created by TransactionScope is not a substitute for a NHibernate transaction.

This recipe shows a more explicit approach. To ensure that at least all our data access layer calls are wrapped in transactions, we create a private `Transact` function that accepts a delegate, consisting of some data access methods, such as `session.Save` or `session. Get`. This `Transact` function first checks if the session has an active transaction. If it does, `Transact` simply invokes the delegate. If it doesn't, it creates an explicit NHibernate transaction, then invokes the delegate, and finally commits the transaction. If the data access method throws an exception, the transaction will be rolled back automatically as the exception bubbles up through the `using` block.

There's more...

This transactional auto-wrapping can also be set up using `SessionWrapper` from the unofficial NHibernate AddIns project at `http://code.google.com/p/unhaddins`. This class wraps a standard NHibernate session. By default, it will throw an exception when the session is used without an NHibernate transaction. However, it can be configured to check for and create a transaction automatically, much in the same way I've shown you here. This is the same `SessionWrapper` we used in the *Conversation per Business Transaction* recipe in *Chapter 3*.

See also

▶ *Setting up an NHibernate repository*

Setting up an NHibernate Repository

Many developers prefer the repository pattern over data access objects. In this recipe, I'll show you how to set up the repository pattern with NHibernate.

Getting ready

Set up the `Eg.Core` project with the model and mappings from *Chapter 1*.

How to do it...

1. Create a new, empty class library project named `Eg.Core.Data`.
2. Add a reference to `Eg.Core` project in *Chapter 1*.
3. Add the following `IRepository` interface:

```
public interface IRepository<T>: IEnumerable<T>
where T : Entity
{
  void Add(T item);
  bool Contains(T item);
  int Count { get; }
```

```
  bool Remove(T item);
}
```

4. Create a new, empty class library project named `Eg.Core.Data.Impl`.

5. Add references to `Eg.Core` and `Eg.Core.Data`

6. Add a new abstract class named `NHibernateBase` using the following code:

```
protected readonly ISessionFactory _sessionFactory;

protected virtual ISession session
{
  get
  {
    return _sessionFactory.GetCurrentSession();
  }
}

public NHibernateBase(ISessionFactory sessionFactory)
{
  _sessionFactory = sessionFactory;
}

protected virtual TResult Transact<TResult>(
Func<TResult> func)
{
  if (!session.Transaction.IsActive)
  {
    // Wrap in transaction
    TResult result;
    using (var tx = session.BeginTransaction())
    {
      result = func.Invoke();
      tx.Commit();
    }
    return result;
  }
  // Don't wrap;
  return func.Invoke();
}

protected virtual void Transact(Action action)
{
  Transact<bool>(() =>
  {
```

```
    action.Invoke();
    return false;
  });
}
```

7. Add a new class named NHibernateRepository using the following code:

```
public class NHibernateRepository<T> :
  NHibernateBase,
  IRepository<T> where T : Entity
{
  public NHibernateRepository(ISessionFactory sessionFactory)
    : base(sessionFactory)
  {
  }

  public void Add(T item)
  {
    Transact(() => session.Save(item));
  }

  public bool Contains(T item)
  {
    if (item.Id == default(Guid))
      return false;
    return Transact(() => session.Get<T>(item.Id)) != null;
  }

  public int Count
  {
    get
    {
      return Transact(() => session.Query<T>().Count());
    }
  }

  public bool Remove(T item)
  {
    Transact(() => session.Delete(item));
    return true;
  }

  public IEnumerator<T> GetEnumerator()
  {
    return Transact(() => session.Query<T>()
```

```
                .Take(1000).GetEnumerator());
     }

     IEnumerator IEnumerable.GetEnumerator()
     {
       return Transact(() => GetEnumerator());
     }

   }
```

How it works...

The repository pattern, as explained in `http://martinfowler.com/eaaCatalog/repository.htm`, has two key features:

- ► It behaves as an in-memory collection
- ► Query specifications are submitted to the repository for satisfaction.

In this recipe, we are concerned only with the first feature, behaving as an in-memory collection. The remaining recipes in this chapter will build on this base, and show various methods for satisfying the second point.

Because our repository should act like an in-memory collection, it makes sense that our `IRepository<T>` interface should resemble `ICollection<T>`.

Our NHibernateBase class provides both contextual session management and the automatic transaction wrapping explained in the previous recipe.

`NHibernateRepository` simply implements the members of `IRepository<T>`.

There's more...

The Repository pattern reduces data access to its absolute simplest form, but this simplification comes with a price. We lose much of the power of NHibernate behind an abstraction layer. Our application must either do without even basic session methods like `Merge`, `Refresh`, and `Load`, or allow them to leak through the abstraction.

See also

- ► *Transaction Auto-wrapping for the data access layer*
- ► *Using Named Queries in the data access layer*
- ► *Using ICriteria in the data access layer*
- ► *Using Paged Queries in the data access layer*
- ► *Using LINQ specifications in the data access layer*

Using Named Queries in the data access layer

Named Queries encapsulated in query objects is a powerful combination. In this recipe, I'll show you how to use Named Queries with your data access layer.

Getting ready

Download the latest release of the Common Service Locator from `http://commonservicelocator.codeplex.com`, and extract `Microsoft.Practices.ServiceLocation.dll` to your solution's `libs` folder.

Complete the previous recipe, *Setting up an NHibernate repository*.

Following the *Fast testing with SQLite in-memory database recipe* in *Chapter 5*, create a new NHibernate test project named `Eg.Core.Data.Impl.Test`.

Include the `Eg.Core.Data.Impl` assembly as an additional mapping assembly in your test project's `App.Config` with the following xml:

```
<mapping assembly="Eg.Core.Data.Impl"/>
```

How to do it...

1. In the `Eg.Core.Data` project, add a folder for the `Queries` namespace.
2. Add the following `IQuery` interfaces:

    ```
    public interface IQuery
    {
    }

    public interface IQuery<TResult> : IQuery
    {

      TResult Execute();

    }
    ```

3. Add the following `IQueryFactory` interface:

    ```
    public interface IQueryFactory
    {

      TQuery CreateQuery<TQuery>() where TQuery :IQuery;

    }
    ```

4. Change the `IRepository` interface to implement the `IQueryFactory` interface, as shown in the following code:

```
public interface IRepository<T>
 : IEnumerable<T>, IQueryFactory
   where T : Entity
{
  void Add(T item);
  bool Contains(T item);
  int Count { get; }
  bool Remove(T item);
}
```

5. In the `Eg.Core.Data.Impl` project, change the `NHibernateRepository` constructor and add the `_queryFactory` field, as shown in the following code:

```
private readonly IQueryFactory _queryFactory;

public NHibernateRepository(ISessionFactory sessionFactory,
  IQueryFactory queryFactory)
   : base(sessionFactory)
{
  _queryFactory = queryFactory;
}
```

6. Add the following method to `NHibernateRepository`:

```
public TQuery CreateQuery<TQuery>() where TQuery : IQuery
{
  return _queryFactory.CreateQuery<TQuery>();
}
```

7. In the `Eg.Core.Data.Impl` project, add a folder for the `Queries` namespace.

8. To the `Eg.Core.Data.Impl` project, add a reference to `Microsoft.Practices.ServiceLocation.dll`.

9. To the `Queries` namespace, add this `QueryFactory` class:

```
public class QueryFactory : IQueryFactory
{

  private readonly IServiceLocator _serviceLocator;

  public QueryFactory(IServiceLocator serviceLocator)
  {
    _serviceLocator = serviceLocator;
  }

  public TQuery CreateQuery<TQuery>() where TQuery : IQuery
  {
```

```
      return _serviceLocator.GetInstance<TQuery>();
    }
  }
```

10. Add the following `NHibernateQueryBase` class:

```
public abstract class NHibernateQueryBase<TResult>
  : NHibernateBase, IQuery<TResult>
{
  protected NHibernateQueryBase(
    ISessionFactory sessionFactory)
    : base(sessionFactory) { }

  public abstract TResult Execute();
}
```

11. Add an empty `INamedQuery` interface, as shown in the following code:

```
public interface INamedQuery
{
  string QueryName { get; }
}
```

12. Add a `NamedQueryBase` class, as shown in the following code:

```
public abstract class NamedQueryBase<TResult>
  : NHibernateQueryBase<TResult>, INamedQuery
{
  protected NamedQueryBase(ISessionFactory sessionFactory)
    : base(sessionFactory) { }

  public override TResult Execute()
  {
    var nhQuery = GetNamedQuery();
    return Transact(() => Execute(nhQuery));
  }

  protected abstract TResult Execute(IQuery query);

  protected virtual IQuery GetNamedQuery()
  {
    var nhQuery = session.GetNamedQuery(
      ((INamedQuery) this).QueryName);
    SetParameters(nhQuery);
    return nhQuery;
  }

  protected abstract void SetParameters(IQuery nhQuery);
```

```
  public virtual string QueryName
  {
    get { return GetType().Name; }
  }
}
```

13. In `Eg.Core.Data.Impl.Test`, add a test fixture named `QueryTests` inherited from `NHibernateFixture`.

14. Add the following test and three helper methods:

```
[Test]
public void NamedQueryCheck()
{
  var errors = new StringBuilder();

  var queryObjectTypes = GetNamedQueryObjectTypes();
  var mappedQueries = GetNamedQueryNames();

  foreach (var queryType in queryObjectTypes)
  {
    var query = GetQuery(queryType);

    if (!mappedQueries.Contains(query.QueryName))
    {
      errors.AppendFormat(
        "Query object {0} references non-existent " +
        "named query {1}.",
        queryType, query.QueryName);
      errors.AppendLine();
    }
  }

  if (errors.Length != 0)
    Assert.Fail(errors.ToString());
}

private IEnumerable<Type> GetNamedQueryObjectTypes()
{
  var namedQueryType = typeof(INamedQuery);
  var queryImplAssembly = typeof(BookWithISBN).Assembly;

  var types = from t in queryImplAssembly.GetTypes()
              where namedQueryType.IsAssignableFrom(t)
              && t.IsClass
              && !t.IsAbstract
```

```
              select t;
    return types;
  }

  private IEnumerable<string> GetNamedQueryNames()
  {
    var nhCfg = NHConfigurator.Configuration;

    var mappedQueries = nhCfg.NamedQueries.Keys
      .Union(nhCfg.NamedSQLQueries.Keys);

    return mappedQueries;
  }

  private INamedQuery GetQuery(Type queryType)
  {
    return (INamedQuery) Activator
      .CreateInstance(queryType,
      new object[] { SessionFactory });
  }
```

15. For our example query, in the `Queries` namespace of `Eg.Core.Data`,
    add the following interface:

```
public interface IBookWithISBN : IQuery<Book>
{
    string ISBN { get; set; }
}
```

16. Add the implementation to the `Queries` namespace of `Eg.Core.Data.Impl`
    using the following code:

```
public class BookWithISBN :
  NamedQueryBase<Book>, IBookWithISBN
{
    public BookWithISBN(ISessionFactory sessionFactory)
      : base(sessionFactory) { }

    public string ISBN { get; set; }

    protected override void SetParameters(
      NHibernate.IQuery nhQuery)
    {
      nhQuery.SetParameter("isbn", ISBN);
    }

    protected override Book Execute(NHibernate.IQuery query)
    {
```

```
        return query.UniqueResult<Book>();
    }

}
```

17. Finally, add the embedded resource mapping, `BookWithISBN.hbm.xml`, to `Eg.Core.Data.Impl` with the following xml code:

```xml
<?xml version="1.0" encoding="utf-8" ?>
<hibernate-mapping xmlns="urn:nhibernate-mapping-2.2">
  <query name="BookWithISBN">
    <![CDATA[
    from Book b where b.ISBN = :isbn
    ]]>
  </query>
</hibernate-mapping>
```

How it works...

As we learned in the previous recipe, according to the repository pattern, the repository is responsible for fulfilling queries, based on the specifications submitted to it. These specifications are limiting. They only concern themselves with whether a particular item matches the given criteria. They don't care for other necessary technical details, such as eager loading of children, batching, query caching, and so on. We need something more powerful than simple `where` clauses. We lose too much to the abstraction.

The query object pattern defines a query object as a group of criteria that can self-organize in to a SQL query. The query object is not responsible for the execution of this SQL. This is handled elsewhere, by some generic query runner, perhaps inside the repository. While a query object can better express the different technical requirements, such as eager loading, batching, and query caching, a generic query runner can't easily implement those concerns for every possible query, especially across the half-dozen query APIs provided by NHibernate.

These details about the execution are specific to each query, and should be handled by the query object. This enhanced query object pattern, as *Fabio Maulo* has named it, not only self-organizes into SQL but also executes the query, returning the results. In this way, the technical concerns of a query's execution are defined and cared for with the query itself, rather than spreading into some highly complex, generic query runner.

According to the abstraction we've built, the repository represents the collection of entities that we are querying. Since the two are already logically linked, if we allow the repository to build the query objects, we can add some context to our code. For example, suppose we have an application service that runs product queries. When we inject dependencies, we could specify `IQueryFactory` directly. This doesn't give us much information beyond "This service runs queries." If, however, we inject `IRepository<Product>`, we have a much better idea about what data the service is using.

The IQuery interface is simply a marker interface for our query objects. Besides advertising the purpose of our query objects, it allows us to easily identify them with reflection.

The IQuery<TResult> interface is implemented by each query object. It specifies only the return type and a single method to execute the query.

The IQueryFactory interface defines a service to create query objects. For the purpose of explanation, the implementation of this service, QueryFactory, is a simple service locator. IQueryFactory is used internally by the repository to instantiate query objects.

The NamedQueryBase class handles most of the plumbing for query objects, based on named HQL and SQL queries. As a convention, the name of the query is the name of the query object type. That is, the underlying named query for BookWithISBN is also named BookWithISBN. Each individual query object must simply implement SetParameters and Execute(NHibernate.IQuery query), which usually consists of a simple call to query. List<SomeEntity>() or query.UniqueResult<SomeEntity>().

The INamedQuery interface both identifies the query objects based on Named Queries, and provides access to the query name. The NamedQueryCheck test uses this to verify that each INamedQuery query object has a matching named query.

Each query has an interface. This interface is used to request the query object from the repository. It also defines any parameters used in the query. In this example, IBookWithISBN has a single string parameter, ISBN. The implementation of this query object sets the :isbn parameter on the internal NHibernate query, executes it, and returns the matching Book object.

Finally, we also create a mapping containing the named query BookWithISBN, which is loaded into the configuration with the rest of our mappings.

There's more...

The code used in the query object setup would look like the following code:

```
var query = bookRepository.CreateQuery<IBookWithISBN>();
query.ISBN = "12345";
var book = query.Execute();
```

See also

- ▶ *Transaction Auto-wrapping for the data access layer*
- ▶ *Setting up an NHibernate repository*
- ▶ *Using ICriteria in the data access layer*
- ▶ *Using Paged Queries in the data access layer*
- ▶ *Using LINQ specifications in the data access layer*

Using ICriteria in the data access layer

For queries where the criteria are not known in advance, such as a website's advanced product search, `ICriteria` queries are more appropriate than named HQL queries. In this recipe, I'll show you how to use the same DAL infrastructure with `ICriteria` and `QueryOver` queries.

Getting ready

Complete the previous recipe, *Using Named Queries in the data access layer*.

How to do it...

1. In `Eg.Core.Data.Impl.Queries`, add a new, empty, public interface named `ICriteriaQuery`.

2. Add a class named `CriteriaQueryBase` with the following code:

```
public abstract class CriteriaQueryBase<TResult> :
  NHibernateQueryBase<TResult>, ICriteriaQuery
{
  public CriteriaQueryBase(ISessionFactory sessionFactory)
    : base(sessionFactory) { }

  public override TResult Execute()
  {
    var criteria = GetCriteria();
    return Transact(() => Execute(criteria));
  }

  protected abstract ICriteria GetCriteria();

  protected abstract TResult Execute(ICriteria criteria);

}
```

3. In `Eg.Core.Data.Queries`, add the following enum:

```
public enum AdvancedProductSearchSort
{
  PriceAsc,
  PriceDesc,
  Name
}
```

4. Add a new interface named `IAdvancedProductSearch` with the following code:

```
public interface IAdvancedProductSearch
  : IQuery<IEnumerable<Product>>
{

  string Name { get; set; }
  string Description { get; set; }
  decimal? MinimumPrice { get; set; }
  decimal? MaximumPrice { get; set; }
  AdvancedProductSearchSort Sort { get; set; }

}
```

5. In `Eg.Core.Data.Impl.Queries`, add the following class:

```
public class AdvancedProductSearch
  : CriteriaQueryBase<IEnumerable<Product>>,
    IAdvancedProductSearch
{

  public AdvancedProductSearch(ISessionFactory sessionFactory)
    : base(sessionFactory) { }

  public string Name { get; set; }
  public string Description { get; set; }
  public decimal? MinimumPrice { get; set; }
  public decimal? MaximumPrice { get; set; }
  public AdvancedProductSearchSort
    Sort { get; set; }

  protected override ICriteria GetCriteria()
  {
    return GetProductQuery().UnderlyingCriteria;
  }

  protected override IEnumerable<Product> Execute(
    ICriteria criteria)
  {
    return criteria.List<Product>();
  }

  private IQueryOver GetProductQuery()
  {
    var query = session.QueryOver<Product>();
    AddProductCriterion(query);
    return query;
  }
}
```

```
    private void AddProductCriterion<T>(
      IQueryOver<T, T> query) where T : Product
    {
      if (!string.IsNullOrEmpty(Name))
        query = query.WhereRestrictionOn(p => p.Name)
          .IsInsensitiveLike(Name, MatchMode.Anywhere);

      if (!string.IsNullOrEmpty(Description))
        query.WhereRestrictionOn(p => p.Description)
          .IsInsensitiveLike(Description, MatchMode.Anywhere);

      if (MinimumPrice.HasValue)
        query.Where(p => p.UnitPrice >= MinimumPrice);

      if (MaximumPrice.HasValue)
        query.Where(p => p.UnitPrice <= MaximumPrice);

      switch (Sort)
      {
        case AdvancedProductSearchSort.PriceDesc:
          query = query.OrderBy(p => p.UnitPrice).Desc;
          break;
        case AdvancedProductSearchSort.Name:
          query = query.OrderBy(p => p.Name).Asc;
          break;
        default:
          query = query.OrderBy(p => p.UnitPrice).Asc;
          break;
      }
    }
}
```

How it works...

In this recipe, we reuse the same repository and query infrastructure from the *Using Named Queries in The Data Access Layer* recipe. Our simple base class for ICriteria-based query objects splits query creation from query execution and handles transactions for us automatically.

The example query we use is typical for an "advanced product search" use case. When a user fills in a particular field on the UI, the corresponding criterion is included in the query. When the user leaves the field blank, we ignore it.

We check each search parameter for data. If the parameter has data, we add the appropriate criterion to the query. Finally, we set the order by clause based on the `Sort` parameter and return the completed `ICriteria` query. The query is executed inside a transaction, and the results are returned.

There's more...

For this type of query, typically, each query parameter would be set to the value of some field on your product search UI. On using this query, your code looks like this:

```
var query = repository.CreateQuery<IAdvancedProductSearch>();
query.Name = searchCriteria.PartialName;
query.Description = searchCriteria.PartialDescription;
query.MinimumPrice = searchCriteria.MinimumPrice;
query.MaximumPrice = searchCriteria.MaximumPrice;
query.Sort = searchCriteria.Sort;
var results = query.Execute();
```

See also

▶ *Transaction Auto-wrapping for The Data Access Layer*

▶ *Setting up an NHibernate Repository*

▶ *Using Named Queries in The Data Access Layer*

▶ *Using Paged Queries in The Data Access Layer*

▶ *Using LINQ specifications in The Data Access Layer*

Using Paged Queries in the data access layer

In an effort to avoid overwhelming the user, and increase application responsiveness, large result sets are commonly broken into smaller pages of results. In this recipe, I'll show you how we can easily add paging to a QueryOver query object in our DAL.

Getting ready

Complete the recipe, *Using Named Queries in the data access layer*.

How to do it...

1. In `Eg.Core.Data.Queries`, add a class using the following code:

```
public class PagedResult<T>
{

  public int TotalItems { get; set; }
  public IEnumerable<T> PageOfResults { get; set; }

}
```

2. Add an interface using the following code:

```
public interface IPagedQuery<T>
  : IQuery<PagedResult<T>>
{

  int PageNumber { get; set; }
  int ItemsPerPage { get; set; }

}
```

3. In `Eg.Core.Data.Impl.Queries`, add the following class:

```
public abstract class PagedQueryOverBase<T>
  : NHibernateQueryBase<PagedResult<T>>,
    IPagedQuery<T>
{

  public PagedQueryOverBase(ISessionFactory sessionFactory)
    : base(sessionFactory) { }

  public int PageNumber { get; set; }
  public int ItemsPerPage { get; set; }

  public override PagedResult<T> Execute()
  {
    var query = GetQuery();
    SetPaging(query);
    return Transact(() => Execute(query));
  }

  protected abstract IQueryOver<T, T> GetQuery();

  protected virtual void SetPaging(
    IQueryOver<T, T> query)
  {
    int maxResults = ItemsPerPage;
    int firstResult = (PageNumber - 1) * ItemsPerPage;
    query.Skip(firstResult).Take(maxResults);
```

```
    }

    protected virtual PagedResult<T> Execute(
      IQueryOver<T, T> query)
    {
      var results = query.Future<T>();
      var count = query.ToRowCountQuery().FutureValue<int>();
      return new PagedResult<T>()
      {
        PageOfResults = results,
        TotalItems = count.Value
      };
    }

  }
```

4. In `Eg.Core.Data.Queries`, add an interface for the example query:

```
public interface IPagedProductSearch
  : IPagedQuery<Product>
{

  string Name { get; set; }
  string Description { get; set; }
  decimal? MinimumPrice { get; set; }
  decimal? MaximumPrice { get; set; }
  PagedProductSearchSort Sort { get; set; }

}
```

5. Add the following enumeration for choosing the sort option:

```
public enum PagedProductSearchSort
{
  PriceAsc,
  PriceDesc,
  Name
}
```

6. In `Eg.Core.Data.Impl.Queries`, implement the interface using the following class:

```
public class PagedProductSearch
  : PagedQueryOverBase<Product>,
    IPagedProductSearch
{

  public PagedProductSearch(ISessionFactory sessionFactory)
    : base(sessionFactory) { }
```

```
public string Name { get; set; }
public string Description { get; set; }
public decimal? MinimumPrice { get; set; }
public decimal? MaximumPrice { get; set; }
public PagedProductSearchSort
  Sort { get; set; }

protected override IQueryOver<Product, Product> GetQuery()
{
  var query = session.QueryOver<Product>();
  if (!string.IsNullOrEmpty(Name))
    query = query.WhereRestrictionOn(p => p.Name)
      .IsInsensitiveLike(Name, MatchMode.Anywhere);

  if (!string.IsNullOrEmpty(Description))
    query.WhereRestrictionOn(p => p.Description)
      .IsInsensitiveLike(Description, MatchMode.Anywhere);

  if (MinimumPrice.HasValue)
    query.Where(p => p.UnitPrice >= MinimumPrice);

  if (MaximumPrice.HasValue)
    query.Where(p => p.UnitPrice <= MaximumPrice);

  switch (Sort)
  {
    case PagedProductSearchSort.PriceDesc:
      query = query.OrderBy(p => p.UnitPrice).Desc;
      break;
    case PagedProductSearchSort.Name:
      query = query.OrderBy(p => p.Name).Asc;
      break;
    default:
      query = query.OrderBy(p => p.UnitPrice).Asc;
      break;
  }
  return query;
  }
}
```

How it works...

In this recipe, we've defined a common `PagedResult<T>` return type for all paged queries. We've also defined the `IPagedQuery<T>` interface, which specifies the paging parameters and a return type of `PagedResult<T>`.

As defined in `PagedQueryOverBase`, each subclassed query object must return a standard `IQueryOver<T, T>` query from `GetQuery()`. The `PagedQueryOverBase` class sets the appropriate `Skip` and `Take` values based on the specified page number and items per page. Then it uses futures to get the results. The row count query is created from the result set query using the new `ToRowCountQuery()` method. The future queries are executed when the count query result is put into the `PagedResult<T>` object.

See also

- ▸ *Transaction Auto-wrapping for the data access layer*
- ▸ *Setting up an NHibernate repository*
- ▸ *Using Named Queries in the data access layer*
- ▸ *Using ICriteria in the data access layer*
- ▸ *Using LINQ specifications in the data access layer*

Using LINQ Specifications in the data access layer

With the completion of LINQ to NHibernate for NHibernate 3.0, we can easily implement the specification pattern. In this recipe, I'll show you how to set up and use the specification pattern with the NHibernate repository.

Getting ready

Download the LinqSpecs library from `http://linqspecs.codeplex.com`. Copy `LinqSpecs.dll` from the `Downloads` folder to your solution's `libs` folder.

Complete the *Setting up an NHibernate Repository* recipe.

How to do it...

1. In `Eg.Core.Data` and `Eg.Core.Data.Impl`, add a reference to `LinqSpecs.dll`.

2. Add these two methods to the `IRepository` interface.

   ```
   IEnumerable<T> FindAll(Specification<T> specification);
   T FindOne(Specification<T> specification);
   ```

3. Add the following three methods to `NHibernateRepository`:

```
public IEnumerable<T> FindAll(Specification<T> specification)
{
  var query = GetQuery(specification);
  return Transact(() => query.ToList());
}

public T FindOne(Specification<T> specification)
{
  var query = GetQuery(specification);
  return Transact(() => query.SingleOrDefault());
}

private IQueryable<T> GetQuery(
  Specification<T> specification)
{
  return session.Query<T>()
    .Where(specification.IsSatisfiedBy());
}
```

4. Add the following specification to `Eg.Core.Data.Queries`:

```
public class MoviesDirectedBy : Specification<Movie>
{
  private readonly string _director;

  public MoviesDirectedBy(string director)
  {
    _director = director;
  }

  public override
    Expression<Func<Movie, bool>> IsSatisfiedBy()
  {
    return m => m.Director == _director;
  }
}
```

5. Add another specification to `Eg.Core.Data.Queries`, using the following code:

```
public class MoviesStarring : Specification<Movie>
{
  private readonly string _actor;

  public MoviesStarring(string actor)
  {
```

```
        _actor = actor;
    }

    public override
        Expression<Func<Movie, bool>> IsSatisfiedBy()
    {
        return m => m.Actors.Any(a => a.Actor == _actor);
    }

}
```

How it works...

The specification pattern allows us to separate the process of selecting objects from the concern of which objects to select. The repository handles selecting objects, while the specification objects are concerned only with the objects that satisfy their requirements.

In our specification objects, the `IsSatisfiedBy` method of the specification objects returns a LINQ expression to determine which objects to select.

In the repository, we get an `IQueryable` from the session, pass this LINQ expression to the `Where` method, and execute the LINQ query. Only the objects that satisfy the specification will be returned.

For a detailed explanation of the specification pattern, check out `http://martinfowler.com/apsupp/spec.pdf`.

There's more...

To use our new specifications with the repository, use the following code:

```
var movies = repository.FindAll(
    new MoviesDirectedBy("Stephen Spielberg"));
```

Specification composition

We can also combine specifications to build more complex queries. For example, the following code will find all movies directed by *Steven Speilberg* starring *Harrison Ford*:

```
var movies = repository.FindAll(
            new MoviesDirectedBy("Steven Spielberg")
            & new MoviesStarring("Harrison Ford"));
```

This may result in expression trees that NHibernate is unable to parse. Be sure to test each combination.

See also

- ▸ *Transaction Auto-wrapping for the data access layer*
- ▸ *Setting up an NHibernate repository*
- ▸ *Using Named Queries in the data access layer*
- ▸ *Using ICriteria in the data access layer*
- ▸ *Using Paged Queries in the data access layer*

7
Extending NHibernate

In this chapter, we will cover the following topics:

- ▶ Creating an encrypted string type
- ▶ Using well-known instance types
- ▶ Using dependency injection with entities
- ▶ Creating an audit-event listener
- ▶ Creating and changing stamping entities
- ▶ Generating trigger-based auditing
- ▶ Setting Microsoft SQL's `CONTEXT_INFO`
- ▶ Using dynamic connection strings

Introduction

NHibernate is incredibly extensible. The recipes in this chapter demonstrate ways to extend NHibernate to accomplish common tasks such as data encryption and auditing.

Creating an encrypted string type

In this age of identity theft, data security is more important than ever. Sensitive data such as credit card numbers should always be encrypted. In this recipe, I'll show you how to use NHibernate to encrypt a single property.

How to do it...

1. Create a new class library project named `EncryptedStringExample`.

2. Add references to `NHibernate.dll`, `log4net.dll`, and `NHibernate.Castle. ByteCode.dll`.

3. Add a new public interface named `IEncryptor` with the following three method definitions:

```
public interface IEncryptor
{
  string Encrypt(string plainText);
  string Decrypt(string encryptedText);
  string EncryptionKey { get; set; }
}
```

4 Create an implementation of `IEncryptor` named `SymmetricEncryptorBase` using the following code:

```
public abstract class SymmetricEncryptorBase : IEncryptor
{
  private readonly SymmetricAlgorithm _cryptoProvider;
  private byte[] _myBytes;

  protected SymmetricEncryptorBase(
    SymmetricAlgorithm cryptoProvider)
  {
    _cryptoProvider = cryptoProvider;
  }

  public string EncryptionKey { get; set; }

  public string Encrypt(string plainText)
  {
    var bytes = GetEncryptionKeyBytes();
    using (var memoryStream = new MemoryStream())
    {
      ICryptoTransform encryptor = _cryptoProvider
        .CreateEncryptor(bytes, bytes);

      using (var cryptoStream = new CryptoStream(
        memoryStream, encryptor, CryptoStreamMode.Write))
      {
        using (var writer = new StreamWriter(cryptoStream))
        {
          writer.Write(plainText);
```

```
            writer.Flush();
            cryptoStream.FlushFinalBlock();
            return Convert.ToBase64String(
              memoryStream.GetBuffer(),
              0,
              (int) memoryStream.Length);
          }
        }
      }
    }

    private byte[] GetEncryptionKeyBytes()
    {
      if (_myBytes == null)
        _myBytes = Encoding.ASCII.GetBytes(EncryptionKey);

      return _myBytes;
    }

    public string Decrypt(string encryptedText)
    {
      var bytes = GetEncryptionKeyBytes();
      using (var memoryStream = new MemoryStream(
        Convert.FromBase64String(encryptedText)))
      {
        ICryptoTransform decryptor = _cryptoProvider
          .CreateDecryptor(bytes, bytes);
        using (var cryptoStream = new CryptoStream(
          memoryStream, decryptor, CryptoStreamMode.Read))
        {
          using (var reader = new StreamReader(cryptoStream))
          {
            return reader.ReadToEnd();
          }
        }
      }
    }
  }
```

5. Create a concrete implementation named DESEncryptor with the following code:

```
public class DESEncryptor : SymmetricEncryptorBase
{

  public DESEncryptor()
```

```
        : base(new DESCryptoServiceProvider())
    { }
}
```

6. Add an implementation of `IUserType` named `EncryptedString` using the following code:

```
public class EncryptedString : IUserType, IParameterizedType
{
    private IEncryptor _encryptor;
    public object NullSafeGet(
        IDataReader rs,
        string[] names,
        object owner)
    {
        //treat for the posibility of null values
        object passwordString =
            NHibernateUtil.String.NullSafeGet(rs, names[0]);
        if (passwordString != null)
        {
            return _encryptor.Decrypt((string)passwordString);
        }
        return null;
    }
    public void NullSafeSet(
        IDbCommand cmd,
        object value,
        int index)
    {
        if (value == null)
        {
            NHibernateUtil.String.NullSafeSet(cmd, null, index);
            return;
        }
        string encryptedValue = _encryptor.Encrypt((string)value);
        NHibernateUtil.String.NullSafeSet(
            cmd, encryptedValue, index);
    }
    public object DeepCopy(object value)
    {
```

```
    return value == null ? null :
      string.Copy((string)value);
  }

  public object Replace(object original,
    object target, object owner)
  {
    return original;
  }

  public object Assemble(object cached, object owner)
  {
    return DeepCopy(cached);
  }

  public object Disassemble(object value)
  {
    return DeepCopy(value);
  }

  public SqlType[] SqlTypes
  {
    get
    {
      return new[] { new SqlType(DbType.String) };
    }
  }

  public Type ReturnedType
  {
    get { return typeof(string); }
  }

  public bool IsMutable
  {
    get { return false; }
  }

  public new bool Equals(object x, object y)
  {
    if (ReferenceEquals(x, y))
    {
      return true;
    }
    if (x == null || y == null)
```

```
    {
      return false;
    }
    return x.Equals(y);
  }

  public int GetHashCode(object x)
  {
    if (x == null)
    {
      throw new ArgumentNullException("x");
    }
    return x.GetHashCode();
  }

  public void SetParameterValues(
    IDictionary<string, string> parameters)
  {
    if (parameters != null)
    {
      var encryptorTypeName = parameters["encryptor"];
      _encryptor = !string.IsNullOrEmpty(encryptorTypeName)
                  ? (IEncryptor) Instantiate(encryptorTypeName)
                  : new DESEncryptor();
      var encryptionKey = parameters["encryptionKey"];
      if (!string.IsNullOrEmpty(encryptionKey))
        _encryptor.EncryptionKey = encryptionKey;
    }
    else
    {
      _encryptor = new DESEncryptor();
    }
  }

  private static object Instantiate(string typeName)
  {
    var type = Type.GetType(typeName);
    return Activator.CreateInstance(type);
  }
}
```

7. Add an entity class named `Account` with the following properties:

```
public virtual Guid Id { get; set; }
public virtual string EMail { get; set; }
public virtual string Name { get; set; }
public virtual string CardNumber { get;  set; }
public virtual int ExpirationMonth { get; set; }
public virtual int ExpirationYear { get; set; }
public virtual string ZipCode { get; set; }
```

8. Add a mapping document with the following XML. Don't forget to set the **Build Action** to **Embedded Resource**:

```xml
<?xml version="1.0" encoding="utf-8" ?>
<hibernate-mapping xmlns="urn:nhibernate-mapping-2.2"
    assembly="EncryptedStringExample"
    namespace="EncryptedStringExample">
  <typedef
    name="encrypted"
    class="EncryptedStringExample.EncryptedString,
EncryptedStringExample">
    <param name="encryptor">
      EncryptedStringExample.DESEncryptor,
      EncryptedStringExample
    </param>
    <param name="encryptionKey">12345678</param>
  </typedef>
  <class name="Account">
    <id name="Id">
      <generator class="guid.comb" />
    </id>
    <property name="Name" not-null="true" />
    <property name="EMail" not-null="true" />
    <property name="CardNumber" not-null="true" type="encrypted"
/>
    <property name="ExpirationMonth" not-null="true" />
    <property name="ExpirationYear" not-null="true" />
    <property name="ZipCode" not-null="true" />
  </class>
</hibernate-mapping>
```

How it works...

As we saw in the *Mapping Enumerations* recipe in *Chapter 1*, we can set the type attribute on a property to specify a class used for converting data between our application and the database. We'll use this to encrypt and decrypt our credit card number.

Our `Account` class mapping defined a type using the `<typedef>` element. The `name` attribute defines a nickname for our `encryption` type. This nickname matches the `type` attribute on our `CardNumber` property's mapping. The `class` attribute specifies the .NET class that will be used to convert our data in standard `namespace.typeName, assemblyName` format.

Our `EncryptedString` type happens to use two parameters—`encryptor` and `encryptionKey`. These are set in the mapping as well.

`DESEncryptor`, our implementation of `IEncryptor`, uses `DESCryptoServiceProvider` to encrypt and decrypt our data. This is one of the symmetric encryption algorithms available in the .NET framework.

Our `EncryptedString` type implements `IUserType`, NHibernate's interface for defining custom types. When implementing `IUserType`, `NullSafeGet` is responsible for reading data from the ADO.NET data reader and returning an appropriate object, in this case, a string. In our `EncryptedString`, we read the encrypted data, use `IEncryptor` to decrypt it, and return the unencrypted string, which is used to set the `CardNumber` property. `NullSafeSet` takes some value, in this case, our unencrypted `CardNumber`, and sets a parameter on the ADO.NET `command`. In `EncryptedString`, we encrypt the card number before setting it on the `command`. The `SqlTypes` property returns an array representing the types of each database field used to store this user type. In our case, we have a single string field. The `ReturnedType` property returns the .NET type. Since our `CardNumber` is a string, we return the string type.

`EncryptedString` also implements `IParameterizedType`. The `SetParameterValues` method provides a dictionary of parameters from the mapping document. From that dictionary, we get the `IEncryptor` implementation to use, as well as the encryption key.

 The class mapping is not the best place to store encryption keys. This recipe can easily be adapted to read the encryption keys from a properly secured location.

There's more...

There are three categories of encryption algorithms. A symmetric algorithm uses the same key to encrypt and decrypt the data. Because our application is responsible for the encryption and decryption, this type of algorithm makes the most sense.

An asymmetric algorithm encrypts data using a pair of keys—one public and one private. The key pairs are generated in such a way that the public key used to encrypt the data gives no hint as to the private key required to decrypt that data. It's not necessary to keep the public key a secret. This type of algorithm is typically used when the data is encrypted in one location and decrypted in another. System A generates the keys, holds onto the private key, and shares the public key with the System B. System B encrypts data with the public key. Only System A has the private key necessary to decrypt the data.

Finally, a hash algorithm is used when the data doesn't need to be decrypted. With a hash algorithm, the original data can't be calculated from the hash value, the chance of finding different data with the same hash value is extremely small, and even a slight change in the data produces a wildly different hash value. This type of algorithm is typically used for passwords. We store the hash of the real password. When a user logs in, we don't need to know what the real password is, only that the attempted password matches the real password. We hash the attempted password. If the hash of the attempted password matches the previously stored hash of the real password, we know that the passwords match.

See also

▸ *Using well-known instance type*

▸ *Using dependency injection with entities*

Using well-known instance type

Most applications contain some set of static relational data, such as a list of countries, states, credit card types, and others. The application doesn't need to waste time retrieving this static data from the database. It never changes. In this recipe, I'll show you how we can use the well-known instance type from the Unofficial NHibernate AddIns project to avoid this unnecessary work.

How to do it...

1. Create a new class library project named `WKITExample` and add a reference to `NHibernate.dll`.

2. Add the following `GenericWellKnownInstanceType` class:

```
[Serializable]
public abstract class GenericWellKnownInstanceType<T, TId> :
    IUserType where T : class
{

    private Func<T, TId, bool> findPredicate;
    private Func<T, TId> idGetter;
    private IEnumerable<T> repository;
```

```csharp
protected GenericWellKnownInstanceType(
  IEnumerable<T> repository,
  Func<T, TId, bool> findPredicate,
  Func<T, TId> idGetter)
{
  this.repository = repository;
  this.findPredicate = findPredicate;
  this.idGetter = idGetter;
}

public Type ReturnedType
{
  get { return typeof(T); }
}

public bool IsMutable
{
  get { return false; }
}

public new bool Equals(object x, object y)
{
  if (ReferenceEquals(x, y))
  {
    return true;
  }
  if (ReferenceEquals(null, x) ||
    ReferenceEquals(null, y))
  {
    return false;
  }

  return x.Equals(y);
}

public int GetHashCode(object x)
{
  return (x == null) ? 0 : x.GetHashCode();
}

public object NullSafeGet(IDataReader rs,
  string[] names, object owner)
{
  int index0 = rs.GetOrdinal(names[0]);
```

```csharp
    if (rs.IsDBNull(index0))
    {
      return null;
    }
  var value = (TId)rs.GetValue(index0);
  return repository.FirstOrDefault(x =>
    findPredicate(x, value));
}
public void NullSafeSet(IDbCommand cmd,
  object value, int index)
{
  if (value == null)
  {
    ((IDbDataParameter)cmd.Parameters[index])
      .Value = DBNull.Value;
  }
  else
  {
    ((IDbDataParameter)cmd.Parameters[index])
      .Value = idGetter((T)value);
  }
}
public object DeepCopy(object value)
{
  return value;
}
public object Replace(object original,
  object target, object owner)
{
  return original;
}
public object Assemble(object cached, object owner)
{
  return cached;
}
public object Disassemble(object value)
{
  return value;
}
```

```csharp
/// <summary>
/// The SQL types for the columns
/// mapped by this type.
/// </summary>
public abstract SqlType[] SqlTypes { get; }

}
```

3. Add the following `StateType` class:

```csharp
public class StateType
  : GenericWellKnownInstanceType<State, string>
{

  private static readonly SqlType[] sqlTypes =
    new[] { SqlTypeFactory.GetString(2) };

  public StateType()
    : base(new States(),
    (entity, id) => entity.PostalCode == id,
    entity => entity.PostalCode)
  { }

  public override SqlType[] SqlTypes
  {
    get { return sqlTypes; }
  }

}
```

4. Add the following `State` class:

```csharp
[Serializable]
public class State
{

  public virtual string PostalCode { get; private set; }
  public virtual string Name { get; private set; }

  internal State(string postalCode, string name)
  {
    PostalCode = postalCode;
    Name = name;
  }

}
```

5. Add the following `States` collection class:

```
public class States : ReadOnlyCollection<State>
{
  public static State Arizona = new State("AZ", "Arizona");
  public static State California =
    new State("CA", "California");
  public static State Colorado = new State("CO", "Colorado");
  public static State Oklahoma = new State("OK", "Oklahoma");
  public static State NewMexico =
    new State("NM", "New Mexico");
  public static State Nevada = new State("NV", "Nevada");
  public static State Texas = new State("TX", "Texas");
  public static State Utah = new State("UT", "Utah");

  public States()
    : base(new State[] { Arizona, California, Colorado,
      Oklahoma, NewMexico, Nevada, Texas, Utah })
  { }

}
```

6. Add an `Address` class using the following properties:

```
public virtual Guid Id { get; set; }
public virtual string Line1 { get; set; }
public virtual string Line2 { get; set; }
public virtual string City { get; set; }
public virtual State State { get; set; }
public virtual string Zip { get; set; }
```

7. Add the following mapping document:

```
<?xml version="1.0" encoding="utf-8" ?>
<hibernate-mapping xmlns="urn:nhibernate-mapping-2.2"
    assembly="WKITExample"
    namespace="WKITExample">
  <typedef
    class="WKITExample.StateType, WKITExample"
    name="State"/>
  <class name="Address">
    <id name="Id">
      <generator class="guid.comb" />
    </id>
    <property name="Line1" not-null="true" />
```

```
        <property name="Line2" />
        <property name="City" not-null="true" />
        <property name="State" type="State" not-null="true" />
        <property name ="Zip" not-null="true" />
    </class>
</hibernate-mapping>
```

How it works...

In this recipe, we have an Address entity with a State property. Suppose we have a requirement to print the state's postal abbreviation on shipping labels, but we need to display the full state name when the user completes an order. It would be a waste of resources to fetch these State entities from the database each time.

GenericWellKnownInstanceType allows us to create a static list of States in our application, and use them with our Address entity. We use the PostalCode property to uniquely identify it in the list. In the database, this postal code value is stored in the State field of Address. When NHibernate loads an Address from the database, it attaches the appropriate State instance to the State property. In this way, State works just like an entity. This is handled by the StateType class, which implements IUserType. When loading an Address, the StateType class is responsible for reading the abbreviation from the raw data and returning the correct State instance. Similarly, when we save an address, it translates the State instance to the abbreviation stored in the Address table.

When inheriting from GenericWellKnownInstanceType, we must provide the following four items:

1. A collection of all the well-known instances. This is our states collection.
2. A predicate to locate the correct well-known instance given a database value.
3. A delegate that returns the database value from a well-known instance.
4. The type of database field used to store this database value, in this case, a two-character string field.

The Unofficial NHibernate AddIns project also includes a WellKnownInstanceType, which specifies a 32-bit integer database value.

See also

  ▶ *Creating an encrypted string type*
  ▶ *Mapping enumerations*

Using dependency injection with entities

In this recipe, I'll show you how we can inject services into our entities to separate implementation details from our real business logic.

Getting ready

Download `uNHAddIns.CommonServiceLocatorAdapters.dll` from the Unofficial NHibernate AddIns project at `http://code.google.com/p/unhaddins/`.

Download `Ninject.dll` and `CommonServiceLocator.NinjectAdapter.dll` from the Ninject project at `http://ninject.org`.

Download `Microsoft.Practices.ServiceLocation.dll` from the Microsoft Patterns and Practices team available at `http://commonservicelocator.codeplex.com/`.

Put these three assemblies in your solution's `Lib` folder.

How to do it...

1. Create a new console application project named `IoCByteCode`.

2. Add a reference to `NHibernate.dll`, `NHibernate.ByteCode.Castle.dll`, `Ninject.dll`, `CommonServiceLocator.NinjectAdapter.dll`, `uNHAddIns.CommonServiceLocatorAdapters.dll`, and `Microsoft.Practices.ServiceLocation.dll`.

3. Add an interface named `IPasswordHasher` with the following method definition:
   ```
   string HashPassword(string email, string password);
   ```

4. Add an implementation named `PasswordHasher` using the following code:
   ```
   public class PasswordHasher : IPasswordHasher
   {

     private readonly HashAlgorithm _algorithm;

     public PasswordHasher(HashAlgorithm algorithm)
     {
       _algorithm = algorithm;
     }

     public string HashPassword(string email, string password)
     {
       var plainText = email + password;
       var plainTextData = Encoding.Default.GetBytes(plainText);
       var hash = _algorithm.ComputeHash(plainTextData);
   ```

```
      return Convert.ToBase64String(hash);
    }

  }
```

5. Add a `UserAccount` entity class using the following code:

```csharp
public class UserAccount
{

  private readonly IPasswordHasher _passwordHasher;

  public UserAccount(IPasswordHasher passwordHasher)
  {
    _passwordHasher = passwordHasher;
  }

  public virtual Guid Id { get; protected set; }
  public virtual string EMail { get; protected set; }
  public virtual string HashedPassword { get; protected set; }

  public virtual void SetCredentials(
    string email, string plainTextPassword)
  {
    EMail = email;
    SetPassword(plainTextPassword);
  }

  public virtual void SetPassword(string plainTextPassword)
  {
    HashedPassword = _passwordHasher.HashPassword(
      EMail, plainTextPassword);
  }

}
```

6. Add the following mapping document:

```xml
<?xml version="1.0" encoding="utf-8" ?>
<hibernate-mapping xmlns="urn:nhibernate-mapping-2.2"
    assembly="IoCByteCode"
    namespace="IoCByteCode">
  <class name="UserAccount">
    <id name="Id">
      <generator class="guid.comb" />
    </id>
    <natural-id>
      <property name="EMail" not-null="true" />
```

```
      </natural-id>
      <property name="HashedPassword" not-null="true" />
    </class>
</hibernate-mapping>
```

7. Add an `App.config` with the standard NHibernate and log4net configurations.

8. Set the `proxyfactory.factory_class` property to `uNHAddIns.CommonServiceLocatorAdapters.ProxyFactoryFactory, uNHAddIns.CommonServiceLocatorAdapters`

9. In `Program.cs`, add the following methods:

```csharp
private static void ConfigureServiceLocator()
{
  var kernel = BuildKernel();
  var sl = new NinjectServiceLocator(kernel);
  ServiceLocator.SetLocatorProvider(() => sl);
}

private static IKernel BuildKernel()
{
  var kernel = new StandardKernel();

  kernel.Bind<NHibernate.Proxy.IProxyFactory>()
    .To<NHibernate.ByteCode.Castle.ProxyFactory>()
    .InSingletonScope();

  kernel.Bind<IPasswordHasher>()
    .To<PasswordHasherImpl>()
    .InSingletonScope();

  kernel.Bind<HashAlgorithm>()
    .To<MD5CryptoServiceProvider>()
    .InSingletonScope();

  return kernel;
}
```

10. In `Program.cs`, add the following code to the `Main` method:

```csharp
ConfigureServiceLocator();
NHibernate.Cfg.Environment.BytecodeProvider =
  new BytecodeProvider();
var cfg = new Configuration().Configure();
var sessionFactory = cfg.BuildSessionFactory();
```

How it works...

An NHibernate bytecode provider is responsible for building several factories, including the **reflection optimizer**, which NHibernate uses to instantiate entity classes. The particular reflection optimizer included with this bytecode provider uses Microsoft's common service locator to instantiate our entity classes. This allows us to use dependency injection to inject services into our entities. It also disables NHibernate's checks for a default constructor. Because we're using dependency injection, we'll need constructor parameters.

A typical bytecode provider also provides a factory for creating proxies. Because common service locator isn't a proxy framework, we need to get this functionality from somewhere else. To fill this requirement, the `ProxyFactoryFactory` included with this bytecode provider fetches an `IProxyFactory` instance from the service locator. We register Castle Dynamic Proxy factory as the implementation for the `IProxyFactory` service.

Additionally, we must register implementations for the services required for our entities, and all of their dependencies. In this case, we register `PasswordHasher` for `IPasswordHasher`, and register .NET's implementation of MD5 as our hash algorithm.

There's more...

uNHAddIns also includes inversion of control bytecode providers specifically for Ninject, Castle Windsor, and Spring IoC, though any of these may also be used through the common service locator.

Bland passwords need salt

As we learned in the *Creating an encrypted string type* recipe, a hashing algorithm is used to generate a hash value from the data. The hash value can't be reverse-engineered to calculate the original data, but a hash of the same data with the same key will always result in the same hash value. Also, any change in the original data results in a wildly different hash value. Finally, there is a near zero chance of two different strings of data resulting in the same hash value.

If your database is compromised, the passwords are hashed. It's a one-way algorithm, so it's safe, right? Wrong. This is not as secure as you may think. Let's say 14 of your accounts have the same password hash value. You don't know what their password is, but you know it's the same across all 14 accounts. Two of those accounts have *Twilight*-related e-mail addresses: sparklyVampire32@yahoo.com and JealousBella1974@gmail.com. Could you guess the password in 42 attempts or less? Easily. That's three chances for each of the 14 accounts. Congratulations. You now know the password for e-mail accounts, FaceBook, Twitter, and countless other websites for nearly all of those 14 people. Only two of them used a password that was easy to guess, but they led to the downfall of the others.

When hashing data for storage in the database, you should always salt the data. Append some non-secret data to the secret data before hashing. In this recipe, we prepend the e-mail address to the password. The e-mail is the salt. Now, those 14 accounts will each have a different hash value. A hacker won't know which passwords are the same, which makes it much more difficult. When a user attempts to log in, prepend the e-mail and calculate the hash value in exactly the same way. If the hashes match, log them in. In a real application, you'll most likely want to clean up the e-mail address and convert it to lowercase. The slightest difference will change the hash value.

See also

- ▸ *Creating an encrypted string type*
- ▸ *Creating an audit-event listener*

Creating an audit-event listener

Auditing is another common security-related task. An audit log is an append-only record of changes in a system that allows you to trace a particular action back to its source. In this recipe, I'll show you how we can easily create an audit log to track changes to our entities.

How to do it...

1. Create a new console application project named `AuditEventListener`.
2. Add a reference to our `Eg.Core` model from *Chapter 1*, along with `NHibernate.dll` and `log4net.dll`.
3. Add an `App.config` with a standard NHibernate and log4net configuration.
4. Just before the end of the `sessionfactory` element, add the following three event elements:

```
<event type="pre-insert">
  <listener class="AuditEventListener.EventListener,
          AuditEventListener" />
</event>
<event type="pre-update">
  <listener class="AuditEventListener.EventListener,
          AuditEventListener" />
</event>
<event type="pre-delete">
  <listener class="AuditEventListener.EventListener,
          AuditEventListener" />
</event>
```

5. Add the following `IAuditLogger` interface:

```
public class AuditLogger : IAuditLogger
{

  private readonly ILog log =
    LogManager.GetLogger(typeof(AuditLogger));

  public void Insert(Entity entity)
  {
    log.DebugFormat("{0} #{1} inserted.",
      entity.GetType(), entity.Id);
  }

  public void Update(Entity entity)
  {
    log.DebugFormat("{0} #{1} updated.",
      entity.GetType(), entity.Id);
  }

  public void Delete(Entity entity)
  {
    log.DebugFormat("{0} #{1} deleted.",
      entity.GetType(), entity.Id);
  }

}
```

6. Add the following event listener class:

```
public class EventListener :
  IPreInsertEventListener,
  IPreUpdateEventListener,
  IPreDeleteEventListener
{

  private readonly IAuditLogger _logger;

  public EventListener()
    : this(new AuditLogger())
  { }

  public EventListener(IAuditLogger logger)
  {
    _logger = logger;
  }

  public bool OnPreInsert(PreInsertEvent e)
  {
```

```
    _logger.Insert(e.Entity as Entity);
    return false;
  }

  public bool OnPreUpdate(PreUpdateEvent e)
  {
    _logger.Update(e.Entity as Entity);
    return false;
  }

  public bool OnPreDelete(PreDeleteEvent e)
  {
    _logger.Delete(e.Entity as Entity);
    return false;
  }

}
```

7. In `Program.cs`, configure NHibernate and log4net, and build a session factory just like we did in *Chapter 2* and *Chapter 3*.

8. Finally, in `Main`, add code to save a new entity, update it, and then delete it.

9. Build and run your application.

How it works...

NHibernate uses an event model to allow applications to hook into the NHibernate pipeline and change behavior. In this case, we simply write a message to the log4net log whenever an entity is inserted, updated, or deleted. The `pre-insert`, `pre-update`, and `pre-delete` event listeners are called just before each change. We set these events with the `event` element in our NHibernate configuration. They can also be set programmatically through the `Configuration` object.

> Log4net includes appenders capable of writing to different types of permanent storage, such as files and databases. We can use active context properties to record additional information such as the user who caused the change. More information, about these advanced log4net configurations is available in the log4net manual at `http://logging.apache.org/log4net`.

There's more...

NHibernate provides the following events:

- auto-flush
- merge
- create
- create-onflush
- delete
- dirty-check
- evict
- flush
- flush-entity
- load
- load-collection
- lock
- refresh
- replicate
- save
- save-update
- pre-update
- update
- pre-load
- pre-delete
- pre-insert
- post-load
- post-insert
- post-update
- post-delete
- post-commit update
- post-commit insert
- post-commit delete
- pre-collection recreate
- pre-collection remove

- pre-collection delete
- post-collection recreate
- post-collection remove
- post-collection update

See also

- *Creating and changing stamping entities*
- *Generating trigger-based auditing*

Creating and changing stamping entities

Although it doesn't track the full history of an entity, another option for auditing is to record information about the entity's creation and the most recent change directly in the entity. In this recipe, I'll show you how to use NHibernate's events to create and change stamp entities.

How to do it...

1. Create a new class library project named `Changestamp`.
2. Add a reference to `NHibernate.dll`.
3. Create an interface named `IStampedEntity` with the following code:

   ```
   public interface IStampedEntity
   {
     string CreatedBy { get; set; }
     DateTime CreatedTS { get; set; }
     string ChangedBy { get; set; }
     DateTime ChangedTS { get; set; }
   }
   ```

4. Create an interface named `IStamper` with the following code:

   ```
   public interface IStamper
   {
     void Insert(IStampedEntity entity, object[] state,
       IEntityPersister persister);
     void Update(IStampedEntity entity, object[] oldState,
       object[] state, IEntityPersister persister);
   }
   ```

5. Create a new `EventListener` class as follows:

```csharp
public class EventListener :
  IPreInsertEventListener,
  IPreUpdateEventListener
{

  private readonly IStamper _stamper;

  public EventListener()
    : this(new Stamper())
  { }

  public EventListener(IStamper stamper)
  {
    _stamper = stamper;
  }

  public bool OnPreInsert(PreInsertEvent e)
  {
    _stamper.Insert(e.Entity as IStampedEntity,
      e.State, e.Persister);
    return false;
  }

  public bool OnPreUpdate(PreUpdateEvent e)
  {
    _stamper.Update(e.Entity as IStampedEntity,
      e.OldState, e.State, e.Persister);
    return false;
  }

}
```

6. Create a base `Entity` class with the following code:

```csharp
public abstract class Entity : IStampedEntity
{

  public virtual Guid Id { get; protected set; }

  public virtual string CreatedBy { get; set; }
  public virtual DateTime CreatedTS { get; set; }
  public virtual string ChangedBy { get; set; }
  public virtual DateTime ChangedTS { get; set; }

}
```

7. Create a `Product` class with the following code:

```
public class Product : Entity
{
  public virtual string Name { get; set; }
  public virtual string Description { get; set; }
  public virtual Decimal UnitPrice { get; set; }
}
```

8. Create a mapping with the following XML:

```
<?xml version="1.0" encoding="utf-8" ?>
<hibernate-mapping xmlns="urn:nhibernate-mapping-2.2"
    assembly="Changestamp"
    namespace="Changestamp">
  <class name="Product">
    <id name="Id">
      <generator class="guid.comb" />
    </id>
    <discriminator column="ProductType" />
    <natural-id>
      <property name="Name" not-null="true" />
    </natural-id>
    <property name="Description" />
    <property name="UnitPrice" not-null="true" />
    <property name="CreatedBy" />
    <property name="CreatedTS" />
    <property name="ChangedBy" />
    <property name="ChangedTS" />
  </class>
</hibernate-mapping>
```

9. Create an implementation of `IStamper` with the following code:

```
public class Stamper : IStamper
{
  private const string CREATED_BY = "CreatedBy";
  private const string CREATED_TS = "CreatedTS";
  private const string CHANGED_BY = "ChangedBy";
  private const string CHANGED_TS = "ChangedTS";

  public void Insert(IStampedEntity entity, object[] state,
    IEntityPersister persister)
  {
```

```csharp
    if (entity == null)
      return;
  SetCreate(entity, state, persister);
  SetChange(entity, state, persister);
}

public void Update(IStampedEntity entity, object[] oldState,
  object[] state, IEntityPersister persister)
{
  if (entity == null)
    return;
  SetChange(entity, state, persister);
}

private void SetCreate(IStampedEntity entity,
  object[] state,
  IEntityPersister persister)
{
  entity.CreatedBy = GetUserName();
  SetState(persister, state, CREATED_BY, entity.CreatedBy);
  entity.CreatedTS = DateTime.Now;
  SetState(persister, state, CREATED_TS, entity.CreatedTS);
}

private void SetChange(IStampedEntity entity,
  object[] state, IEntityPersister persister)
{
  entity.ChangedBy = GetUserName();
  SetState(persister, state, CHANGED_BY,
    entity.ChangedBy);
  entity.ChangedTS = DateTime.Now;
  SetState(persister, state, CHANGED_TS,
    entity.ChangedTS);
}

private void SetState(IEntityPersister persister,
  object[] state, string propertyName, object value)
{
  var index = GetIndex(persister, propertyName);
  if (index == -1)
    return;
  state[index] = value;
}
```

```
    private int GetIndex(IEntityPersister persister,
      string propertyName)
    {
      return Array.IndexOf(persister.PropertyNames,
        propertyName);
    }

    private string GetUserName()
    {
      return WindowsIdentity.GetCurrent().Name;
    }

  }
```

10. Set the `pre-insert` and `pre-update` event listeners in the `App.config`, just like we did in the previous recipe.

How it works...

In this recipe, we've added four additional properties to our standard entity. Our `pre-insert` and `pre-update` event listener is responsible for setting the values of these properties. The task of setting these properties is handed over to our `IStamper` implementation. The `pre-` entity listeners happen fairly late in the process of updating the database. NHibernate has already read our entity's property values into the object array `state`. This object array provides the actual values written to the database. However, failing to keep the object in sync with the state array can lead to a number of strange and unexpected behaviors later, so we must update both the state array and the object properties.

When an object is inserted, we set the create and change properties to the current user and date / time. When an object is updated, we update these change properties with the current user and date / time.

The `GetUserName` method of `Stamper` uses `WindowsIdentity.GetCurrent()`. This may not return a meaningful user identity, but rather the identity of some service account. The correct implementation of the `GetUserName` method depends on your application's architecture.

See also

▶ *Creating an audit-event listener*

▶ *Generating trigger-based auditing*

Generating trigger-based auditing

Another approach to auditing involves tracking each change to an entity in a separate audit table. In this recipe, I'll show you how to use NHibernate to generate audit triggers for our entity tables.

Getting ready

Download uNHAddIns.dll from the Unofficial NHibernate AddIns project at http://code.google.com/p/unhaddins/. Save the file to your solution's Lib folder.

How to do it...

1. Create a new console application project with all standard NHibernate references, the standard NHibernate and log4net configuration, and the Eg.Core model from *Chapter 1*.

2. Add a reference to uNHAddIns.dll.

3. Set the dialect to uNHAddIns.Audit.TriggerGenerator. ExtendedMsSql2008Dialect, uNHAddIns

4. Add the following code to the Main method of Program.cs:

```
var cfg = new Configuration().Configure();

var namingStrategy = new NamingStrategy();
var auditColumnSource = new AuditColumnSource();
new TriggerAuditing(cfg, namingStrategy,
   auditColumnSource).Configure();

var sessionFaculty = cfg.BuildSessionFactory();

var se = new NHibernate.Tool.hbm2ddl.SchemaExport(cfg);
se.Execute(true, true, false);
```

5. Build and run your application.

How it works...

NHibernate has three distinct levels of mapping. First, NHibernate simply deserializes the mapping documents into their equivalent .NET objects. Second, NHibernate transforms these mapping objects into a second, more detailed set of classes named mapping metadata. Finally, NHibernate transforms these detailed classes into the final persisters. We have an opportunity to manipulate this second-level mapping up to the point where we build the session factory.

The uNHAddIns trigger generator code reads the structure of each table from the mapping metadata and constructs a matching audit table and set of triggers.

We can use the standard `NamingStrategy` or provide our own. When naming the audit tables, the default naming strategy simply appends `Audit` to the name of data table. For trigger names, it appends `_onInsert`, `_onUpdate`, or `_onDelete` to the data table name.

An implementation of `IAuditColumnSource` should return a list of `AuditColumns` to be added to each audit table. For example, to record the current date and time when an entity is changed, we would use this `AuditColumn`:

```
new AuditColumn()
{
  Name = "AuditTimestamp",
  Value = new SimpleValue()
  {
    TypeName = NHibernateUtil.DateTime.Name
  },
  IsNullable = false,
  IncludeInPrimaryKey = true,
  ValueFunction = delegate(TriggerActions action)
  {
    return "getdate()";
  }
};
```

The default implementation returns three audit columns: `AuditUser`, `AuditTimestamp`, and `AuditOperation`. This is sufficient to answer "what changed", "who changed it", and "when". Unfortunately, SQL doesn't have a handy function to answer "why". The trigger generator also defines an interface `IExtendedDialect`, which adds some additional trigger-related SQL dialect functions to the standard dialects. A Microsoft SQL Server 2008 and SQLite implementation are both included. This recipe uses the `ExtendedMsSql2008Dialect`.

The `TriggerAuditing Configure()` method adds the appropriate objects to our second-level mapping to be included in our database schema output from `hbm2ddl`. This diagram shows the resulting schema.

The objects added to our mapping all implement `IAuxiliaryDatabaseObject`. This interface is used by `hbm2ddl` to include `drop` and `create` SQL statements for database objects outside the scope of NHibernate, such as triggers and non-entity tables. As we will see in the next recipe, these can also be defined using xml mappings.

Because we get the current username from SQL's `system_user` to get meaningful audit logs using this method, you must use one SQL or Windows account per user when logging into the SQL server. This effectively disables connection pooling, because most connections use different credentials.

In the next recipe, I'll show you how we can use SQL's `CONTEXT_INFO` as our username source, avoiding the account maintenance overhead and relieve the stress on the connection pool.

See also

- *Creating an audit-event listener*
- *Setting MS Sql's* `Context Info`

Setting MS Sql's Context Info

In this recipe, I'll show you how to use Microsoft SQL Server's `Context_Info` to provide the current username to our audit triggers.

Getting ready

Complete the previous recipe, *Generating trigger-based auditing*.

Download `Ninject.dll` and `CommonServiceLocator.NinjectAdapter.dll` from the Ninject project at `http://ninject.org`.

Download `Microsoft.Practices.ServiceLocation.dll` from the Microsoft Patterns and Practices team available at `http://commonservicelocator.codeplex.com/`.

How to do it...

1. Add a reference to `Ninject.dll`, `CommonServiceLocator.NinjectAdapter.dll`, and `Microsoft.Practices.ServiceLocation.dll`.

2. Add the following `IAuditColumnSource` implementation:

```
public class CtxAuditColumnSource : IAuditColumnSource
{

  public IEnumerable<AuditColumn>
    GetAuditColumns(Table dataTable)
  {
    var userStamp = new AuditColumn()
    {
      Name = "AuditUser",
      Value = new SimpleValue()
      {
        TypeName = NHibernateUtil.String.Name
      },
      Length = 127,
      IsNullable = false,
      IncludeInPrimaryKey = true,
      ValueFunction = delegate(TriggerActions action)
      {
        return "dbo.fnGetContextData()";
      }
    };
```

```
var timeStamp = new AuditColumn()
{
  Name = "AuditTimestamp",
  Value = new SimpleValue()
  {
    TypeName = NHibernateUtil.DateTime.Name
  },
  IsNullable = false,
  IncludeInPrimaryKey = true,
  ValueFunction = delegate(TriggerActions action)
  {
    return "getdate()";
  }
};
var operation = new AuditColumn()
{
  Name = "AuditOperation",
  Value = new SimpleValue()
  {
    TypeName = NHibernateUtil.AnsiChar.Name
  },
  Length = 1,
  IsNullable = false,
  IncludeInPrimaryKey = false,
  ValueFunction = delegate(TriggerActions action)
  {
    switch (action)
    {
      case TriggerActions.INSERT:
        return "'I'";
      case TriggerActions.UPDATE:
        return "'U'";
      case TriggerActions.DELETE:
        return "'D'";
      default:
        throw new ArgumentOutOfRangeException("action");
    }
  }
};
```

```
      return new AuditColumn[] {
        userStamp, timeStamp, operation
      };
    }
  }
```

3. Add the following `IContextDataProvider` interface:

```
public interface IContextDataProvider
{
  string GetData();
  string GetEmptyData();
}
```

4. Add the following implementation:

```
public class UsernameContextDataProvider :
  IContextDataProvider
{
  public string GetData()
  {
    return WindowsIdentity.GetCurrent().Name;
  }
  public string GetEmptyData()
  {
    return string.Empty;
  }
}
```

5. Add the following `ContextConnectionDriver`:

```
public class ContextInfoConnectionDriver :
  DriverConnectionProvider
{
  private const string COMMAND_TEXT =
    "declare @length tinyint\n" +
    "declare @ctx varbinary(128)\n" +
    "select @length = len(@data)\n" +
    "select @ctx = convert(binary(1), @length) + " +
    "convert(binary(127), @data)\n" +
    "set context_info @ctx";

  public override IDbConnection GetConnection()
```

```
  {
    var conn = base.GetConnection();
    SetContext(conn);
    return conn;
  }

  public override void CloseConnection(IDbConnection conn)
  {
    EraseContext(conn);
    base.CloseConnection(conn);
  }

  private void SetContext(IDbConnection conn)
  {
    var sl = ServiceLocator.Current;
    var dataProvider = sl.GetInstance<IContextDataProvider>();
    var data = dataProvider.GetData();
    SetContext(conn, data);
  }

  private void EraseContext(IDbConnection conn)
  {
    var sl = ServiceLocator.Current;
    var dataProvider = sl.GetInstance<IContextDataProvider>();
    var data = dataProvider.GetEmptyData();
    SetContext(conn, data);
  }

  private void SetContext(IDbConnection conn, string data)
  {
    var cmd = conn.CreateCommand();
    cmd.CommandType = CommandType.Text;
    cmd.CommandText = COMMAND_TEXT;

    var param = cmd.CreateParameter();
    param.ParameterName = "@data";
    param.DbType = DbType.AnsiString;
    param.Size = 127;
    param.Value = data;
    cmd.Parameters.Add(param);

    cmd.ExecuteNonQuery();
  }
}
```

6. Add the following mapping document:

```xml
<?xml version="1.0" encoding="utf-8" ?>
<hibernate-mapping xmlns="urn:nhibernate-mapping-2.2">
  <database-object>
    <create>
      CREATE FUNCTION dbo.fnGetContextData()
      RETURNS varchar(127)
      AS
      BEGIN
        declare @data varchar(127)
        declare @length tinyint
        declare @ctx varbinary(128)
        select @ctx = CONTEXT_INFO()
        select @length = convert(tinyint,
            substring(@ctx, 1, 1))
        select @data = convert(varchar(127),
            substring(@ctx, 2, 1 + @length))
        return @data
      END
    </create>
    <drop>DROP FUNCTION dbo.fnGetContextData</drop>
  </database-object>
</hibernate-mapping>
```

7. In the `Main` method of `Program.cs`, use the following code:

```csharp
var kernel = new StandardKernel();
kernel.Bind<IContextDataProvider>()
  .To<UsernameContextDataProvider>();
var sl = new NinjectServiceLocator(kernel);
ServiceLocator.SetLocatorProvider(() => sl);

var namingStrategy = new NamingStrategy();
var auditColumnSource = new CtxAuditColumnSource();
var cfg = new Configuration().Configure();
new TriggerAuditing(cfg, namingStrategy,
  auditColumnSource).Configure();

var sessionFaculty = cfg.BuildSessionFactory();

var se = new NHibernate.Tool.hbm2ddl.SchemaExport(cfg);
se.Execute(true, true, false);
```

8. Set the NHibernate property `connection.provider` to `<namespace>`. `ContextInfoConnectionDriver, <assembly>`, to set the namespace and assembly according to the name of your project.

9. Add a mapping element for this assembly so that the `fnGetContextData` mapping document is loaded.

10. Build and run the program.

How it works...

Starting with Microsoft SQL Server 2000, SQL Server provides 128 bytes of context data for each database connection. This data is set using the SQL statement `SET CONTEXT_INFO @ContextData` where `@ContextData` may be a `binary(128)` variable or constant. It can be read using the `CONTEXT_INFO()` SQL function, which returns `binary(128)` data.

In this recipe, we store the current username in the `CONTEXT_INFO`. It's important to note that the `CONTEXT_INFO` is a fixed-length `binary` array, not a variable-length `varbinary`. When placing data into `CONTEXT_INFO`, any leftover bytes may contain trash.

Similar to storing strings in memory, when storing variable-length data in this fixed-length field, we must have some way to determine where the real data ends. The two possible ways to do this are as follows:

1. Taking the Pascal strings approach, we can use the first byte to determine the length of the data. This limits the amount of data that can be stored to 255 characters. This is fine, because SQL Server only allows half that amount.

2. Using the C string approach, we place a null terminator (zero byte) at the end of the string. The data can be any length, but we have to search for the null terminator to find the end.

In this recipe, we use the Pascal string approach. The `fnGetContextData` SQL function uses the first byte to determine the correct `substring` parameters to get our username string from the `CONTEXT_INFO()`.

Because the `Context Info` is tied to the database connection, we need to set it every time we open a database connection. Additionally, because our application will most likely use connection pooling, we should also clear the `Context Info` when the application releases the connection back to the pool.

NHibernate's `DriverConnectionProvider` is responsible for providing a database connection as needed, and for closing those connections when they're no longer needed. This is the perfect place to set our `Context Info`. The custom connection provider will set the `Context Info` after the connection is opened, but before it's passed back to NHibernate. It also clears the `Context Info` just before calling `conn.Close()` to return the connection to the connection pool.

The `AuditUser` column has been changed from our previous recipe so that our triggers call `fnGetContextData()` instead of using `system_user`.

Finally, we've added `fnGetContextData` as an auxiliary database object with our `database-object` mapping. This mapping provides the drop and create scripts used by `hbm2ddl`.

All of this allows us to use the application's current username in our audit logs. We can use any SQL credentials we like, including plain old SQL accounts. Of course, just as with the *Creating and changing stamping entities* recipe, you will likely need to replace `WindowsIdentity.GetCurrent()` with the correct implementation for your application.

See also

▸ *Generating trigger-based auditing*

▸ *Using dynamic connection strings*

▸ *Creating and changing stamping entities*

Using dynamic connection strings

There are cases where an application may need to change connection strings depending on some condition. This can be in the context of a multi-tenant application, or perhaps a database failover scenario. In this recipe, I'll show you how to switch NHibernate connection strings at runtime.

How to do it...

1. Start a new console application project named `DynamicConnectionString`.
2. Add references to `NHibernate.dll`, `NHibernate.ByteCode.Castle.dll`, `log4net.dll`, and the `Eg.Core` model from *Chapter 1*.
3. Add a reference to `System.Configuration` from the .NET framework.
4. Set up the `App.config` with a standard NHibernate and log4net configuration.
5. Add the following `DynamicConnectionProvider` class:

```
public class DynamicConnectionProvider :
  DriverConnectionProvider
{

  private const string ANON_CONN_NAME = "db";
  private const string AUTH_CONN_NAME = "auth_db";

  protected override string ConnectionString
  {
    get
```

```
      {
        var connstrs = ConfigurationManager.ConnectionStrings;
        var connstr = connstrs[ANON_CONN_NAME];
        if (IsAuthenticated())
          connstr = connstrs[AUTH_CONN_NAME];
        return connstr.ConnectionString;
      }
    }

    private bool IsAuthenticated()
    {
      var identity = WindowsIdentity.GetCurrent();
      return identity != null && identity.IsAuthenticated;
    }

  }
```

6. Add the following two connection strings to the `App.config`:

```
<add name="db" connectionString=
"Server=.\SQLExpress; Database=NHCookbook;
User Id=AnonymousUser; Password=p455w0rd"/>
<add name="auth_db" connectionString=
"Server=.\SQLExpress; Database=NHCookbook;
Trusted_Connection=SSPI"/>
```

7. Set the NHibernate property `connection.provider` to
`DynamicConnectionString.DynamicConnectionProvider,`
`DynamicConnectionString`

8. Build and run the program.

How it works...

Just like we did in our previous recipe, we are using a custom connection provider. However, this time, we only override the `ConnectionString` property to return different connection strings for anonymous and authenticated users. We set the NHibernate configuration property `connection.provider` to the assembly qualified name of our custom connection provider, and NHibernate handles the rest.

See also

▶ *Setting Microsoft SQL's* `CONTEXT_INFO`

8
NHibernate Contribution Projects

In this chapter, we will cover the following topics:

- ► Configuring the cache
- ► Property validation with attributes
- ► Creating validator classes
- ► Using the Burrows framework
- ► Setting up full-text search
- ► Sharing databases for performance
- ► Using NHibernate Spatial

Introduction

The NHibernate Contribution projects, available at `http://sourceforge.net/projects/nhcontrib/`, provide a number of very useful extensions to NHibernate. The recipes in this chapter introduce some of these extremely powerful add-ons to projects.

Configuring the cache

Caching frequently used, rarely updated data can greatly improve the performance of websites and other high traffic applications. In this recipe, we'll configure NHibernate's cache, just as we would for a typical public facing website.

Getting ready

1. Complete the *Configuring NHibernate with App.config* recipe from *Chapter 1*.

2. Download the NHibernate Caches binary files from SourceForge at `http://sourceforge.net/projects/nhcontrib/files/`.

3. Extract `NHibernate.Caches.SysCache.dll` to your solution's `Lib` folder.

How to do it...

1. Add a reference to `NHibernate.Caches.SysCache.dll`.

2. Open the `App.config` file.

3. In the `configSections` element, declare a section for the cache configuration:

```
<section name="syscache"
    type="NHibernate.Caches.SysCache.SysCacheSectionHandler,
        NHibernate.Caches.SysCache" />
```

4. Add the following three properties to the `hibernate-configuration` section.

```
<property name="cache.provider_class">
  NHibernate.Caches.SysCache.SysCacheProvider,
  NHibernate.Caches.SysCache
</property>

<property name="cache.use_second_level_cache">
  true
</property>

<property name="cache.use_query_cache">
  true
</property>
```

5. After the mapping element, add the following cache elements:

```
<class-cache class="Eg.Core.Product, Eg.Core"
    region="hourly" usage="read-only"/>

<class-cache class="Eg.Core.ActorRole, Eg.Core"
    region="hourly" usage="read-only"/>

<collection-cache collection="Eg.Core.Movie.Actors"
    region="hourly" usage="read-only "/>
```

6. After the `hibernate configuration` section, add the `syscache` section declared in the first step:

```
<syscache>
  <cache region="hourly" expiration="60" priority="3" />
</syscache>
```

7. Build and run your application.

How it works...

The `cache.provider_class` configuration property defines the cache provider to use. In this case, we're using `syscache`, NHibernate's wrapper for ASP.NET's `System.Web.Caching.Cache`.

The `cache.use_second_level_cache` enables the second-level cache. If the second-level cache is enabled, setting `cache.use_query_cache` will allow query results to be cached.

Caching must still be set up on a per-class hierarchy, per-collection, and per-query basis. That is, you must also set up caching for each specific item to be cached. In this recipe, we've set up caching for the `Product` entity class, which, because they're in the same class hierarchy, implicitly sets up caching for `Book` and `Movie` with the same settings. In addition, we've set up caching for our `ActorRole` entity class. Finally, because caching for collections is configured separately from entities, we set up caching for the `Movie's Actors` collection.

We've set up each of these to use a region of the cache named `hourly`. A cache region separates the cached data and defines a set of rules governing when that data will expire. In this case, our hourly region is set to remove an item from the cache after 60 minutes or under stress, such as low memory. `priority` can be set to a value from 1 to 5, with 1 being the lowest priority, and thus the first to be removed from the cache.

The cache concurrency strategy for each item, set with the `usage` attribute, defines how an object's cache entry may be updated. In this recipe, we've set all of our product data to `read-only`. Our public-facing website only displays our products. It doesn't change them. In other scenarios, it may be appropriate to use `read-write` or, when concurrency isn't a concern, `nonstrict-read-write`.

Caching is only meant to improve the performance of a properly designed NHibernate application. Your application shouldn't depend on the cache to function properly. Before adding caching, you should correct poorly performing queries and issues like SELECT N+1. This will usually give a significant performance boost, eliminating the need for caching and its added complexity.

There's more...

NHibernate allows us to configure a cache with the same scope as the session factory. Logically, this cache is divided into three parts.

Entity cache

The entity cache stores persistent objects or the values of persistent objects. These objects are stored as a dictionary of POIDs to arrays of values, as shown in the following diagram:

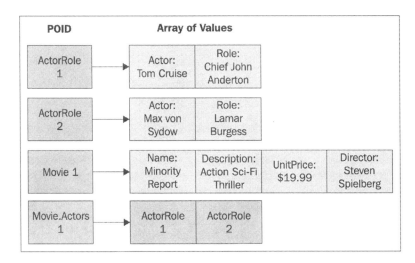

Notice in the previous image that the **Movie.Actors** collection has a cache entry of its own. Also notice that in this entry, we're storing the POIDs of the **ActorRole** objects, not the **ActorRole** data. There is no data duplication in the cache. From the cached data shown in the diagram, we can easily rehydrate the entire object graph for the movie without the chance of any inconsistent results.

Query cache

In addition to caching entities, NHibernate can also cache query results. In the cache, each query is associated with an array of POIDs for the entities of the query returns, similar to the way our movie actor collection is stored in the previous image. The entity data is stored in the entity cache. Again, this eliminates the chance of inconsistent results.

Update timestamp cache

The third part of the cache stores a last-updated timestamp for each table. When data is first placed in the cache, the timestamp is set to a value in the future, ensuring the cache will never return uncommitted data from a pending transaction. Once the transaction is committed, the timestamp is set back to the present, allowing that data to be read from the cache.

The rules

There are some basic requirements when using the cache:

- Always explicitly begin a transaction before any database interaction, even when reading data from the database. This is a required practice with NHibernate in general, but it is especially important for interacting with the cache. Without an explicit transaction, caching is bypassed.

- When opening a session, don't provide your own database connection. This also affects caching. Instead, implement your own IConnectionProvider, and set the `connection.provider` configuration property as in the *Using dynamic connection strings* recipe in *Chapter 7*.

See also

- *Configuring NHibernate with App.config*
- *Using dynamic connection strings*
- *Configuring the cache with code*

Configuring the cache with code

NHibernate also provides an option for cache configuration with the NHibernate.Cfg. `Loquacious namespace`. In this recipe, I'll show you how to configure the second level cache with code.

Getting ready

1. Complete the *Configuring NHibernate with App.config* recipe from *Chapter 1*.
2. Download the NHibernate Caches binary files from SourceForge at `http://sourceforge.net/projects/nhcontrib/files/`.
3. Extract `NHibernate.Caches.SysCache.dll` to your solution's Lib folder.

How to do it...

1. In the configSections element of App.config, declare a section for our cache provider's configuration:

   ```
   <section name="syscache"
       type="NHibernate.Caches.SysCache.SysCacheSectionHandler,
           NHibernate.Caches.SysCache" />
   ```

2. After the hibernate-configuration section, add the syscache section we just declared:

   ```
   <syscache>
     <cache region="hourly" expiration="60" priority="3" />
   </syscache>
   ```

3. In `Program.cs`, add the following using statements:

```
using System;
using Eg.Core;
using NHibernate.Caches.SysCache;
using NHibernate.Cfg;
using NHibernate.Cfg.Loquacious;
using Environment = NHibernate.Cfg.Environment;
```

4. In `Program.cs`, add the following method:

```
static void ConfigureCaching(Configuration nhConfig)
{
  nhConfig
    .SetProperty(Environment.UseSecondLevelCache, "true")
    .SetProperty(Environment.UseQueryCache, "true")
    .Cache(c => c.Provider<SysCacheProvider>())
    .EntityCache<Product>(c =>
        {
          c.Strategy = EntityCacheUsage.Readonly;
          c.RegionName = "hourly";
        })
    .EntityCache<ActorRole>(c =>
        {
          c.Strategy = EntityCacheUsage.Readonly;
          c.RegionName = "hourly";
        })
    .EntityCache<Movie>(c => c.Collection(
        movie => movie.Actors,
        coll =>
        {
          coll.Strategy = EntityCacheUsage.Readonly;
          coll.RegionName = "hourly";
        }));
}
```

5. Use the following code in `Main`:

```
var nhConfig = new Configuration().Configure();
ConfigureCaching(nhConfig);
var sessionFactory = nhConfig.BuildSessionFactory();
Console.WriteLine("NHibernate cache configured!");
Console.ReadKey();
```

6. Build and run your application. You will see NHibernate cache configured!

How it works...

In this recipe, we use the `NHibernate.Cfg.Loquacious` namespace to configure the second level cache. Our configuration is identical to the one used in the previous recipe, *Configuring the cache*. The relevant items from the XML configuration are as follows:

```xml
<property name="cache.use_second_level_cache">
  true
</property>

<property name="cache.use_query_cache">
  true
</property>

<property name="cache.provider_class">
  NHibernate.Caches.SysCache.SysCacheProvider,
  NHibernate.Caches.SysCache
</property>

<class-cache class="Eg.Core.Product, Eg.Core"
            region="hourly" usage="read-only"/>

<class-cache class="Eg.Core.ActorRole, Eg.Core"
            region="hourly" usage="read-only"/>

<collection-cache collection="Eg.Core.Movie.Actors"
                  region="hourly" usage="read-only"/>
```

We begin by setting `cache.use_second_level_cache` and `cache.use_query_cache` to true with the following code:

```
nhConfig
  .SetProperty(Environment.UseSecondLevelCache, "true")
  .SetProperty(Environment.UseQueryCache, "true")
```

We set `cache.provider_class` with the following code:

```
nhConfig
  .Cache(c => c.Provider<SysCacheProvider>())
```

We configure the class cache for our Product hierarchy and ActorRole entities with the following code:

```
nhConfig
  .EntityCache<Product>(c =>
     {
        c.Strategy = EntityCacheUsage.Readonly;
        c.RegionName = "hourly";
     })
  .EntityCache<ActorRole>(c =>
```

```
      {
        c.Strategy = EntityCacheUsage.Readonly;
        c.RegionName = "hourly";
      })
```

Finally, we configure the collection cache for our Actors collection with the following code:

```
nhConfig
  .EntityCache<Movie>(c => c.Collection(
      movie => movie.Actors,
      coll =>
      {
        coll.Strategy = EntityCacheUsage.Readonly;
        coll.RegionName = "hourly";
      }));
```

Notice how we call Collection(), passing an expression for our Actors collection, as well as the settings for our collection cache.

See also

▶   *Configuring the cache*

Property validation with attributes

Another NHibernate Contribution project, NHibernate Validator, provides data validation for classes. In this recipe, I'll show you how to use NHibernate Validator attributes to validate your entities.

Getting ready

1.   Download the NHibernate Validator binary files from SourceForge at `http://sourceforge.net/projects/nhcontrib/files/`.

2.   Extract `NHibernate.Validator.dll`, `nhv-configuration.xsd`, and `nhv-mapping.xsd` from the downloaded ZIP file to your solution's `Lib` folder.

3.   Add both `xsd` files to the `Schema` folder of your solution, just as we did with the NHibernate xml schema files in the *Mapping a class with XML* recipe in *Chapter 1.*

4.   Complete the `Eg.Core` model and mappings from *Chapter 1.*

How to do it...

1.   Create a new class library project named `Eg.AttributeValidation`.

2.   Copy the `Eg.Core` model and mappings from *Chapter 1* to this new project.

3. Change the namespace and assembly references in the mappings to
   `Eg.AttributeValidation`.

4. Change the namespaces for the entity classes to `Eg.AttributeValidation`.

5. In your `Eg.AttributeValidation` project, add a reference to `NHibernate.Validator`.

6. Create a new attribute class named `NotNegativeDecimalAttribute`
   with the following code:

```
[AttributeUsage(AttributeTargets.Field |
   AttributeTargets.Property)]
[Serializable]
public class NotNegativeDecimalAttribute
   : DecimalMinAttribute
{

  public NotNegativeDecimalAttribute()
     : base(0M)
  {
  }

}
```

7. Open `Product.cs` and add the following attributes:

```
public class Product : Entity
{

   [NotNull, Length(Min=1, Max=255)]
   public virtual string Name { get; set; }

   [NotNullNotEmpty]
   public virtual string Description { get; set; }

   [NotNull, NotNegativeDecimal]
   public virtual Decimal UnitPrice { get; set; }

}
```

8. Create a new console project named `Eg.AttributeValidation.Runner`.

9. Add references to the `Eg.AttributeValidation` model project, `log4net.dll`,
   `NHibernate.dll`, `NHibernate.ByteCode.Castle.dll`, and `NHibernate.Validator.dll`.

10. Set up an `App.config` with the standard `log4net` and `hibernate-configuration` sections, just as we did in the *Configuring NHibernate with App.config* and *Configuring NHibernate Logging* recipes of *Chapter 2*.

11. In the `<configSections>` element, add an additional section declaration named `nhv-configuration` with the following xml:

```xml
<section name="nhv-configuration" type="NHibernate.Validator.Cfg.
ConfigurationSectionHandler, NHibernate.Validator" />
```

12. Add the `<nhv-configuration>` section with the following xml:

```xml
<nhv-configuration xmlns="urn:nhv-configuration-1.0">
  <property name='apply_to_ddl'>true</property>
  <property name='autoregister_listeners'>true</property>
  <property name='default_validator_mode'>
OverrideExternalWithAttribute</property>
  <mapping assembly='Eg.AttributeValidation'/>
</nhv-configuration>
```

13. Add a new class named `BasicSharedEngineProvider` using the following code:

```csharp
public class BasicSharedEngineProvider :
  ISharedEngineProvider
{


  private readonly ValidatorEngine ve;
  public BasicSharedEngineProvider(ValidatorEngine ve)
  {
    this.ve = ve;
  }
  public ValidatorEngine GetEngine()
  {
    return ve;
  }
  public void UseMe()
  {
    Environment.SharedEngineProvider = this;
  }

}
```

14. In `Program.cs`, use the following code:

```csharp
class Program
{
  static void Main(string[] args)
  {
    XmlConfigurator.Configure();
    var log = LogManager.GetLogger(typeof(Program));
```

```
SetupNHibernateValidator();

var cfg = new Configuration().Configure();
cfg.Initialize();

var sessionFactory = cfg.BuildSessionFactory();

var schemaExport = new SchemaExport(cfg);
schemaExport.Execute(true, true, false);

var junk = new Product
            {
                Name = "Spiffy Junk",
                Description = "Stuff we can't sell.",
                UnitPrice = -1M
            };

using (var session = sessionFactory.OpenSession())
{
  using (var tx = session.BeginTransaction())
  {
    try
    {
      session.Save(junk);
      tx.Commit();
    }
    catch (InvalidStateException validationException)
    {
      var errors = validationException.GetInvalidValues();
      foreach (var error in errors)
        log.ErrorFormat("Error with property {0}: {1}",
          error.PropertyName, error.Message);
      tx.Rollback();
    }
  }
}
}

private static ValidatorEngine GetValidatorEngine()
{
  var validatorEngine = new ValidatorEngine();
  validatorEngine.Configure();
  return validatorEngine;
}
```

```
        private static void SetupNHibernateValidator()
        {
          var validatorEngine = GetValidatorEngine();
          new BasicSharedEngineProvider(validatorEngine).UseMe();
        }

    }
```

15. Build and run your program.

How it works...

NHibernate Validator, or NHV, has a few major components. `ValidatorEngine` is the main class used to interact with NHV. Like the session factory, applications typically have only one instance. NHV uses an implementation of `ISharedEngineProvider` to find the singleton instance of the `ValidatorEngine`. NHV may be used independently from NHibernate to validate any class. When integrated with NHibernate, it validates each entity before inserting or updating data. This integration is accomplished through `ValidatePreInsertEventListener` and `ValidatePreUpdateEventListener` event listeners.

To integrate NHV with NHibernate, we begin by creating a `ValidatorEngine`. The call to `ValidatorEngine.Configure()` loads our NHV configuration from the `App.config`. Next, we create an `ISharedEngineProvider` to return our `ValidatorEngine`. We configure NHV to use this shared engine provider by setting the static property `Environment.SharedEngineProvider`. Finally, after configuring NHibernate, but before creating the session factory, we call `Initialize()`, an NHV extension method for the NHibernate configuration object.

Our NHV configuration in `App.config` contains the following four configuration settings:

▶ `apply_to_ddl`: When this property is set to true, `hbm2ddl` will generate database constraints to enforce many of our validation attributes. For example, the script to create our `UnitPrice` column, shown next, now has a check constraint to enforce our `NotNegativeDecimal` rule.

  `UnitPrice DECIMAL(19,5) not null check( UnitPrice>=0)`

▶ `autoregister_listeners`: This property determines if the `Initialize` extension method will add the `pre-insert` and `pre-update` event listeners to the NHibernate configuration.

▶ `default_validator_mode`: This property determines the priority of validation rules when using a mix of XML validation definitions, validation classes, or attributes.

▶ The NHV mapping element behaves similar to the NHibernate mapping element. It defines an assembly containing our entities decorated with attributes.

In this recipe, we attempt to save a new product with a negative `UnitPrice`. This violates our `NotNegativeDecimal` validation rule. Without NHibernate Validator, our application would silently accept the invalid data, leading to potentially larger problems later. If we had simply added a constraint in the database, our application would attempt to insert the bad data, then throw an unwieldy `SQLException` that gives us no information about which property is invalid and why. With NHibernate Validator, the event listeners validate each entity before any data is written to the database. If they find invalid data, they throw an `InvalidStateException` that tells us exactly which properties of the entity are invalid and why.

 When a validation event listener throws an `InvalidStateException`, the session is in an undefined state. Once this happens, the only operation that can be safely performed on the session is `Dispose`.

You may be wondering why we created a separate `NotNegativeDecimalAttribute` class. Couldn't we just decorate our `UnitPrice` property with `[DecimalMin(0M)]`? As it turns out, we can't do this. In C#, we can't use `decimal` parameters in this way. To work around this limitation, we subclass the `DecimalMinAttribute` and hardcode the zero inside `NotNegativeDecimalAttribute` class.

In our assemblies, attribute decorations are not stored as Intermediate Language (IL) instructions, but as metadata. This limits the types we can use as parameters. The C# specification at `http://msdn.microsoft.com/en-us/library/aa664615(v=VS.71).aspx` defines the types we can use as `bool`, `byte`, `char`, `double`, `float`, `int`, `long`, `short`, `string`, `object`, `System.Type`, `enum`, or any one-dimensional array of these types. `decimal` is not on the list.

There's more...

If you check your entities for invalid data prior to saving them, you don't run the risk of blowing up the NHibernate session. To validate an object explicitly, your code might look like this:

```
var ve = Environment.SharedEngineProvider.GetEngine();
var invalidValues = ve.Validate(someObject);
```

`invalidValues` is an array of `InvalidValue` objects describing each failed validation rule. If it's empty, the object is valid. If not, you can easily display the validation messages to the user without risking the session.

NHibernate Validator can be used to validate any class, not just NHibernate entities. You can easily adapt this sort of explicit validation to integrate with ASP.NET MVC's model validation.

See also

▸   *Creating validator classes*

Creating validator classes

In the previous recipe, we saw how to decorate our entity classes with NHibernate Validator. A better practice is to extract your validation rules to separate classes and avoid this dependency. In this recipe, I'll show you how to create validator classes, as well as an alternative method for configuring NHibernate Validator.

Getting ready

1.   Download the NHibernate Validator binary files from SourceForge at `http://sourceforge.net/projects/nhcontrib/files/`.

2.   Extract `NHibernate.Validator.dll` from the downloaded ZIP file to your solution's `Lib` folder.

3.   Complete the `Eg.Core` model and mappings from *Chapter 1*.

How to do it...

1.   Create a new class library project named `Eg.ClassValidation`.

2.   Add a reference to the `Eg.Core` model and `NHibernate.Validator.dll`.

3.   Add the following `ProductValidation` class:

```
public class ProductValidator :
  ValidationDef<Product>
{

  public ProductValidator()
  {
    Define(p => p.Name)
      .NotNullableAndNotEmpty()
      .And.MaxLength(255);

    Define(p => p.Description)
      .NotNullableAndNotEmpty();

    Define(p => p.UnitPrice)
      .GreaterThanOrEqualTo(0M)
      .WithMessage("Unit price can't be negative.");

  }

}
```

4. Create a new console application named `Eg.ClassValidation.Runner`.

5. Add references to `log4net.dll`, `NHibernate.dll`, `NHibernate.ByteCode.Castle.dll`, and `NHibernate.Validator.dll`.

6. Set up an `App.config` with the standard `log4net` and `hibernate-configuration` sections, following the *Configuring NHibernate with App.config* and *Configuring NHibernate Logging* recipes from *Chapter 2*.

7. Add a new class named `BasicSharedEngineProvider` using the following code:

```
public class BasicSharedEngineProvider :
  ISharedEngineProvider
{


  private readonly ValidatorEngine ve;

  public BasicSharedEngineProvider(ValidatorEngine ve)
  {
    this.ve = ve;
  }

  public ValidatorEngine GetEngine()
  {
    return ve;
  }

  public void UseMe()
  {
    Environment.SharedEngineProvider = this;
  }

}
```

8. In `Program.cs`, use the following code:

```
private static void Main(string[] args)
{
  XmlConfigurator.Configure();
  var log = LogManager.GetLogger(typeof (Program));

  SetupNHibernateValidator();

  var nhibernateConfig = new Configuration().Configure();
  nhibernateConfig.Initialize();

  ISessionFactory sessionFactory = nhibernateConfig.
BuildSessionFactory();

  var schemaExport = new SchemaExport(nhibernateConfig);
  schemaExport.Execute(false, true, false);
```

```
        var junk = new Product
                   {
                   Name = "Spiffy Junk",
                   Description = string.Empty,
                   UnitPrice = -1M
                   };

      var ve = Environment.SharedEngineProvider.GetEngine();
      var invalidValues = ve.Validate(junk);
      foreach (var invalidValue in invalidValues)
        log.InfoFormat("{0} {1}",
          invalidValue.PropertyName,
          invalidValue.Message);
    }

    private static FluentConfiguration GetNhvConfiguration()
    {
      var nhvConfiguration = new FluentConfiguration();
      nhvConfiguration
        .SetDefaultValidatorMode(ValidatorMode.UseExternal)
        .Register(Assembly.Load("Eg.ClassValidation")
                   .ValidationDefinitions())
        .IntegrateWithNHibernate
        .ApplyingDDLConstraints()
        .And
        .RegisteringListeners();
      return nhvConfiguration;
    }

    private static ValidatorEngine GetValidatorEngine()
    {
      var cfg = GetNhvConfiguration();
      var validatorEngine = new ValidatorEngine();
      validatorEngine.Configure(cfg);
      return validatorEngine;
    }

    private static void SetupNHibernateValidator()
    {
      var validatorEngine = GetValidatorEngine();
      new BasicSharedEngineProvider(validatorEngine).UseMe();
    }
```

9. Build and run your application.

How it works...

In this recipe, we've separated our validation rules into a separate class named `ProductValidation`. Just as we did in our previous recipe, we've decided that each valid `Product` must have a non-null, non-empty `Name` and `Description` no more than 255 characters long and must have a non-negative `UnitPrice`.

As we learned in the previous recipe, we use an `ISharedEngineProvider` to locate our validation engine.

Unlike the previous recipe, we use the loquacious, or fluent, syntax to configure NHibernate Validator.

We validate our `junk Product`. It fails two validation rules. First, the `Description` can't be empty. Second, the `UnitPrice` can't be negative. As we see in the log4net output, we get the following validation error messages:

Description may not be null or empty

UnitPrice must be greater than or equal to 0

There's more...

We can also use NHibernate Validator to validate an entire object graph. Let's take our Movie entity as an example. Suppose we want to ensure that the movie entity is valid, as well as all of its ActorRole children. Our validation class would appear as shown:

```
Define(m => m.Director)
  .NotNullableAndNotEmpty()
  .And.MaxLength(255);
Define(m => m.Actors)
  .HasValidElements();
```

The `HasValidElements` runs the ActorRole validation rules on each object in the `Actors` collection.

See also

▸ *Property validation with attributes*

Using the Burrows framework

The NHibernate Burrows framework works especially well for ASP.NET Web Forms applications. In this recipe, I'll show you how we can use Burrows to build an ASP.NET Web Forms application quickly.

Getting ready

1. Download the latest NHibernate Burrows binaries from SourceForge at `http://sourceforge.net/projects/nhcontrib/files/`.

2. Extract `NHibernate.Burrow.dll`, `NHibernate.Burrow.AppBlock.dll`, and `NHibernate.Burrow.WebUtil.dll` to your solution's `Lib` folder.

3. Complete the `Eg.Core` model and mappings from *Chapter 1*.

4. In the `NHCookbook` database, create at least 12 `Product` rows either by hand or by running the following SQL script at least 12 times:

```
DECLARE @Count int;
SELECT @Count = COUNT(*)+1 FROM Product

INSERT INTO Product
VALUES (
NEWID(), 'Eg.Core.Product',
'Product #' + CAST(@Count as VarChar(255)),
'Description of Product #' + CAST(@Count as VarChar(255)),
CAST(@Count AS Decimal) * 0.99,
null, null, null);
```

How to do it...

1. Create a new ASP.NET Web Forms project named `Eg.Burrows`.

2. Add a reference to the `Eg.Core` model, `log4net.dll`, `NHibernate.dll`, `NHibernate.ByteCode.Castle.dll`, `NHibernate.Burrows.dll`, `NHIbernate.Burrows.AppBlock.dll`, and `NHibernate.Burrows.WebKit.dll`.

3. In the `Web.Config`, add the standard `log4net` and `hibernate-configuration` sections as done in *Chapter 2*.

4. In the `<configSections>` element, add the following section declaration:

```
<section name="NHibernate.Burrow" type= "NHibernate.Burrow.
Configuration.NHibernateBurrowCfgSection, NHibernate.Burrow"/>
```

5. Add the `NHibernate.Burrow` section to `Web.Config`:

   ```
   <NHibernate.Burrow customConfigurator= "Eg.Burrows.
   BurrowsConfigurator, Eg.Burrows" />
   ```

6. Inside `<system.web>`, find the `<httpModules>` element and add the following Burrows http module:

   ```
   <add name= "NHibernate.Burrow.WebUtil.HttpModule" type=
   "NHibernate.Burrow.WebUtil.WebUtilHTTPModule, NHibernate.Burrow.
   WebUtil"/>
   ```

7. Create a new class named `BurrowsConfigurator` using the following code:

   ```
   public class BurrowsConfigurator : IConfigurator
   {
     public void Config(IPersistenceUnitCfg puCfg,
       Configuration nhCfg)
     {
       nhCfg.Configure();
     }

     public void Config(IBurrowConfig val)
     {
       var unit = new PersistenceUnitElement
                    {
                        Name = "persistenceUnit1",
                        NHConfigFile = null
                    };
       val.PersistenceUnitCfgs.Add(unit);
     }
   }
   ```

8. Create a new class named `ProductDAO` with the following code:

   ```
   public class ProductDAO : GenericDAO<Product>
   {
   }
   ```

9. Open the design view of `Default.aspx`, and drag in a `GridView` control.

10. In the `Properties` pane, change the ID to `ProductGridView`.

11. Drag an `ObjectDataSource` control onto the page.

12. Name it `ProductDataSource`.

13. From **ObjectDataSource Tasks**, choose **Configure Data Sourc** as shown in the next screenshot:

14. Choose **Eg.Burrows.ProductDAO** from the drop-down, and click on **Next**.

15. On the **SELECT** tab, choose **FindAll(Int32 startRow, Int32 pageSize, String sortExpression), returns IList<Product>**, and click on **Finish**.

16. On the **Properties** pane, set **MaximumRowsParameterName** to **pageSize**.

17. Set **SelectCountMethod** to **CountAll**.

18. Set **StartRowIndexParameterName** to **startRow**.

19. Set **SortParameterName** to **sortExpression**.

20. From **GridView Tasks** for **ProductGridView** shown in the next screenshot, Choose **ProductDataSource** and check **Enable Paging** and **Enable Selection**.

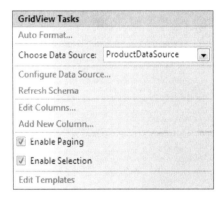

21. Click on **Edit Columns** to bring up the **Fields** window as shown in the next screenshot:

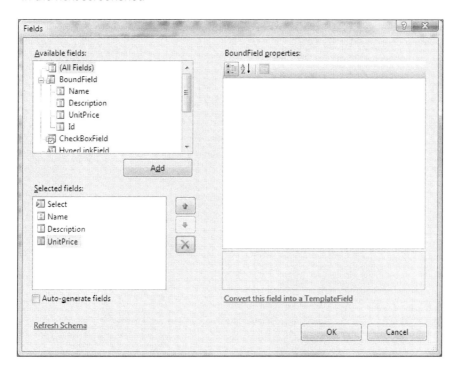

22. Delete the **Id** field.

23. On the **UnitPrice** field, set the **DataFormatString** to **{0:c}** and click on **OK**.

24. From **DataGrid task**, click on **Auto-Format** and choose the **Colorful** scheme. The result should look like the next screenshot:

25. On the **Properties** tab, set **AllowSorting** to **true**.

26. Double-click on **ProductGridView**, and add this code to the `SelectIndexChanged` event:

```
var productId = (Guid) ProductGridView
    .SelectedDataKey.Value;
var url = string.Format(
    "~/ViewProduct.aspx?ProductId={0}",
    productId.ToString());
Response.Redirect(url);
```

27. Add a new ASP.NET Web Forms page named `ViewProduct.aspx`.

28. Add an ASP.NET UserControl named `EditProduct.aspx`.

29. Add the following markup to the control:

```
<fieldset>
    <legend>Edit Product</legend>
    <table border="0">
        <tr>
            <td>
                <asp:Label
                ID="lblProductName" runat="server"
                Text="Name:"
                AssociatedControlID="txtProductName">
                </asp:Label>
            </td>
        </tr>
        <tr>
            <td>
                <asp:TextBox ID="txtProductName"
                runat="server"></asp:TextBox>
            </td>
        </tr>
        <tr>
            <td>
                <asp:Label ID="lblDescription" runat="server"
                Text="Description:"
                    AssociatedControlID="txtDescription">
                    </asp:Label>
            </td>
        </tr>
        <tr>
            <td>
```

```
                    <asp:TextBox ID="txtDescription"
                    runat="server" TextMode="MultiLine">
                    </asp:TextBox>
                </td>
            </tr>
            <tr>
                <td>
                    <asp:Label ID="Label1" runat="server"
                    Text="Unit Price:"
                        AssociatedControlID="txtUnitPrice">
                        </asp:Label>
                </td>
            </tr>
            <tr>
                <td>
                    <asp:TextBox ID="txtUnitPrice"
                    runat="server"></asp:TextBox>
                </td>
            </tr>
        </table>
        <asp:Button ID="btnSave"
        runat="server" Text="Save"
        onclick="btnSave_Click" />
        <asp:Button ID="btnCancel"
            runat="server" Text="Cancel"
            onclick="btnCancel_Click" />
    </fieldset>
```

30. The design view should look like the following screenshot:

31. In the code-behind for `EditProduct`, add the following code:

```
public partial class EditProduct
  : UserControl
{

  [EntityField]
  protected Product product;

  public event EventHandler Updated;
  public event EventHandler Cancelled;

  public void Bind(Product product)
  {
    this.product = product;
    if (product == null) return;
    txtProductName.Text = product.Name;
    txtDescription.Text = product.Description;
    txtUnitPrice.Text = product.UnitPrice.ToString();
  }

  protected void btnSave_Click(object sender,
    EventArgs e)
  {
    product.Name = txtProductName.Text;
    product.Description = txtDescription.Text;
    product.UnitPrice = decimal.Parse(txtUnitPrice.Text);
    if (Updated != null)
      Updated(this, new EventArgs());
  }

  protected void btnCancel_Click(object sender,
    EventArgs e)
  {
    product = null;
    if (Cancelled != null)
      Cancelled(this, new EventArgs());
  }
}
```

32. On the second line of `ViewProduct.aspx`, register the `EditProduct` control with the following markup:

```
<%@ Register Src="EditProduct.ascx"
TagName="EditProduct" TagPrefix="uc1" %>
```

33. In the `<form>` tag, add the `EditProduct` control with the following markup:

```
<ucl:EditProduct ID="editProduct" runat="server"
OnUpdated="editProduct_Updated"
OnCancelled="editProduct_Cancelled">
</ucl:EditProduct>
```

34. In the code-behind for `ViewProduct`, use the following code:

```
public partial class ViewProduct : System.Web.UI.Page
{
  protected void Page_Load(object sender, EventArgs e)
  {
    if (!IsPostBack)
    {
      Guid Id = new Guid(Request
        .QueryString["ProductId"]);
      editProduct.Bind(new ProductDAO().Get(Id));
    }
  }

  protected void editProduct_Updated(
    object sender, EventArgs e)
  {
    Response.Redirect("~/");
  }

  protected void editProduct_Cancelled(
    object sender, EventArgs e)
  {
    Response.Redirect("~/");
  }
}
```

35. Build and run your web application.

How it works...

In this recipe, we've built a small web application to display and edit `Product` data. Thanks to the Burrows `http` module, Burrows will automatically handle session-per-request and transaction management.

In our `web.config`, we told the Burrows framework that the `BurrowsConfigurator` class would supply the Burrows configuration. Burrows supports multiple NHibernate configurations in the same application. Each of these is named a persistence unit. In this recipe, we only need one database. We load the `Web.Config` NHibernate configuration into our one and only persistence unit.

Burrows also provides a base class for data access objects that follow the common patterns of ASP.NET Web Forms data access controls. Our ProductDAO class uses this GenericDAO class.

The `Default.aspx` page wires an instance of `ProductDAO` to an `ObjectDataSource`, which is used to data-bind the `GridView`. When a user clicks on a column header, the data source calls `ProductDAO.FindAll` with `sortExpression` set to the field name. Burrows adds this as sort to the query. Similarly, paging through the `GridView` sets the `startRow` to the page number times the page size, minus one.

When a user clicks on the **Select** link, the `SelectedIndexChanged` event fires and redirects the user to `ViewProduct.aspx`, passing the `Product Id` on the query string of the URL.

The first time we load the `ViewProduct` page, we get the `Product Id` from the query string, get the `Product` instance from the database, and bind it to our `EditProduct` control.

In `EditProduct`, our `Product` field is decorated with the Burrows `EntityFieldAttribute`. This attribute tells Burrows that this field contains an entity and the ID of that entity should be remembered from one postback to the next. Burrows automatically loads the `Product` instance from the database and sets this field with each postback request. Any changes to the entity are automatically persisted at the end of each request. We can code our user control almost as if the entity was held in memory from one request to the next.

When a user clicks on the **Save** button, we copy the field data back to the entity instance and redirect to the `Default.aspx` page. When a user clicks on the **Cancel** button, we simply redirect without writing any data.

There's more...

Burrows also provides a method for providing long-running conversations, essentially stateful business transactions using NHibernate sessions that can span several web requests. For more information on this feature, check out the conversation explained in the article at `http://nhforge.org/wikis/burrow/conversation-explained.aspx`.

See also

▸ *Setting up session per web request*

Setting up full-text search

While most relational databases provide some mechanism for full-text search, these databases are optimized for online transaction processing (OLTP) type workloads. Document databases, on the other hand, are designed specifically for full-text search queries, and excel at them. In this recipe, I'll show you how to use NHibernate Search and Lucene.Net to provide full-text search capabilities for your entities.

Getting ready

1. Download the NHibernate Search binary files from SourceForge at `http://sourceforge.net/projects/nhcontrib/files/`.

2. Extract `NHibernate.Search.dll` and `Lucene.Net.dll` from the downloaded ZIP file to your solution's `Lib` folder.

3. Complete the `Eg.Core` model and mappings from *Chapter 1*.

How to do it...

1. In `Eg.Core`, add a reference to `NHibernate.Search.dll`.

2. On the `Entity` base class, decorate the `Id` property with the `DocumentId` attribute from `NHibernate.Search.Attributes`.

3. On the `Product` class, add the following attributes:
    ```
    [Indexed]
    public class Product : Entity
    {

      [Field]
      public virtual string Name { get; set; }

      [Field]
      public virtual string Description { get; set; }
      public virtual Decimal UnitPrice { get; set; }

    }
    ```

4. On the book class, add the following attributes:
    ```
    [Indexed]
    public class Book : Product
    {

      [Field(Index = Index.UnTokenized)]
      public virtual string ISBN { get; set; }

      [Field]
      public virtual string Author { get; set; }

    }
    ```

5. Create a new console project named `Eg.Search.Runner`.

6. Add references to the `Eg.Core` model, `log4net.dll`, `Lucene.Net.dll`, `NHibernate.dll`, and `NHibernate.ByteCode.dll`.

7. Add an `App.config` file with the standard `log4net` and `hibernate-configuration` sections.

8. Add a new class named `SearchConfiguration` using the following code:

```
public class SearchConfiguration
{
  public ISessionFactory BuildSessionFactory()
  {
    var cfg = new Configuration().Configure();
    SetSearchPropscfg);
    AddSearchListeners(cfg);
    var sessionFactory = cfg.BuildSessionFactory();
    return new SessionFactorySearchWrapper(
      sessionFactory);
  }

  private void SetSearchProps(Configuration cfg)
  {
    cfg.SetProperty(
      "hibernate.search.default.directory_provider",
      typeof(FSDirectoryProvider)
      .AssemblyQualifiedName);

    cfg.SetProperty(
      "hibernate.search.default.indexBase",
      "~/Index");
  }

  private void AddSearchListeners(Configuration cfg)
  {
    cfg.SetListener(ListenerType.PostUpdate,
      new FullTextIndexEventListener());
    cfg.SetListener(ListenerType.PostInsert,
      new FullTextIndexEventListener());
    cfg.SetListener(ListenerType.PostDelete,
      new FullTextIndexEventListener());
    cfg.SetListener(ListenerType.PostCollectionRecreate,
      new FullTextIndexCollectionEventListener());
    cfg.SetListener(ListenerType.PostCollectionRemove,
      new FullTextIndexCollectionEventListener());
    cfg.SetListener(ListenerType.PostCollectionUpdate,
      new FullTextIndexCollectionEventListener());
  }
}
```

9. Create a new class named `SessionFactorySearchWrapper` using the following code:

```
public class SessionFactorySearchWrapper
: ISessionFactory
{
  private readonly ISessionFactory _sessionFactory;

  public SessionFactorySearchWrapper(
    ISessionFactory sessionFactory)
  {
    _sessionFactory = sessionFactory;
  }

  public ISession OpenSession()
  {
    var session = _sessionFactory.OpenSession();
    return WrapSession(session);
  }

  public ISession OpenSession(
    IDbConnection conn,
    IInterceptor sessionLocalInterceptor)
  {
    var session = _sessionFactory
      .OpenSession(conn, sessionLocalInterceptor);
    return WrapSession(session);
  }

  public ISession OpenSession(
    IInterceptor sessionLocalInterceptor)
  {
    var session = _sessionFactory
      .OpenSession(sessionLocalInterceptor);
    return WrapSession(session);
  }

  public ISession OpenSession(
    IDbConnection conn)
  {
    var session = _sessionFactory.OpenSession(conn);
    return WrapSession(session);
  }

  private static ISession WrapSession(
```

```
      ISession session)
  {
    return NHibernate.Search
      .Search.CreateFullTextSession(session);
  }


}
```

10. Implement the remaining `ISessionFactory` methods and properties in `SessionFactorySearchWrapper` by passing the call to the `_sessionFactory` field, as shown in the following code:

```
public IClassMetadata GetClassMetadata(string entityName)
{
    return _sessionFactory.GetClassMetadata(entityName);
}
```

11. In `Program.cs`, use the following code:

```
class Program
{
  static void Main(string[] args)
  {

    XmlConfigurator.Configure();
    var log = LogManager.GetLogger(typeof(Program));

    var cfg = new SearchConfiguration();
    var sessionFactory = cfg.BuildSessionFactory();

    var theBook = new Book()
                    {
                      Name = @"Gödel, Escher, Bach: An Eternal
Golden Braid",
                      Author = "Douglas Hofstadter",
                      Description =
                      @"This groundbreaking Pulitzer Prize-
winning book sets the standard for interdisciplinary writing,
exploring the patterns and symbols in the thinking of
mathematician Kurt Godel, artist M.C. Escher, and composer Johann
Sebastian Bach.",
                      ISBN = "978-0465026562",
                      UnitPrice = 22.95M
                    };

    var theOtherBook = new Book()
                    {
```

```
                                Name = "Technical Writing",
                                Author = "Joe Professor",
                                Description = "College text",
                                ISBN = "123-1231231234",
                                UnitPrice = 143.73M
                             };

      var thePoster = new Product()
                         {
                            Name = "Ascending and Descending",
                            Description = "Poster of famous Escher
print",
                            UnitPrice = 7.95M
                         };

      using (var session = sessionFactory.OpenSession())
      {
        using (var tx = session.BeginTransaction())
        {
          session.Delete(«from Product»);
          tx.Commit();
        }
      }

      using (var session = sessionFactory.OpenSession())
      {
        using (var tx = session.BeginTransaction())
        {
          session.Save(theBook);
          session.Save(theOtherBook);
          session.Save(thePoster);
          tx.Commit();
        }
      }

      var products = GetEscherProducts(sessionFactory);
      OutputProducts(products, log);

      var books = GetEscherBooks(sessionFactory);
      OutputProducts(books.Cast<Product>(), log);
    }

    private static void OutputProducts(
      IEnumerable<Product> products,
```

```
    ILog log)
{

  foreach (var product in products)
  {
    log.InfoFormat("Found {0} with price {1:C}",
                    product.Name, product.UnitPrice);
  }

}

private static IEnumerable<Product>
  GetEscherProducts(
  ISessionFactory sessionFactory)
{
  IEnumerable<Product> results;
  using (var session = sessionFactory.OpenSession()
                        as IFullTextSession)
  {
    using (var tx = session.BeginTransaction())
    {
      var queryString = "Description:Escher";
      var query = session
        .CreateFullTextQuery<Product>(queryString);
      results = query.List<Product>();
      tx.Commit();
    }
  }
  return results;
}

private static IEnumerable<Book> GetEscherBooks(
  ISessionFactory sessionFactory)
{
  IEnumerable<Book> results;
  using (var session = sessionFactory.OpenSession()
                        as IFullTextSession)
  {
    using (var tx = session.BeginTransaction())
    {
      var queryString = "Description:Escher";
      var query = session
        .CreateFullTextQuery<Book>(queryString);
```

```
            results = query.List<Book>();
            tx.Commit();
        }
    }
    return results;

  }
}
```

12. Build and run your application

How it works...

In this recipe, we've offloaded our full-text queries to a Lucene index in the `bin/Debug/Index` folder.

First, let's quickly discuss some Lucene terminology. The Lucene database is referred to as an **Index**. Each record in the Index is referred to as a **Document**. In the case of NHibernate Search, each Document in the Index has a corresponding entity in the relational database. Each Document has **Fields**, and each field comprises a name and value. By default, fields are **tokenized** or broken up into **terms**. A term can best be described as a single, significant, lower-case word from some string of words. For example, the string "Bag of Cats" would be tokenized into the terms "bag" and "cat". Additionally, Lucene maintains a map of terms in a field, which documents contain a given term, and the frequency of that term in the document. This makes keyword searches extremely fast.

Entity classes with the `Indexed` attribute will be included as documents in the Lucene index. The remaining attributes are used to determine what properties from these entities should be included in the document, and how that data will be stored. Automatically, the `_hibernate_class` field stores the entity type. Each searchable entity must have a field or property decorated with the `DocumentId` attribute. This is stored in the ID field, and is used to maintain the relationship between entities and documents. In our case, the ID property on `Entity` will be used.

To be useful, we should include additional data in our documents using the `Field` attribute. For keyword searches, we've included the tokenized name and description of every product, and the author of every book. We've also included the ISBN of every book, but have chosen not to tokenize it because a partial ISBN match is useless.

The `SearchConfiguration` class is responsible for building an NHibernate configuration, adding the necessary NHibernate Search settings to the configuration, building an NHibernate session factory, and wrapping the session factory in our search wrapper.

The `SessionFactorySearchWrapper` wraps the standard NHibernate session factory and returns `IFullTextSearchSession` from calls to `OpenSession`. These sessions behave as normal NHibernate sessions, and provide additional methods for creating full-text search queries against the Lucene index. The `CreateFullTextQuery` method of the session takes a Lucene query in string or query object form and returns a familiar NHibernate `IQuery` interface, the same interface used for HQL and SQL queries. When we call `List` or `UniqueResult`, the query is executed against our Lucene index. For example, the query in our `GetEscherProduct` query will search Lucene for documents with a `Description` containing the term `escher`. This query returns two results: the GEB book and the M. C. Escher poster. The IDs of each of those search results are gathered up and used to build a SQL database query similar to the next query.

```
SELECT this_.Id          as Id0_0_,
       this_.Name        as Name0_0_,
       this_.Description as Descript4_0_0_,
       this_.UnitPrice   as UnitPrice0_0_,
       this_.Director    as Director0_0_,
       this_.Author      as Author0_0_,
       this_.ISBN        as ISBN0_0_,
       this_.ProductType as ProductT2_0_0_
FROM   Product this_
WHERE  (this_.Id in ('5933e3ba-3092-4db7-8d19-9daf014b8ce4' /* @p0
*/,'05058886-8436-4a1d-8412-9db1010561b5' /* @p1 */))
```

Because this database query is performed on the primary key, it is amazingly fast. The Lucene query is fast because the database was specially designed for that purpose. This has the potential for huge performance and functionality gains over the weak full-text search capabilities in most relational databases.

There's more...

This is just the most basic example of what we can do with NHibernate Search. We can also choose to store the original value of a field in the document. This is useful when we want to display Lucene query results without querying the SQL database. Additionally, Lucene has many more features, like search-term highlighting and spell-checking. Although Lucene is a very capable document database, remember that it is not relational. There is no support for relationships or references between documents stored in a Lucene index.

Sharding databases for performance

There are a few scenarios where it may be appropriate to partition data horizontally across several servers, with performance being the most obvious. In this recipe, I'll show you how we can use NHibernate Shards to split our data set across three databases.

Getting ready

1. Download the latest NHibernate Shards binary from SourceForge at `http://sourceforge.net/projects/nhcontrib/files/`.

2. Extract `NHibernate.Shards.dll` from the downloaded ZIP file to your solution's `Lib` folder.

3. Complete the `Eg.Core` model and mappings from _Chapter 1_.

4. In SQL Server, create three new, blank databases named `Shard1`, `Shard2`, and `Shard3`.

How to do it...

1. In the `Entity` base class, change the type of the `Id` property from `Guid` to `String`.

2. In `Product.hbm.xml`, change the `Id` generator from `guid.comb` to `NHibernate.Shards.Id.ShardedUUIDGenerator, NHibernate.Shards`.

3. Follow the same procedure for `ActorRole.hbm.xml`.

4. Use the NHibernate Schema Tool explained in _Chapter 2_ to build the database schema for each of the three databases.

5. Create a new class library project named `Eg.Shards.Runner`.

6. Add a reference to the `Eg.Core` model, `log4net.dll`, `NHibernate.dll`, `NHibernate.ByteCode.dll`, and `NHibernate.Shards.dll`.

7. Add an `App.config` file with the following connection strings:

```xml
<?xml version="1.0" encoding="utf-8" ?>
<configuration>
  <connectionStrings>
    <add name="Shard1" connectionString="Server=.\SQLExpress;
Database=Shard1; Trusted_Connection=SSPI"/>
    <add name="Shard2" connectionString="Server=.\SQLExpress;
Database=Shard2; Trusted_Connection=SSPI"/>
    <add name="Shard3" connectionString="Server=.\SQLExpress;
Database=Shard3; Trusted_Connection=SSPI"/>
  </connectionStrings>
</configuration>
```

8. Add a new class named `ShardConfiguration` with the following code:

```csharp
public class ShardConfiguration
{
  private Configuration GetConfiguration(
    string connStrName,
    int shardId)
```

```
  {
    var cfg = new Configuration()
      .SessionFactoryName("SessionFactory"
          + shardId.ToString())
      .Proxy(p =>
        p.ProxyFactoryFactory<ProxyFactoryFactory>())
      .DataBaseIntegration(db =>
          {
            db.Dialect<MsSql2008Dialect>();
            db.ConnectionStringName = connStrName;
          })
      .AddAssembly("Eg.Core")
      .SetProperty(
        ShardedEnvironment.ShardIdProperty,
        shardId.ToString());
    return cfg;
  }

  private IShardConfiguration GetShardCfg(
    string connStrName,
    int shardId)
  {
    var cfg = GetConfiguration(connStrName, shardId);
    return new ConfigurationToShardConfigurationAdapter(
      cfg);
  }

  private IList<IShardConfiguration> GetShardCfg(
    IEnumerable<string> connStrNames)
  {
    var cfg = new List<IShardConfiguration>();
    int shardId = 1;
    foreach (var connStrName in connStrNames)
      cfg.Add(GetShardCfg(connStrName, shardId++));
    return cfg;
  }

  public IShardedSessionFactory GetSessionFactory(
    IEnumerable<string> connStrNames,
    IShardStrategyFactory shardStrategyFactory)
  {
    var prototypeCfg = GetConfiguration(
      connStrNames.First(), 1);
```

```
      var cfg = new ShardedConfiguration(
        prototypeCfg,
        GetShardCfg(connStrNames),
        shardStrategyFactory);

      return cfg.BuildShardedSessionFactory();
    }

  }
```

9. Add a new class named `ShardStrategyFactory` with the following code:

```
public class ShardStrategyFactory : IShardStrategyFactory
{

  public IShardStrategy NewShardStrategy(
    ICollection<ShardId> shardIds)
  {

    return new ShardStrategyImpl(
      GetSelectionStrategy(shardIds),
      GetResolutionStrategy(shardIds),
      GetAccessStrategy(shardIds));
  }

  private static IShardSelectionStrategy
    GetSelectionStrategy(
      ICollection<ShardId> shardIds)
  {

    var loadBalancer =
      new RoundRobinShardLoadBalancer(shardIds);
    return new RoundRobinShardSelectionStrategy(
      loadBalancer);
  }

  private static IShardResolutionStrategy
    GetResolutionStrategy(
      ICollection<ShardId> shardIds)
  {

    return new AllShardsShardResolutionStrategy(
      shardIds);
  }

  private static IShardAccessStrategy
    GetAccessStrategy(
      ICollection<ShardId> shardIds)
```

```
    {
      return new SequentialShardAccessStrategy();
    }

  }
```

10. In `Program.cs`, use the following code:

```
static void Main(string[] args)
{

  NHibernateProfiler.Initialize();

  var connStrNames = new List<string>();
  connStrNames.Add("Shard1");
  connStrNames.Add("Shard2");
  connStrNames.Add("Shard3");

  var shardStrategy = new ShardStrategy();

  var sessionFactory = new ShardConfiguration()
    .GetSessionFactory(connStrNames, shardStrategy);

  ClearDB(sessionFactory);

  var p1 = new Product()
             {
               Name = "Water Hose",
               Description = "50 ft.",
               UnitPrice = 17.46M
             };

  var p2 = new Product()
             {
               Name = "Water Sprinkler",
               Description = "Rust resistant plastic",
               UnitPrice = 4.95M
             };

  var p3 = new Product()
             {
               Name = "Beach Ball",
               Description = "Hours of fun",
               UnitPrice = 3.45M
             };

  using (var session = sessionFactory.OpenSession())
  {
```

```
    using (var tx = session.BeginTransaction())
    {
      session.Save(p1);
      session.Save(p2);
      session.Save(p3);
      tx.Commit();
    }
    session.Close();
  }

  using (var session = sessionFactory.OpenSession())
  {
    using (var tx = session.BeginTransaction())
    {
      var query =
        "from Product p where upper(p.Name) " +
        "like '%WATER%'";
      var products = session.CreateQuery(query)
        .List();

      foreach (Product p in products)
        Console.WriteLine(p.Name);

      tx.Commit();
    }
    session.Close();
  }

  Console.ReadKey();
}

private static void ClearDB(ISessionFactory sessionFactory)
{
  using (var s = sessionFactory.OpenSession())
  {
    using (var tx = s.BeginTransaction())
    {
      var products = s.CreateQuery("from Product")
        .List();
      foreach (Product product in products)
        s.Delete(product);
      tx.Commit();
    }
    s.Close();
```

```
        }
    }
```

11. Build and run the application.

12. Inspect the product table in each of the three databases. You should find one product in each.

How it works...

NHibernate Shards allows you to split your data across several databases, named shards, while hiding this additional complexity behind the familiar NHibernate APIs. In this recipe, we use the sharded UUID POID generator, which generates UUIDs with a four-digit shard ID, followed by a 28 hexadecimal digit unique ID. A typical ID looks like this: `0001000069334c47a07afd3f6f46d587`. You can provide your own POID generator, provided the shard ID is somehow encoded in the persistent object's IDs.

The `ShardConfiguration` class configures a session factory for each shard. These session factories are grouped together with an implementation of `IShardStrategyFactory` to build an `IShardedSessionFactory`. A sharded session factory implements the familiar `ISessionFactory` interface, so the impact on your larger application is minimal.

An implementation of `IShardStrategyFactory` must return three strategies to control the operation of NHibernate Shards. First, the `IShardSelectionStrategy` assigns each new entity to a shard. In this recipe, we use a simple round-robin technique that spreads the data across each shard equally. The first entity is assigned to shard 1, the second to shard 2, the third to shard 3, the fourth to shard 1, and so on. Next, the `IShardResolutionStrategy` is used to determine the correct shard given an entity name and entity ID. In this example, we use the `AllShardsShardResolutionStrategy`, which doesn't attempt to determine the correct shard. Instead, all shards are queried for an entity. We could provide our own implementation to get the shard ID from the first 4 characters of the entity ID. This would allow us to determine which shard contains the entity we want and query only that shard, reducing the load on each database. Finally, the `IShardAccessStrategy` determines how the shards will be accessed. In this example, we use the `SequentialShardAccessStrategy`, so the first shard will be queried, then the next, and so on. NHibernate Shards also includes a parallel strategy.

Once we've built a sharded session factory, the application code looks like any other NHibernate application. However, there are a few caveats. NHibernate Shards doesn't support many of the lesser-used features of NHibernate. For example, `session.Delete("from Products");` throws a `NotImplementedException`. Additionally, sharded sessions expect to be explicitly `Closed` before being `Disposed`. Finally, NHibernate Shards doesn't support object graphs spread across shard boundaries. The idea of well-defined boundaries between object graphs fits well with the Domain-Driven Design pattern of aggregate roots and is generally considered a good NHibernate practice even without sharding.

Using NHibernate Spatial

NHibernate Spatial brings the spatial capabilities of several relational databases to the NHibernate API. In this recipe, I'll show you how to use NHibernate Spatial with Microsoft SQL Server 2008 to query for a geographic region containing a point.

Getting ready

In SQL Server 2008 Express, create a new, blank database named Spatial.

Download the State shapes from the US Census website by following these steps:

1. Inside the solution directory, create a directory named SpatialData.

2. Download the Shapefile containing all 50 states, D.C. and Puerto Rico from the United States Census website at http://www.census.gov/geo/www/cob/st2000.html or from the code download for this book. The file is named st99_d00_shp.zip.

3. Extract all three files in ZIP to the SpatialData folder. The files are named st99_d00.shp, st99_d00.dbf, and st99_d00.shx.

Import the data from the Shapefile into the Spatial database using the following steps:

1. Inside the solution directory, create a directory named SpatialTools.

2. Download the SQL Spatial Tools from the SharpGIS website at http://www.sharpgis.net/page/SQL-Server-2008-Spatial-Tools.aspx.

3. Extract the files in ZIP to the SpatialTools folder.

4. Run Shape2SQL.exe from the SpatialTools folder.

5. When prompted, enter your database information as shown in the next screenshot, and click **OK**.

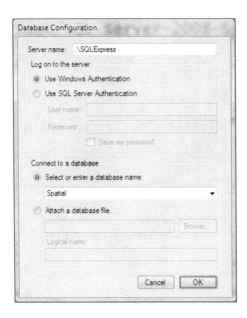

6. Click on the ellipsis next to the **Shapefile** textbox to browse for the Shapefile. Select the **st99_d00.shp** Shapefile we downloaded and extracted in the `SpatialData` folder.

7. Check the **Set SRID** checkbox, and enter **4269** as the SRID.

8. Change the table name to **StatePart,** as shown in the next screenshot:

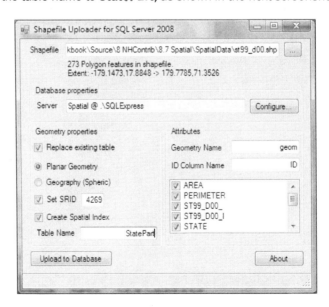

9. Click on **Upload to Database**.
10. When the upload process is complete, close the Shape2SQL tool.

Test your imported data using the following steps:

1. Open the `Spatial` database in Microsoft SQL Server Management Studio 2008.
2. Run the following query:
   ```
   SELECT * FROM StatePart WHERE Name LIKE 'Texas'
   ```
3. The **Results** tab should contain two rows.
4. The **Spatial results** tab should display the following image:

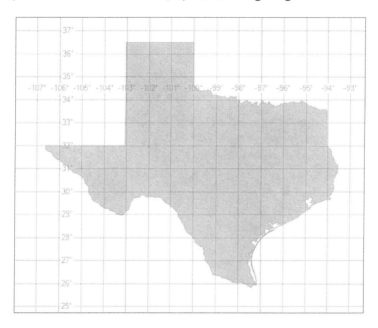

Download the NHibernate Spatial assemblies using the following steps:

1. Create a folder named `Lib` in your solution directory.
2. Download the latest NHibernate Spatial binary files from SourceForge at `http://sourceforge.net/projects/nhcontrib/files/`.
3. Extract the assemblies in ZIP format to the `Lib` folder.

How to do it...

1. Create a new, empty class library project named `Eg.Spatial`.
2. Add a reference to `GeoAPI.dll` in the `Lib` folder.

3. Create a class named `StatePart` with the following code:

```
public class StatePart
{

  public virtual int Id { get; protected set; }
  public virtual string Name { get; protected set; }
  public virtual float Area { get; protected set; }
  public virtual float Perimeter { get; protected set; }
  public virtual IGeometry Geometry { get; protected set; }

}
```

4. Create an embedded resource mapping file for `StatePart` with the following XML:

```xml
<?xml version="1.0" encoding="utf-8" ?>
<hibernate-mapping xmlns="urn:nhibernate-mapping-2.2"
    assembly="Eg.Spatial"
    namespace="Eg.Spatial">
  <typedef name="Geometry"
          class="NHibernate.Spatial.Type.GeometryType,
          NHibernate.Spatial">
    <param name="srid">4269</param>
    <param name="subtype">GEOMETRY</param>
  </typedef>
  <class name="StatePart"
          table="StatePart"
          mutable="false"
          schema-action="none">
    <id name="Id" column="ID">
      <generator class="assigned" />
    </id>
    <property name="Name" column="NAME"/>
    <property name="Area" column="AREA"/>
    <property name="Perimeter" column="PERIMETER"/>
    <property name="Geometry" type="Geometry"
                column="geom" />
  </class>
</hibernate-mapping>
```

4. Create a new console project named `Eg.Spatial.Runner`.

5. Add references to the `Eg.Spatial` model, `GeoAPI.dll`, `log4net.dll`, `NetTopologySuite.dll`, `NHibernate.dll`, `NHibernate.ByteCode.Castle.dll`, `NHibernate.Spatial.dll`, and `NHibernate.Spatial.MsSql2008.dll`.

6. Add an `App.config` file with standard `log4net` and `hibernate-configuration` sections as done in *Chapter 2*.

7. Change the connection string to point to the Spatial database, as shown in the following code:

```
<connectionStrings>
  <add name="db" connectionString="Server=.\SQLExpress;
Database=Spatial; Trusted_Connection=SSPI"/>
</connectionStrings>
```

8. Change the NHibernate dialect property to the `MsSql2008GeometryDialect`:

```
<property name="dialect">
  NHibernate.Spatial.Dialect.MsSql2008GeometryDialect, NHibernate.
Spatial.MsSql2008
</property>
```

9. Use the following code in the `Main` method of `Program.cs`:

```
static void Main(string[] args)
{

    XmlConfigurator.Configure();
    var log = LogManager.GetLogger(typeof (Program));

    NHibernateProfiler.Initialize();

    var cfg = new Configuration().Configure();

    cfg.AddAuxiliaryDatabaseObject(
      new SpatialAuxiliaryDatabaseObject(cfg));

    var sessionFactory = cfg.BuildSessionFactory();

    //Houston, TX
    var houstonTX = new Point(-95.383056, 29.762778);

    using (var session = sessionFactory.OpenSession())
    {
      using (var tx = session.BeginTransaction())
      {
        var query = session.CreateCriteria(
          typeof (StatePart))
          .Add(SpatialExpression.Contains(
            "Geometry", houstonTX));
        var part = query.UniqueResult<StatePart>();
        if (part == null)
        {
```

```
        log.InfoFormat("Houston, we have a problem.");
      }
      else
      {
        log.InfoFormat("Houston is in {0}",
          part.Name);
      }
      tx.Commit();
    }
  }
}
```

10. Build and run the program.

11. Check the log output for the line **Houston is in Texas**.

How it works...

In this recipe, we have simply created a `Point` with the latitude and longitude of Houston, Texas. Then we created an NHibernate criteria query to find the geometries containing that point. The `geom` field in each row of our `StateParts` table has a single polygon representing some distinct landmass. For example, Texas has two rows. The first polygon defines the border of mainland Texas while the other represents Padre Island, the large barrier island that runs along the South Texas shore. When our query returns the `StatePart` entity that contains our point, we output the `Name` field.

To allow for the additional spatial-related SQL keywords and syntax, we use the `MsSql2008GeometryDialect`.

The `Geometry` property on our `StatePart` entity is an `IGeometry`. This is mapped using the user type `GeometryType`. We also provide the **spatial reference identifier**, or SRID, for our datum and a subtype as parameters for this user type. Datums and SRIDs are explained later in this recipe.

There's more...

This recipe barely scratches the surface of what is possible with NHibernate Spatial. With just the basic spatial data, it's possible to query for any number and combination of criteria from the availability of valuable natural resources to the standard "Find the nearest retail location" feature on a website.

Geography or geometry?

To phrase this question differently, should you use a globe or map? Geography corresponds to the round-earth model, much like a globe. It works well for making measurements over great distances, accounting for the curvature of the earth.

Geometry, on the other hand, corresponds with the planar system or flat-earth model, like a map. As with a map, some distortion is tolerated, and this system is best-suited for smaller regions. However, standards for full-featured geometry data types are well established, while standards for geography data types are generally lacking. NHibernate Spatial has full support for geometry, as well as limited support for geography.

What's this SRID?

A **datum** is a model of the shape of the earth, combined with defined points on the surface used to measure accurate latitude and longitude. It's a sort of calibration where an exact location is defined in the datum as being at a precise latitude and longitude, and then everything else is measured from that point. For example, the North American Datum of 1927 (NAD 27) defines a marker on Meades Ranch in Kansas as 39° 13' 26.71218" N, 98° 32' 31.74604" W. Using NAD 27, every other point in North America was measured from this one point.

Each datum has a corresponding spatial reference identifier or SRID. The census Shapefile we used was built with the North American Datum of 1983, or NAD 83, an update to NAD 27. A query of SQL Server's `sys.spatial_reference_systems` table reveals that the corresponding SRID for NAD 83 is 4269.

Incidentally, most GPS devices use the World Geodetic System of 1984 (WGS 84), which corresponds with SQL Server's default SRID of 4326. NAD 83 and WGS 84 are essentially interchangeable for all but the most accurate applications. Given a set of coordinates, the location measured with NAD 83 will be at most, about one meter away from the location measured with WGS 84. That is, the two systems differ by about one meter at most.

Spatial data types

Spatial data can be broken down into three essential data types. First, a **point** consists of a simple X and Y coordinate. It has no length or area. A **Linestring** is simply two or more points in sequence, and the shortest possible line from each point to the next, as shown in the following diagrams. It has length, but no area. There are two special cases of linestring. A simple Linestring is one that doesn't cross itself. A ring is a Linestring whose first point is the same as its last.

Linestring

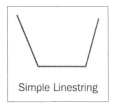

Simple Linestring

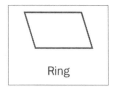

Ring

In its most basic form, a **polygon** is a simple ring. It has length (or rather perimeter), as well as area. As shown in the second diagram, the line string forming the perimeter of the polygon must be simple; it can't cross over itself to form a bow-tie. A polygon may have inner negative areas defined with inner rings. The Linestrings forming these rings may touch, but they can never cross each other or the outside ring. This can best be explained with the following diagrams:

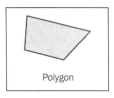

Polygon

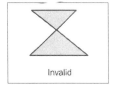

Invalid

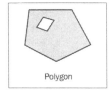

Polygon

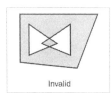

Invalid

Menu

The recipes presented in this book can be combined to build the following types of applications:

- ▸ **ASP.NET MVC** Web applications
- ▸ **ASP.NET Web Forms** applications
- ▸ **Windows Presentation Foundation** (**WPF**) and **WinForms** applications

ASP.NET MVC web applications

To build a complete web application using ASP.NET MVC or MVC 2, first choose a mapping method from the following recipes:

Choose a configuration method from the following recipes:

Create your database from the following recipes:

Choose a session management method from the following recipes:

Choose a query method from the following recipes:

Choose a data access layer style from the following recipes:

Finally, build your ASP.NET MVC application on top of this fully functional data access layer.

ASP.NET Web Forms applications

To build a complete web application using ASP.NET Web Forms, first choose a mapping method from the following list of recipes:

Choose a configuration method from the following recipes:

Create your database from the following list of recipes:

2.8   Generating the database

2.9   Scripting the database

2.10   Using NHibernate Schema Tool

Choose a session management method from the following recipes:

3.1   Setting up session-per-web request

3.5   Using the Conversation-per-Business transaction pattern

8.4   Using the Burrows framework

Choose a query method from the following recipies:

4.1   Using Criteria Queries

4.2   Using QueryOver

4.5   Using the Hibernate Query Language

4.7   Using Named Queries

4.10   Using LINQ to NHibernate

Choose a data access layer style from the following recipes:

6.1   Transaction Auto-wrapping for the data access layer (Data Access Objects)

6.2   Setting up an NHibernate repository

8.3   Using the Burrows framework

Finally, build your Web Forms application on top of this complete data access layer.

WPF and WinForms applications

To build a complete desktop application using Windows Presentation Foundation or WinForms, first choose a mapping method from the following list of recipes:

1.1   Mapping a class with XML

1.7   Creating mappings fluently

1.8   Mapping with ConfORM

Choose a configuration method from the following recipes:

Create your database from the following recipes:

Choose a session management method from the following two recipes:

Choose a query method from the following recipes:

Choose a data access layer style from the following recipes:

Finally, build your application on top of this data access layer.

Index

E

encrypted string type
  creating 217-224
EncryptedString type 224
encryption algorithms
  asymmetric algorithm 225
  hash algorithm 225
  symmetric algorithm 224
encryptionKey parameter 224
encryptor parameter 224
entities
  dependency injection, using 231-233
  fetching, criteria queries used 125-129
entity cache 258
entity class 8
EntityMode.Map 111
enumeration property
  mapping, to string field 43, 44
enum property 189
Equals method 26
events, NHibernate
  auto-flush 238
  create 238
  create-onflush 238
  delete 238
  dirty-check 238
  evict 238
  flush 238
  flush-entity 238
  load 238
  load-collection 238
  lock 238
  merge 238
  post-collection recreate 239
  post-collection remove 239
  post-collection update 239
  post-commit delete 238
  post-commit insert 238
  post-commit update 238
  post-delete 238
  post-insert 238
  post-load 238
  post-update 238
  pre-collection delete 239
  pre-collection recreate 238
  pre-collection remove 238

  pre-delete 238
  pre-insert 238
  pre-load 238
  pre-update 238
  refresh 238
  replicate 238
  save 238
  save-update 238
  update 238
ExampleDataCreator class
  creating 120, 121
extends attribute 16

F

fast testing
  SQLite in-memory database, used 172-177
Field attribute 287
fields 287
Fluent NHibernate
  NHibernate, configuring 58, 59, 60
  Persistence Tester 182, 184
Fluent NHibernate project
  about 31
  binary, downloading 31
  working 33
foreign generator 12
format_sql property 53
full-text search
  setting up 280-286
futures feature
  about 152
  cautions 155
  using 153
  using, with session cache 155-157
  working 154

G

generate_statistics property 53
generator element 9
geography 301
geometry 301
Geometry property 300
geom field 300
Ghostbusters test
  GhostInterceptor 190
  ghost update, issues 189, 190

About Packt Publishing

Packt, pronounced 'packed', published its first book "*Mastering phpMyAdmin for Effective MySQL Management*" in April 2004 and subsequently continued to specialize in publishing highly focused books on specific technologies and solutions.

Our books and publications share the experiences of your fellow IT professionals in adapting and customizing today's systems, applications, and frameworks. Our solution based books give you the knowledge and power to customize the software and technologies you're using to get the job done. Packt books are more specific and less general than the IT books you have seen in the past. Our unique business model allows us to bring you more focused information, giving you more of what you need to know, and less of what you don't.

Packt is a modern, yet unique publishing company, which focuses on producing quality, cutting-edge books for communities of developers, administrators, and newbies alike. For more information, please visit our website: www.packtpub.com.

About Packt Open Source

In 2010, Packt launched two new brands, Packt Open Source and Packt Enterprise, in order to continue its focus on specialization. This book is part of the Packt Open Source brand, home to books published on software built around Open Source licences, and offering information to anybody from advanced developers to budding web designers. The Open Source brand also runs Packt's Open Source Royalty Scheme, by which Packt gives a royalty to each Open Source project about whose software a book is sold.

Writing for Packt

We welcome all inquiries from people who are interested in authoring. Book proposals should be sent to author@packtpub.com. If your book idea is still at an early stage and you would like to discuss it first before writing a formal book proposal, contact us; one of our commissioning editors will get in touch with you.

We're not just looking for published authors; if you have strong technical skills but no writing experience, our experienced editors can help you develop a writing career, or simply get some additional reward for your expertise.

NHibernate 2 Beginner's Guide

ISBN: 978-1-847198-90-7   Paperback: 276 pages

Rapidly retrieve data from your database into .NET objects

1. Incorporate robust, efficient data access into your .Net projects

2. Gain database independence, not tied to any particular technology

3. Avoid spending countless hours developing data access layers

ASP.NET Site Performance Secrets

ISBN: 978-1-84969-068-3   Paperback: 483 pages

Simple and proven techniques to quickly speed up your ASP.NET website

1. Speed up your ASP.NET website by identifying performance bottlenecks that hold back your site's performance and fixing them

2. Tips and tricks for writing faster code and pinpointing those areas in the code that matter most, thus saving time and energy

3. Drastically reduce page load times

4. Configure and improve compression – the single most important way to improve your site's performance

LaVergne, TN USA
01 February 2011
214824LV00005B/50/P